Routledge Revivals

Anger

First published in 1923, *Anger* presents some considerations of anger where it comes close to conduct and religion. It is hoped that the explanation of conscience, and of the origins of religion, and particularly of monotheism has been carried a firm step farther than hitherto, and that interest will be found in the novel grouping of the great faiths with respect to wrath. The spirit of the great religions is drawn from their sacred writings. This book will be of interest to students of philosophy and religion.

Anger
Its Religious and Moral Significance

George Malcolm Stratton

First published in 1923
By George Allen & Unwin Ltd

This edition first published in 2024 by Routledge
4 Park Square, Milton Park, Abingdon, Oxon, OX14 4RN

and by Routledge
605 Third Avenue, New York, NY 10017

Routledge is an imprint of the Taylor & Francis Group, an informa business

© George Allen & Unwin 1923

All rights reserved. No part of this book may be reprinted or reproduced or utilised in any form or by any electronic, mechanical, or other means, now known or hereafter invented, including photocopying and recording, or in any information storage or retrieval system, without permission in writing from the publishers.

Publisher's Note
The publisher has gone to great lengths to ensure the quality of this reprint but points out that some imperfections in the original copies may be apparent.

Disclaimer
The publisher has made every effort to trace copyright holders and welcomes correspondence from those they have been unable to contact.

A Library of Congress record exists under LCCN: 23004742

ISBN: 978-1-032-74867-2 (hbk)
ISBN: 978-1-003-47136-3 (ebk)
ISBN: 978-1-032-74870-2 (pbk)

Book DOI 10.4324/9781003471363

ANGER: ITS RELIGIOUS AND MORAL SIGNIFICANCE

BY
GEORGE MALCOLM STRATTON
PROFESSOR OF PSYCHOLOGY IN THE UNIVERSITY OF CALIFORNIA

LONDON: GEORGE ALLEN & UNWIN, LTD.
RUSKIN HOUSE, 40 MUSEUM STREET, W. C. 1

PRINTED IN THE U. S. A.

To my friend
HARRY ROBERTS MILES
IN APPRECIATION OF HIS
WARM INTEREST IN THESE STUDIES.

PREFACE

For some years the writer has been studying pugnacity in men and in animals, for its immediate importance in psychology and because here lie the roots of war, and help in regard to its control. The psychology of religion has also been long of interest to him.

While busied thus, an invitation was accepted to deliver the Taylor Lectures at the Divinity School of Yale University, and to present some considerations of anger where it comes close to conduct and religion. The writer is more indebted than he can well express, to those who so generously gave him this opportunity, and especially to Dean C. R. Brown and many others for their personal encouragement and criticism when the lectures were delivered. The present account, however, goes far beyond what was possible in even the generous time there offered, making the whole perhaps more worthy of its important theme. It is hoped that the explanation of conscience, and of the origins of religion, and particularly of monotheism has been carried a firm step farther than hitherto, and that interest will be found in the novel grouping of the great faiths with respect to wrath. What is here said of war should be counted as but preliminary and as part of a larger plan for its psychology.

A method employed in the writer's *Psychology of the Religious Life* has here again been used, whereby the spirit of the great religions is drawn from their sacred writings. From this it will be understood that by Buddhism, Jainism, Vishnuism, Taoism, Confucianism, Zarathustrism, Islam, or Christianity, is meant (unless there is special word to the contrary) the religion which dominates the canon used; and there is not meant the religious life which may have preceded or followed the enlargement of faith there recorded. Although loss doubtless comes of following this strict procedure, yet the scientific advantages are clear, since thus we have fairly comparable data from far groups of people who by reason of their remoteness in time or place or tongue are unequally accessible by interview or questionary or by report of travellers. In its scriptures the religious community tells of itself freely, without self-consciousness, as no one can in autobiography or when confronted by a scientific enquirer. In every case the sources of evidence are noted; the numerals within round brackets after a citation indicate volume and page of such works as fall within Max Müller's monumental collection of *The Sacred Books of the East,* translated into English by many experts.

CONTENTS

INTRODUCTION: THE NEW SIGNIFICANCE OF EMOTION 1

PART I
THE PLACE OF ANGER IN MORALS

CHAPTER
I. THE BEGINNINGS OF ANGER 31
II. PUBLIC USES OF PUGNACITY 36
III. ANGER IN CONSCIENCE 50
IV. THE UNCREATIVE CHARACTER OF ANGER . . 62

PART II
THE DILEMMA OF RELIGION: ANGER IN THE GREAT FAITHS

V. THE IRATE AND MARTIAL RELIGIONS:
JUDAISM, ZOROASTRISM, ISLAM . . . 75

VI. THE UNANGRY RELIGIONS:
TAOISM, VISHNUISM, BUDDHISM, JAINISM 96

VII. THE RELIGIONS OF ANGER-SUPPORTED LOVE:
CONFUCIANISM, CHRISTIANITY 119

CONTENTS

PART III

ANGER IN RELIGION'S GROWTH

CHAPTER		PAGE
VIII.	Man's Anger toward the Supernatural .	139
IX.	The Anger of the Gods	147
X.	Curse, Persecution, and War, in Religion	161
XI.	The Worship of Malign Spirits . . .	176
XII.	Anger and the Origin of Religion . . .	187
XIII.	The Geography of Hatred	200
XIV.	Jealousy as a Source of Monotheism .	209

PART IV

THE FUTURE OF ANGER IN THE WEST

XV.	The Historic Trend in the Occident .	233
XVI.	Will and the Native Impulses . . .	243
XVII.	The Right Offices of Anger	252
XVIII.	Rules for the Fighting Mood	259
	Index	269

ANGER: ITS RELIGIOUS
AND MORAL SIGNIFICANCE

ANGER: ITS RELIGIOUS AND MORAL SIGNIFICANCE

INTRODUCTION

THE NEW SIGNIFICANCE OF EMOTION

I

There was a time, and indeed not long ago, when the emotions seemed to have significance chiefly for the intellectual mischief they could do. It was seen that they could disturb the judgment, inclining its sensitive scale by a weight other than the weight of evidence, introducing affection and antipathy where only fact and principle should sway. The intelligence was conceived after the manner of those delicate instruments to be seen in the Bureau of Standards which are shut away and read by telescope through windows from a distance, lest the warmth of the living person should cause them to act untrue.

And instinct, which is all knit together with emotion has been distrusted, although from a different cause. Instinct has been regarded less as a disturber of reason, and more as a rival and substitute for reason, guiding the mind as by an intuition along ways not chosen by our understanding; where the intellect must wait for light, instinct drives on, guided by an independent sense, like birds that make their immense migrations from continent to continent, without chart or compass.

The lovers of intelligence therefore mistrust these strange elements of the mind, our instincts and emotions, discovering in them little but a brute inheritance, almost a dead hand of the past to hold us from what is distinctive of man, his life of reason. And shall we not all feel some spark of this jealous care for knowledge, ready to oppose those who prevent its free course? For there are many who are to-day content with vagary, content to be cut off from the main currents of thought, in part because of some strange arrest of curiosity but also because of some emotional check upon their power to observe, to think, to join in the age-long endeavor of science to see dispassionately into nature and the human mind.

This salutary enthusiasm for the intellect has been of unconscious influence upon psychology in the past. Its treatises and its experiments in the laboratory have dwelt tirelessly on the senses and the cognitive powers; these have been its first love. But in later years a change has come. Although the processes of knowledge have not been abandoned, a new and lively interest has awakened in our life of emotion and of will. An eagerness, almost a fever is to be observed in this new movement, like the rush to some point where gold has been discovered, until the remote spot becomes populous, with claims staked out for miles. The tests of intelligence, centering in Binet's work, with their incalculable range of application, together with the activity in the psychology of learning, mean that workers are bent upon holding the old field of cognition, opening new veins, using new methods. But the instincts, the emotions, invite us more and more.

There is promise here of discovering something of the original nature of men. The interest in our inborn powers is perennial. For generations it ruled the study of the intellect, with its inquiry whether we had innate ideas; and if so, what they were. Curiosity, largely satisfied or baffled in this long and subtle discussion, now turns with hope to the study of behavior, to the natural responses observed in children and animals and uncivilized men. It is peril for peril, in science. In the older days the philosopher took his own mind as the type and standard by which all minds were to be interpreted; the psychologist applied universally whatever stood in the forefront of his own consciousness. The intellectual interest, so powerful in the observer, made him see little but intellectual interests and devices wherever his eye might rest. To-day in the effort to correct his prepossession we have come to a careful study of rudimentary minds, where there is risk that our judgment be distorted in an opposite way, man being now conceived as made in the image not of pure reason but of the beast. But in this way we are attaining to a knowledge, never before had, of the driving forces of inheritance, of the impulses, of the passions of the human mind. When new corrections are made in the light of these, then our intelligence is seen not as a thing apart, moved solely by laws of consistency and evidence, but swept this way and that, by deep currents of longing and anger and fear.

The first fruits of this wider study of the mind are in the realm of morals. We are beginning to see the natural roots of virtue and of vice. There is less thought of profit and loss in this region, less calculation of pleasure and pain, than was the wont of some specialists to believe. Nor, as we now explore farther, does there seem to be a special moral faculty, whose sole function from the beginning is to speak for the right in conduct and against the wrong. Out of deep and primitive impulsions, themselves perhaps neither good nor bad, comes the emphatic attraction and repulsion of certain modes of conduct in ourselves, and the favor and disfavor with which our acts are viewed by others. The original impulsions, it is true, do not remain unchanged; they become of a different quality, and of a different direction as they are pressed upon by our critical attention, by the example of moral genius, and by the steady force of institutions. But into whatever form they are converted, here in these natural forces is their original spring and source. The voice of duty, of conscience, is now seen to be a natural voice that has learned a spiritual language, and its persuasiveness is in part due to the authority and eloquence of nature. It speaks in the name of native impulses and emotions. Vice, too, has the same springs; it is no more and no less natural than is virtue. Out of conduct back in the dim past have come these two great classes of action, the one desired and praised, the other repugnant to the spirit of the community. A knowledge of the source and of the later causes of change in these divergent emotional promptings must be of value to those who would guide the course. That the study of the emotions has this moral bearing gives to it weight, when it might otherwise seem vain and unmuscular.

Further, our native impulses and emotions no longer appear in their old relation to our thinking. They are not mere disturbers of the intellectual peace. It is now recognized that ideas do not have potency of themselves; they derive this from their emotional connections. The promptings of some hunger must favor them. Not until they receive such hidden support do they arouse us, either to antipathy or alarm if they seem threatening, or to advocacy if they appear full of promise, if they seem to lay foundations on which we can build and live. Our emotions we might almost say think for us. The genesis of delusions illustrates as in a morbid satire what is quietly at work even in the healthy mind. A man elated finds the world transformed by his own feelings: he sees only a favoring fortune, with all men well-disposed and admiring, his own poor qualities elevated into talent, so that wealth and fame are within his reach. But let his emotions move toward the opposite pole, let depression now come, then instead of his swelling prospect he sees only ruins; his friends, his family, conspire against him; they would have his property which seems already shrunken; perhaps someone plots to take his life; his powers are felt to be insufficient to meet the misfortunes which crowd in upon him on every side.

I do not mean that every idea we possess can be traced to some distinct emotion, for many of them come by tradition, by dull hearing of our companions' words, by listless watching of their acts and the world of things. But the ideas that lay hold of our will are of a different order; they must first seize the attention, and they do so because of some inner eagerness for them, something within us that answers to them, giving them value and vitality. Some ideas remain unreal, others are real, and the difference lies in the break or making of an electric circuit with our feelings. Attention is little more than a name for interest, and shades off into this region where things tingle and excite. I would not have it understood that emotion itself is intellect; all that I mean is, that the two are not separate faculties as once was thought; the walls are thin between, indeed there are no walls, there are only artificial lines for the purpose of study and exposition. Our emotions will have ideas in them if they have to make them; and an idea without a trace of ardor merely floats by like a bubble, it drives no machinery, it grinds no corn. It is true that we have dream-fancies,—of winged horses, headless giants and the like,—but we do not *believe* in them. They lack the poignancy which brings belief; they do not quicken the heart-beat, or if they do when we give ourselves to them in imaginative mood, this is a stirring only in some side waters, and not in the mind's main currents, not in the great system of interests that controls our voluntary muscles. Even the rules of logical consistency, which require that our ideas conform to one another and to fact, master us because we love such consistency, have indeed a passion for it. Without the buttress-strength of quiet emotion the whole intellectual structure would topple and fall.

II

But if it be now clear that in psychology there has come a great change in our attitude toward emotion, we shall at once wish to know who were the men that wrought the change, and in what way they went about their work.

And the first to be named would be Darwin, and the attempt which he made to trace in the animal's behavior some of the rudiments of the mental life of man. His work on *The Expression of the Emotions in Man and Animals* is the beginning of the present study of emotion; in which, by showing their importance for the life and maintenance of the creature, he gave energy to a part of psychology that was feeble and fit for death. Darwin watched with great care the physical expression of emotion and, after his usual wide gathering of facts, he proposed three principles to explain the confusing variety of these expressions. Some were to be explained as remnants of a form of action that once was of direct use to the animal or man: the clenching of the fist in anger, the unfleshing of the eye-tooth, the erect, stiff and aggressive posture of the whole frame in man, the rising hair along the dog's neck and back. Others were due to the fact that an emotion,—let it be friendliness or affection, which stands *in strong contrast* to anger,—would naturally make itself known *by signs opposite* to those of its opposing emotion; the friendly dog is accordingly unerect, relaxed, crouching, sinuous, his whole posture being the very opposite to all readiness for attack. Still other emotions express themselves by sheer undirected overflow of energy escaping through nervous channels out into action regardless of use,[1]—as when a child jumps up or down with joy.

[1] Darwin: *The Expression of the Emotions in Man and Animals,*— especially Chapters I, II, and III. His own terms for what I have

INTRODUCTION 7

More light has come from the first of these principles than from the others, from the principle that the human emotion utters itself in ways that once were actually needed to meet the crisis. For in those distant times the acts of which we now have only a vestige were carried out to the full; the tension of frame was followed by a spring, the clenched fist was used to strike, the unfleshed tooth was sunk in the enemy's flesh. This doctrine casts a steady light on the emotional expression and prepares us to see as never before into the emotions themselves, into the work they once performed and still perform in the mental and bodily life. All later studies are colored by this idea of the emotion's biological use.

The next great advance is due to William James, whose thought in this field was shared by the Danish scientist Lange. These two men independently and almost at the same time took up where Darwin had left it the study of emotional expression and gave it still farther meaning. James, as all know, would turn from north to south our naïve convictions on this subject, making the last first, and the first last. The emotional expression, in which he would include not the mere externals but the whole deep bodily response, is for him not the effect, but the cause of the emotion. Instead of conceiving that the emotion begins as a purely psychic excitement and then flows over into the body to cause there a commotion in face and limbs and blood and breathing, for James the whole current runs an opposite course: the storm breaks out in the body and thence sweeps over into the mind.

As in Darwin's work so here, one may say that the account is not throughout of equal power to convince. In the precise form in which it left James' hands it has not been generally received as truth. But a permanent

described so briefly above are: (a) "The principle of serviceable associated Habits;" (b) "The principle of Antithesis;" and (c) "The principle of actions due to the constitution of the Nervous System, independently from the first of the Will, and independently to a certain extent of Habit."

reshaping of our thought has come from this theory which he summed up in the famous paradox, that we are afraid because we run, we enjoy a joke because we laugh at it. No one believes this to the letter. Yet everyone feels that the emotion and what we still call the emotion's expression stand in a different relation each to the other from what was theirs in the account before James' day. They have become intimate, mingled; and with this, the bodily state has become significant, appearing of influence upon the mind. Darwin had shown the importance of the expression, by reason of its effect *outward and upon others,* rendering the creature more formidable perhaps or more attractive, and giving him an advantage over his competitors. James showed the importance of the expression, by reason of its effect *upon oneself.* The emotional storm sweeps back upon us from muscle, deepest organ, and skin and joint, invading the mind with sensations from the body's remotest parts. We may still hold that this invasion of organic sensations is not all that there is in emotion, nor does it distinguish one emotion from another; but without it our emotions would surely lack their present substance and depth. The sensory influx from the body is like the resonance given by a reverberating space behind a tuning fork, which makes the thin tone rich and full. If emotions occur that are purely cerebral and without origin in the lower depths of the body, it is perhaps because there is in the brain and ready to be reawakened the dormant traces of the repeated expression of the body's stress and storm.

Our next great advance in the knowledge of emotion is due to several physiologists, among the most important is Cannon. His work tends to restore the balance threatened by the work of James, and it confirms and supplements in unexpected ways Darwin's idea that the emotions add to our power to meet those critical moments when we face the dangerous and the gratifying things of life. Cannon discovered that in certain powerful emotions, notably in fear and rage, there is a strange and hidden process in the body, by which it is temporarily fortified to meet the threat to its welfare. An intricate bodily response in anger—into which I shall feel free to go in some detail because it is central to our theme—calls the bodily forces away from all work that is not of instant service, and rushes them to the front. The blood is summoned from the skin, where it is not needed; and there is pallor. Digestion is stopped because its results would not be available until perhaps hours hence, and after the battle had been lost or won; while with the increased volume of blood now surging back to the heart, the action of this organ upon which all depends is strengthened, a greater amount of oxygen is drawn into the lungs and thence into the blood. And for what farther purpose is this hurried preparation? That the muscles controlled by the will, and which are needed for the combat, may have the fullest measure of strength for their work; that they may have ample oxygen and other substances to supply their increased demand. But in the meantime the liver has been called upon to release sugar from its stores; and this, poured into the blood, is flushed through the muscles to give them added vigor, while the waste substance of the muscles, poisonous to them, is not allowed to remain, but is rushed away and discharged. And then, with a strange prudence, the blood is so changed that it becomes readier to clot than in times of calm, in order that if a wound is received there be less danger of serious bleeding.

In this process, a marvel of sudden coöperation of many distant organs, a chief rôle is played by a portion of the nervous system distinct from the brain and spinal cord, although connected with them. What is called the autonomic system—a double chain of ganglia running parallel to the spinal cord and not far from it—comes into play, and more particularly that portion of this autonomic system known as its sympathetic division.

Moreover a very important part is taken by a pair of small glands near the kidneys, the adrenal glands, the uncovering of the details of whose service is among the most brilliant of Cannon's findings. These adrenal glands pour into the blood a substance which Cannon calls *adrenin;* and this, carried to distant parts of the body, so influences the organs which we have just seen in action that the work begun by the sympathetic nerves is continued and enlarged.

This emotion of anger, then, which is hereafter to be so long in the forefront of our attention, is thus a psychic and bodily response in which we become stronger for the struggle; energy is suddenly transformed and made available for action; reserves are hurried into the trenches, and to what would otherwise have been the maximal effort a still greater strength is added and prolonged. It is a fascinating view which these and the earlier studies give us of the economy of the hostile emotions, how they not only externally render us more fit to bring dismay to our opponent, but within they secretly minister to our vital power, giving an impetus and an endurance to our effort, making us far less ready to fail.

But now let us pass from these studies of the bodily side of emotion to others that deal rather with its mental character and effect. These investigations, latest in our account, are not latest in occurrence, but extend through many decades, culminating in what has been revealed in recent years, particularly by students of what is morbid. From these studies there has come a new insight into the mind in health.

The conditions that have brought most light are not the insanities but those less sinister but still serious and disabling troubles known as the functional diseases, of which hysteria is a good example. All have heard of the work of Prince and of Sidis in America, of Tuke and Bramwell in England, of Charcot and Bernheim and

Janet in France, of Krafft-Ebing and Freud and Jung in the German-speaking lands. And in all investigations of these men and others, spread now the world over, it becomes ever clearer how livingly important are the emotions. The former contempt in which they were held now seems almost unbelievable, seeing them, as we do, at the very center of the mind's health and balance.

But before we go at length into their work let us have illustration of the cases with which these pathologists deal. Of Miss Beauchamp all have heard. Her early years had been distressed by a father without self-control and by a mother who did not love her, until in her later youth she was mentally and physically undone and wholly incapable of those things which her ability and education should have brought forth. At one time she would be over-sensitive and depressed; and then she would suddenly change into an animated and irresponsible creature that despised and hated her other self, and was ready to embarrass her in every way. And against both of these was a third self, yet knowing directly what neither had done or thought. Each of these three selves that in succession ruled her conduct had its separate aim, and a disposition and taste in contrast to the others', whether in food or dress or friendship. So her days were spent in monkey-and-parrot discord until under Prince's care she was finally restored to singleness of mind, becoming rid of the emotional excesses which had marked her partial selves.

Or to take a case less well known, a girl whose sister has married feels herself attracted to this sister's husband. The girl and her mother now leave home and while they are travelling a sudden summons reaches them to return home, with no full explanation given them of the cause of this request. On their arrival they find that the married sister is dead; and as the girl stands by the death-bed the thought flashes into her startled mind, "Now he will be free to marry me!" She instantly turns in horror

12 ANGER: ITS RELIGIOUS AND MORAL SIGNIFICANCE

from this idea, and becomes thereafter deeply sick. She forgets the distressing scene and her suppressed wish, and these are with difficulty discovered and brought to her recognition. But when this is fully done and the experience is lived over until it ceases to have any longer its deep emotional effect, the girl is restored to health. These may serve as examples of a new and curative achievement which is of an importance difficult to estimate for all who, whether as parent or physician or priest, are charged with the care of minds distressed.

In looking farther into these deep effects of emotion, let us picture some fierce engagement in which a man is buried by the explosion of a shell. His comrades unearth him still living and indeed without a wound. Yet, strange to say, from that time and for long he is unable to use his legs and has lost all power of speech; he is paralyzed and dumb. Or at some other part of the wide front a soldier sees with horror his boon companion blown into fragments while he himself is unscathed. But this man living and without a gash cannot control himself, he trembles violently, and further he is stricken blind.

There is no cut or break or bruise of the body of these men; they are wounded of mind. The experience of war has torn their emotions, setting their inner powers against one another. On this side fight patriotism, duty, self-respect, regard for the opinion of officers and men of the ranks, and of friends at home; our soldiers would bear themselves like men. Opposed to all this is the revulsion from the inhuman work, the filth, the stench, the ghastly protruding members, the horror of the killing, the horror of being slain. The mind unable to endure this inner warfare added to the outer, has without intention sought refuge in surrender. Without willing it, the man has found a torturing release by incapacity, by some form of nervous and mental collapse. The paralysis, the loss of speech, the blindness, the tremors are not simulated, they are real; the man is not a malingerer, he can in truth no longer do his soldier's work. Under the emotional stress and strain his mind has broken apart and into rebellion, and the one side stands there defiant of the other. And he can be cured only when this inner strife is quieted, when his impulses can be brought to some manner of harmony, when his will can assert itself again single and one.

Never have men in numbers had to endure, in pitiless fatigue, protracted and benumbing agony like that of the World War. When the war was upon us, and morale must be looked to at home and at the front, we shut our eyes to all but the dogged courage, the cheer, the inexhaustible humor of our men. But now we can face the facts which were not wholly thus. One of the stoutest hearts in all our service, an officer intelligent and devoted and sound to the very core, told me that his moment of supreme satisfaction came when a machine-gun brought him down and he knew that, for the time at least, he was out of the nightmare and could rest. Just back from France he picked up a book which happened to be lying near us, *The Glory of the Trenches,* and the very title offended him. He in his uniform bright with gold stripes for his foreign service and his wound pushed the volume away: "The trenches will never look that way to me," was all he said.

What has been called shell-shock, then, came from the moral insult of this hideous experience, and not from the physical concussion, which no earlier war had given. The war-neuroses were unknown, it is said, in the Boer War; they began to show their face in the war between Russia and Japan. In the World War they became truly ominous in their severity. Should another World War not be prevented by the outraged nations, exceeding as it will the late one as that out-topped all others, what will not be its emotional impact, its grinding and rending power upon the substance of human passion!

III

But if one is to recognize this new importance of impulse and emotion must he also accept the word of some of their students as to what are the ruling impulses and emotions in men? It is a matter of moment for all who hold fast to the interests of morals and of religion. For in the work of Freud and others there is a dark effect along with the enlightenment which their studies bring. There is the assumption, rather than the cautious inference from abundant fact, that man is driven only by his animal desires; that in anyone who seems to have high aims, the conscious purpose recognized by himself is only a veil drawn over his primitive lust and self-seeking, thrown before his eyes because he has become unwilling to look upon his own naked shame. Such an account comes more readily from those whose attention has long been fixed on the diseased forms of human emotion. And it is seized gratefully by those who find it a handy tool. It goes with the thought that progress in life generally is only by undiluted self-interest, by struggle, and by the domination of the strong,—a thought attractive to statesmen of blood and iron but which is perhaps less favored to-day than it was some years ago. The pain of war caused many to re-examine this grinning lie and to thrust it from them. But part of its wide brood is still with us, especially the thought that human emotion and human impulse are at core but animal desire.

There is just enough truth in this to give it credence and danger. For we have to admit a connection between man's mind and the mind of animals. And in our passions we find nothing that is not intimated in the impulses of the higher brutes. But it is to the honor of the human spirit that it cannot be content with its brute inheritance; it works upon these ancient things until it gives them another form. By selecting from among his animal passions, by encouraging here and repressing there, by patiently devising institutions—the family, for example, and the state and the church,—man has reshaped his crude endowment. He has turned defiantly upon the brute within him, using the better parts of this old nature against the worse, until the code of the jungle is elevated to that of the commonwealth. Yet even the animal is not so low as the man described by the Viennese school of philosophy. For the animal is not all selfishness and lust. There is in the higher beasts a strain of disinterested affection, of pugnacity for a few others of their kind, an activity of attention undriven by sex, an attachment to the mate and to kindred that has in it a tinge of companionableness in addition to whatever there may be of craving appetite. In the monkeys and in other higher animals the impulses and emotions of self-seeking are checked and supplemented by the impulses and emotions of friendliness and by a curiosity that plays beyond the limits of purely sensual desire. If these traits are in animals, we may perhaps be less skeptical of their existence in men. Indeed these are the traits which, reappearing in man, are used by him as a club to subdue his other passions. The error of the strictest sect of the Freudians is not that they find in us the emotional traits of animals, but that they fail to find in us all the animal traits there are. The beast has more range of emotion than they discover in man.

But the blind spot in Freud's own vision has been detected by many who have nevertheless been greatly in his debt. The Zürich school of psychoanalysts, led by Jung, see that our emotional life heads up in many streams besides that of sex. And the war has helped to correct Freud's error. For it was a part of his general view, that all the neuroses are erotic at their source. And this the war has openly disproved. It has shown that man is affected, and affected deeply, by more than one emotion. Shell-shock, that strange form of mental collapse already described, makes us know that a man may be sick not in love alone, the love of woman, but in that web of affections which run through the warrior, in the feelings stirred by self and friend and country, by the eyes of all observers. The doctrine then is absurd that would find in man but the one mastering emotion. Those who propose it are misled by their desire not to appraise human nature too high, and they fall on the other side. Their teaching is one of those intellectual adversities which challenge us to turn them to sweet use. Otherwise the effect is bitter and bewildering. The great aims of mankind then lose substance and solidity: what is real seems to lie no longer both before and behind and above, but only behind,—in fur and fang and claw. The rest appears to belong to the world of dreams.

Those who are concerned with morals and religion will therefore welcome the facts that correct this sordid picture, strengthening our confidence in the power of generosity, of good-will. And yet we need not overlook the tangled mass of self-interest that is there. Indeed it is there so unmistakable and not to be up-torn, that we may always expect to have with us those who can see nothing else. But however honest they be, their doctrine takes the heart out of moral effort. They are enemies of the good. From their direction comes no bugle call for the great advance. The erotic type of resistance to moral idealism is but the day's form of what is always found. In its more general character this resistance has to be met and corrected by all who believe in Darwin's great work. It will take many decades for us to adjust ourselves to his fresh perception of our animal antecedents, and not to draw from it a false inference. The crass realist in literature, in painting, in politics, in business, in psychotherapy, draws strength and comfort from this discovery in the natural history of the human mind. But there is in it a latent strength also for the lover of fine morals and of reverence; he may still press on with his work, helped now with new truth. Although his work may not primarily be to make or to unmake science, yet with all openmindedness he does well, I believe, to keep a high heart, confident that on second thought his own idealism is not made foolish.

IV

We have just seen that our emotions are varied and are of deepest effect. Shall we now press a step farther, to see something of what can be done to direct them into a right course? One might in this way hope for some lifting of that terrible weight of mental disease, which seems to become greater year by year. For when the mind is awry, when intelligence can no longer do its work, the seat of the trouble is amazingly often found to be here,—indeed some have gone so far as to declare that all mental disease has its seat and focus in the emotions.

Without assent to so extreme a doctrine, we may find ample evidence that from the emotions comes not only an access of strength to muscle and to will, but an added power to resist the invasion of disease. This is not to deny that some men and women need, not more, but less emotion, need most of all a psychic toughening, so that their nerves do not lie raw and exposed to every contact. Yet this is not for us all the one thing needed. We must see that more truly there are emotions which we cannot spare,—that all alike are not condemned.

For emotions are of two qualities, of opposite trend: those that invigorate, and those that sap our strength. The strengthening, the sthenic, emotions are those among which we find good-will, confidence, cheer. Among the emotions that weaken, that are asthenic, are anxiety, dismay, and lasting self-accusation. Homely wisdom, in agreement with psychology and the newer therapy, is

against this brood of gloom. A sage friend tells me of a
saying in her family, that it is idle to worry about whatever belongs to either of two groups,—first, the things
that cannot be helped, and second the things that can.
Physicians assure us that few persons break down from
work; they break from worry. And we might add that
comparatively few worry themselves sick over others; we
shall all be well when we are all sick in that wise. There
is in our worries an excessive, a morbid self-attention; the
natural and wholesome ratio of outward to inward interest has been lost. In spite of those who find the mind
ruled now and from all antiquity by self-regard, the facts
point originally to a great interest in an opposite way.
The attention, the interest, like the eye, normally looks
outward; it functions healthily if in the main it be kept
in that direction. In our American life especially we
shall be wise if we keep free the channels of strengthening
emotion. In the face of business anxiety and of minds
tense for success, we have not too much healthful recreation. What passes for recreation is often close to a goad
or an anodyne; it lacks hearty and lasting cheer. For
we must in the end look to the psychic cost of our refreshment. No pleasures are worth the having that leave a
great seeded field of discontent to choke the steady enjoyment of work and family and friends. And yet contentment need not be bovine; it always calls for some noble
dissatisfaction. This latter, then, is reorganizing, not
crippling, and without it there settles on the mind a
cankering discontent.

It is evident then that we are dealing with something
which touches our mental balance and clarity, and not
merely our body's health. The mind through its emotional tone affects the body, but it affects still more itself.
From mind there may come numberless physical ills, not
imaginary but real. And to the mind come ills, from
itself, and by way of the body. We are only at the beginning of our knowledge of these strange interlacings

of mind and body, and especially of the energizing power
which comes from the mind. The energies of men, which
James discussed in his Essay of so wide influence, are
locked or set free by the gates of our emotions. These
are able to release the mind's energy when they can
organize the mind and bring it to a free-moving unity.
Other emotions are disorganizing, and instead of releas-
ing energy they leave it bound. The release of energy
comes when great demands are emotionally recognized,
with whole-hearted surrender, the mind now facing its
purpose with an unwavering look. There now comes an
elation, intense or perhaps moderate, which knits the
mind together; while its opposite, a sense of depression,
unravels and destroys the mind's integrity. Miss Beauchamp, it will be remembered from Prince's report, was
less of a multiple person when her feelings moved to the
side of mild elation; she tended to break into fragments
of her true self when the emotional pendulum swung the
other way.

And to some extent this is true of normal minds. The
immoral passions work poisonously, not alone because
they bring evil fruit into the world about us, the world
of other men, but because they almost of necessity destroy
our own singleness of mind. The mind is at war with
itself, the central government is denied and can do nothing effective or of value until the rebellion is put down,
or else becomes so powerful that it can triumph and can
organize the mind after its own evil way. But the forces
of sympathy and of regard for the opinions of men are
so strong in all normal minds that nothing can be settled
until it is settled right. The mind usually can find no
rest so long as the generous impulses are baffled and suppressed. Not until these come to expression is there
peace and singleness and energy, bringing with them an
outlook cleared and a stout heart. Bitterness, envy, self-
seeking are sinister in their prime character, and their
secondary effect on the self is toward what is ruinous.

The emotional conflict which they commonly introduce in persons accustomed to the inspiring associations of our better communities brings not only their intrinsic moral loss, but often a loss of vigor in mind and body. Their opposites, generosity and a happy confidence, accord with the prudential hygiene of the mind. They are not merely their own reward; they increase the opportunity for our life to be compact and whole.

But in declaring the large office of the emotions, we must try not to exaggerate and conceal, after the manner of advocates. In the past there has been suspicion of the emotions; we must now see to it that in urging a more hospitable bearing toward them they do not alone seem of worth. For they must hold themselves in right relation to knowledge and the will. We must not be sentimental toward them, nor let them usurp the place of thought and stanch resolve. If we are tempted to see the powers of the mind in disproportion, we might recall the words of Marshal Joffre when asked to explain his method of bringing victory to the French. "How, then, did I win the war? I did it by smoking my pipe. I mean to say, in not getting excited, in reducing everything to its essential, in avoiding useless emotions, in concentrating all my strength on my job." He does not claim, however, that as he smoked his pipe he did more than rid himself of *useless* emotions. For there was an emotional impulse, he tells us, maintained throughout the years: "From the age of seventeen," he says, "I dreamed of revenge, after having seen the Germans at Metz."[1]

The emotions then are much, but not everything. There must be maintained in each of us a judge to look coldly on their promptings and to ply them with questions. But at times thought is sluggish, needing to be stung into action, and then is emotion's use clear. Or again, thought has completed its task, the plan is formed, the orders

[1] *New York Times*, January 20, 1920.

written out; and now all fails if there is no zeal, no eager soldiery to follow the orders into action. The emotions are there for work and for halting unsuited work; but they must not get out of hand, they must never be beyond reach of fresh orders from our thinking. They need supplement, although they themselves are needed, in turn, by the other powers of mind. Nothing avails if there be not some control, some directing of them to their proper work.

There will in time come a confidence that we can turn the emotions into right channels. At present we are beset with the idea that, while we may discipline the intellectual powers and through moral instruction may train the will, the emotions are an ungovernable crew; that we must go down to the grave with nearly the emotional constitution received at birth. But in time the emotions will not be thought merely an instrument on which artists play; they will be in the serious charge of all who guide childhood and youth, to be made of right pattern and consonant one with another, brought under a government of the noblest of their kind.

We are misled, as to what is possible, by the failure of a mere resolve to make an end of vanity or rage or dread. We look only to repression and do not come to understand even repression itself. All remember the eager young artist who would have the secret of Sir Joshua Reynolds' skill, asking with what he mixed his paints; and Sir Joshua's quick reply, "With brains, sir." To direct the emotions, will-power must be mingled with intelligence; we must know that the emotions are as subject to habit as are our hands or our ways of thought. If some emotions are to be subdued to others, it will not be by proclamation and a flourish of trumpets; there will be need of battle and guile. When frontal attacks fail, attacks will have to be made on flank and rear, with raids and a questioning of prisoners. Right habits displace bad ones only by steady pressure and a sleepless eye and by never knowing when you are beaten. It is well to know that one's resources here do not lie within the narrow confines of oneself. We can help to circumvent our crafty nature by a choice of companions, of books, and of what is offered on the stage, even on the screen. From children, too, one inhales something of the breath of youth, something of the emotional resplendence which lies between the weather-vane petulance of mere babyhood and the moody querulance of age. A habit of serenity, not neutral but tinged with cheer, must in due time seem as proper to the educated mind as is a stored memory or an attention well in hand. The men and women who have already something of this complete discipline are an earnest of what we may expect will become nearly universal.

V

Our emotions thus lie at a point where work is needed and where the work is full of hope. And whence may we expect the influences to come that will curb and spur these great powers and bring among them a right mastery? Help must come from many quarters. It must come from parents, from physicians, and from teachers, from each of us by himself. But besides, and working in and through all these, I know of no source from which we may be assured of more than from religion; and with this there is an added dignity to religion's service. It now lies with the directors of religion, in a more conscious way than hitherto, to give to the emotions a quality that is invigorating and restorative. It is possible to have a new reason for the confidence that religion has power to make the inner life free from disunion, and integral.

But one will recognize religion's power of an opposite character, its power to be not tonic but toxic, paralyzing,— bolting and sealing the gates through which comes energy.

Those days are happily passing,—in many communities indeed they are completely passed,—when to be religious is to surrender all peace of mind, to cultivate endless and gloomy introspection, to sit circled with dreads. Such a condition belongs to the sins of religion's past, of which it must repent but not too long, and then it must forget and press on with its work of binding up the broken spirit.

For it is in accord with our new studies of the mind that there can be no health for the person through and through until his purpose wins the respect and obedience of all his great impulsions. He is not whole until he finds an idea, a cause that ends his petty self-attention by setting before him something larger than himself, able to master his affections and quiet his misgiving. And this it is the very office of religion to give. Men cannot be content with making and selling, only to make and to sell still more. It is doubtless a great game, as men say; but there is a craving not for a game but for work, for a great objective that without gloss and hoodwink can hold our fealty. Men break down in business, women have nervous prostration in their fashionable living, because of some biting disappointment. Some reasonable hunger unfed consumes their hearts. Their disability is the protest of their souls; it expresses the moral indignity to which they are being subjected and of whose outline they themselves may be only dimly conscious.

Some it is true feel no indignity. They live on stolidly neither sick at heart nor mastered by a high purpose. They easily resist their own mild prompting toward excellence, and all urging from without. To these inert souls the community is not in debt. But at some time and somewhere, it would seem, the universe must crack their hard casings and either require of them pain and readjustment or else that they be cast aside. In a moral universe none can be kept who persists content with a work below his powers.

Such and all other persons are tested by religion. For can we not say that a right religion takes our life and offers to it a man's task? An employment that stands in a suitable relation to the great world which is now disclosed by religion is worth a man's will; all his powers consent and there is no inner revulsion, no revolt. Even failure is only temporary. For the books of the Ideal are never closed; there never comes the time when it is impossible to have some extension of credit. Perhaps at some new and more wisely selected point the man then gives himself afresh to the magnificent enterprise.

And were we to give this thought a local welcome, in what land might it be more heartily received than in America, where in the form of promise and of threat we are perhaps shown the coming spirit of our entire modern life. For there is with us an unwholesome self-importance which it is the very service of religion to correct, leaving a sound self-respect. The larger world to a religious man does not rotate about a particular city, and a particular person, himself. God is the axis of the universe, and not I. Something of the weight and friction, something of the motive power, rests with him. Democracy rightly enlarges the individual in his own eyes and others', but it must stop short of an inflation that comes to the bursting point. In America let a man be mentioned in the next county, and straightway he begins his autobiography. The Oriental mind feels repugnance toward such a display of self-appreciation. And it is the function of religion to lance this swelling which is morally and physically unsound.

In urging the value of the sthenic emotions, one must guard the truth on still another side. There is danger that the new doctrine appear in such guise that the character be not braced to meet the shocks of life. Can one declare that pain and depression are diminishers of

INTRODUCTION 25

strength and are to be supplanted by happiness, and yet give that high place to sorrow assigned it in the wisdom of the race? Are the uses of adversity sweet; does it, as Shakspeare says, really bear within its toad-like head a precious jewel? What of the current warning against fear, against anxiety?

These are for our hurt if they permeate the mind and continue to shadow all our thought and decision. Job lost his great wealth; his family life was broken; his health gave way. But he maintained his confidence that somewhere the apparent wrong could be justified, somewhere his questions could receive their answer; he would trust God even though God slew him. Health and prosperity then flowed back into his life. It is a poetic image of what was real with Sir Thomas More. He too knew loss of station, the loss of a King's favor shown for many years, and the loss of life itself. But he too had a saving confidence. "I thanke our Lord," said More, to his near relative, when at last he had made an unalterable decision to refuse obedience to the king and go willingly the way which led straight to the Tower and the block; "Sonne Roper, I thanke our Lord the feilde is wonne." [1] His misgiving, his inner conflict was ended; his soul was at peace. Adversity when accepted in this spirit, when met also as Socrates met it, knowing that he would be morally ruined should he accept his friends' offer and escape from prison and certain death, clear in his mind that happiness for him lay in accepting whatever pain and loss the laws ordained,—adversity met in this spirit is not weakening, not disintegrating, but gives strength.

We must not then catch at some new psychic rule and apply it pettily. The rule of thumb would proscribe disappointment as always weakening. But anxiety can be transient and can act like a tonic poison, like those threatening cultures of which physicians tell, that injected

[1] Roper's *Life of More*, in the edition of *The Utopia*, ed. Sampson, 1910, p. 253.

into the system increase the very power to down them. The uses of adversity are sweet or bitter, then, according as its emotions bring disruption or a stronger union. All situations that are depressing in their first intention bring a crisis; one's fortune is in some measure decided, and thereafter one finds himself rejoicing, as More, in his victory, or cast down by defeat. These asthenic emotions are for quick consumption, for immediate results, and not to poison the mind and body permanently. The biological function of pain and of the painful emotions is to deter; it comes when action should be checked, bringing us to a full stop, and then, if there be an adversary, at him in rage and with the strength of ten. If it does not pass over into this active phase the deposit of pain works as a poison. The primary check upon action comes to break off the old course, to give a moment for reconsideration; it prepares the way for a second phase, when we are goaded to fresh action in the light of this new view. But if the experience remains at its incomplete stage, adversity has paralyzed and impoverished; while if it passes on to its sthenic phase the mind is left the stronger. Thus the rich character is farther enriched even by outrageous fortune, while from the poor man is taken even the little that he had.

Thus our initial survey must come to its close, and not I hope without some deepening of the conviction that emotions bear upon life and conduct at every point. The man who would be a director of human purpose in himself or others must know the emotions and become an artist in their handling. To them one must turn who would find driving power. The mind needs both light and heat. But heat it is which gives energy, which takes sleepy substances and makes them awaken and unite or tear apart. Everywhere it hastens the slower processes of nature. In our mental life this then is the work of the emotions, creative and destructive. The man who holds of value either right action or right faith must look to them as the forces behind and entering into his suggestions for a sounder world. And for this reason one may have less hesitation in the attempt to trace the effect and promise of one of these emotions, and one that seems so forbidding, namely anger.

PART I

THE PLACE OF ANGER IN MORALS

CHAPTER I

THE BEGINNINGS OF ANGER

We have seen the distrust felt toward our emotions, and how these misgivings in a measure have been quieted by "finds" in many sciences,—in biology, physiology, and psychology. The emotions and instincts have in consequence come to be regarded as among the central forces of human character. More clearly than ever before, we now know that a man cannot be well of body or of spirit if his emotions be not disposed aright. Religion, whose concern is so clearly with these native energies, must in consequence see her own labor in a new light. A heightened dignity is given to all who bring government to our savage passions.

So much by way of preparation; and now we are to look narrowly to one of these impulsions, namely anger, that we may know something of its power in the moral life, keeping our eye as yet away from religion, save as morals are already of religion's flesh and blood. With the reader's consent we shall go for a moment perhaps farther than he would have chosen, to see the place of anger in the early and in the whole growth of mind. For only in this way can we know whether anger's hold upon us promises to tighten or relax.

And first it must become clear that to be angry is an accomplishment, and marks the uplands of mind rather than its plains. For the mind grows into anger and not out of it. This is clearly true at least for the stretches of life below the highest levels. For if we descend the path, down far into animal behavior, we come to regions where nothing properly angry is to be found. And yet anger's preparation is already there; below the beginnings of anger is effort, but effort without emotion, and it is from this emotionless soil that anger grows.

Anger then brings one nearer to the human plane. The incoming of a special psychic quality into effort has made this a shade less purely physical, has led it a step onward toward what is of the spirit.

This early and angerless stage can be noted in new-born animals. A litter of puppies that I recently watched from the time of their birth, if held from the mother on that first day, wriggled with energy and emitted miniature grunts. They struggled, but hardly within the threshold of anger. And a like fact can be seen early in human life. The unborn infant makes violent movements, perhaps in response to some unaccustomed pressure, while yet there can hardly be any psychic resentment or opposition. This action of the *unborn* is probably not very different from what Watson has noticed in the *new-born* babe if one restrains its free movements: then too it struggles against the barriers,—a response which, I have observed, is given also upon occasion by the sleeping child when older. That there exists a stage of angerless effort is suggested likewise by the strange experience of Thomas Hanna who, upon opening his eyes after a fall which rendered him for a time unconscious, struggled violently with those who attempted to restrain him but seems to have felt no anger, according to his own account.[1] His accident had swept his mind of the conscious contents of experience; he knew little of what was *meant;* his condition in this respect resembled that of a new-born babe.

This emotionless form of struggle some think they find in the combats of ants and bees, believing them to be without anger in its psychic sense, their apparently fierce contention being the response of their bodily mechanism wholly without the guidance and enforcement of mind, a view which reminds one of Descartes's denial of all

[1] Sidis and Goodhart: *Multiple Personality*, 1905, 107 ff.

mental life to animals. Yet even when limited to bees and ants the refusal to grant the existence of psychic passion seems unwarranted. For there is an intensity and a richness of expression and a plasticity in much of this insect fighting which makes it probable that the rudiments of psychic and not only physiological disturbance has entered into it. But as we descend still farther, the presence of anger becomes more doubtful—as one watches, for example, in sea-urchins and anemones, the sluggish retraction and closing against the enemy, their fastening upon what they would devour, their increase of hold, bringing the object at last within their body. Even less is anger evident in still lower life; until finally we reach levels where the structure and behavior, though still complex, seem to carry us beyond the horizon not only of emotion but of all mental life whatever.

In regarding anger, whether in the individual or in the race, as something *added* to struggle, entering after instinctive struggle and resistance are already established, one runs counter to such psychologists as James and McDougall. Each of these in his own way would have instinct and emotion tight-riveted together, regarding them indeed as but different aspects of a unit fact. According to these writers, anger cannot well be without the physical expression of attack and defense, nor any instinctive attack and defense without its counterpart emotion. But the evidence seems to point to a looser connection between anger and struggle, struggle having at its early stage the unpsychic, almost mechanical character found in a reflex act, although in other respects the two may differ, since struggle calls the whole body into action and is not so local as are most of the reflexes.

Struggle, then, as I see it, begins without the powerful reinforcement of anger; and when anger enters into it, the reaction is elevated from the plane of the sensory-motor responses, and becomes a more clear expression of mind because a more clear expression of purpose. There have entered into it vague suggestions of desire, organizing the entire mind and body, simple as these may be, into an active attitude toward the object, in a way not found in reflexes like winking or knee-jerk. Even as struggle marks a distinct advance over plant-like absorption and rejection, so pugnacity in which there is anger marks a distinct advance beyond mere struggle. Only by a metaphor can plants be said to struggle; only by a metaphor can the lowest minds be said to fight.

But there is no shadow of a doubt when we come to the higher vertebrates. These forms all display anger and true pugnacity. Such emotional impulses appear not only in the carnivores,—the lion, the cat, the dog,—but in the elephant, the horse, the cow, the man-like apes. The shyest of animals,—mice and rabbits and birds,—will under a suitable excitement turn fiercely on the threatener; their fighting blood is up.

It is doubtless because anger brings us to these higher levels, preparing the way for what is human and spiritual, that cold-blooded cruelty seems retrograde and more revolting than hot and angry violence. And I should include in cruelty not alone the production of suffering in order to enjoy it, but the causing of pain recklessly and because one is so bent upon his purpose that another's pain is to him as dust in the balance. The passionless eating of the living creature by a snake, as I have seen it in the Sierra Nevada, its methodical procedure to engulf even a toad, gives an indescribable chill to the act, which is not all due to our revulsion from the snake itself. And that a human being can calmly plan and thoughtfully complete an outrage on his fellows makes it far blacker than if done in rage. The shudder which the world felt at the German conduct in Belgium in 1914 was in a large measure due to the apparent coolness of its preparation; it was the more frightful because it was a passionless frightfulness. For this reason a community rightly imposes the severer judgment on crime done with a calm mind and not in anger. Many would hold that the milder punishment visited on the angry man is not because he is more a man, but because he is less a man; that his passion has lessened his responsibility and brought him nearer to the level of the insane. But this is a lawyer-like reflection, a learned after-thought, and does not explain the impulsive attitude of common humanity toward cold crime. The community may condemn and deplore the condition and act of the angry man, but in contrast to cold violence it seems more nearly normal and human, and less snake-like. And perhaps in a like way, as by some jealous lover of human reputation, we have had the humorous admonition, which Hocking has transmitted to us, "Never punish a child unless you are angry." In such a state the punishment may be less nicely fitted to the crime, but you and your child will in memory review the act more kindly.

Pugnacity, then, is a psychic possession, a weapon and protection which none of the higher creatures is asked by nature to forego. *Anger, we may say, is an achievement in mental progress. Its coming is preceded by an angerless existence, but when once it comes it is never permitted to disappear. The better kinds of animal life depend upon its powerful aid.*

CHAPTER II

PUBLIC USES OF PUGNACITY

Having thus seen anger and pugnacity established, let us now turn with an undivided mind to human life and observe the rôle which anger there plays, and first as it shows itself in war. Here we shall need to guard our judgment both from coldness and from heat.

I

Warfare is one of the great occasions of coöperative effort not only among civilized men but among savages. But it is false to say that war creates the coöperative spirit; it presupposes it and, by using it intensely, enlarges and deepens this power to work upon a common plan. For without the social impulse, without the coöperative spirit already there, wars could never be waged, an army could never be raised and drilled and disciplined to become an effective weapon.

But the picture of a world in which men were all indifferent to one another, all ignorant of what it means to work with other men, and having in warfare their first taste of a common enterprise,—this would befit the thinking of the eighteenth century rather than of the twentieth. Men in large numbers have never been so centrifugal. We know indeed that armies, both to threaten and to repel, are possible only where some form of union already exists, a union arising ultimately, as we shall see, from another source.

In this, one need not deny that a common object of hatred acts as a bond among men otherwise far opposed. The Irish in America, during the World War, clasped hands with Hindu and German from hate of England. But were such persons to succeed in their vain endeavor, they would view coldly or would turn and rend one another. The union that is to outlast these flashes of animosity, as a stable political structure must do, springs from a common liking, a common attraction. And still earlier, and behind the common attraction, there must be *mutual* attraction. Union from love of the same object is a later and higher form, which Dante and Swedenborg have celebrated as drawing men into a mystic fellowship.

One will the better detect the spirit of the community if he refuse to identify it with the mob or the crowd. To some persons, influenced by what is sometimes offered as the psychology of the crowd, all large bodies of men look alike; they are all "crowds," endlessly suggestible, fierce, cruel, led by the most savage and narrow of their number. But look half-sharply and this which is sometimes true of the mob, is by no means always true of the crowd and is not true at all of the community. A mob may be possessed by a frenzy of fear or anger. But not of necessity a crowd. This may be in holiday mood, contented, mildly well-disposed, cheery, ready to make way for the weak, ready to resist with gibes the self-assertive.

The community has deeper and more lasting bonds than either of these, coming neither from hot passion nor from mere good-nature, but from a recognition of mutual interests that endure, and from the giving and acceptance of tacit pledges. Such men have almost taken vows whereby they erect over themselves and their fellows various institutions to shelter them and their many interests. If we were to say that it is not wholly unlike marriage, this would mislead only as to the warmth and focus, but not as to the central quality, of its feeling. Instead of this, to some blind eyes the relation of the criminal to the community is the type of all wide association; they see the whole to rest on fear and avarice and smothered resentment. But no community, no state, has lived or ever can live in this damp atmosphere. The compulsion of the relatively few who may have such feelings requires the free coöperation of many others, held together by some degree of mutual respect and comradeship,—as war requires some bond with one's fellow-warriors, added to whatever hate may be directed toward the enemy.

While war is being waged, hate may far exceed the forces of attraction, but not in the life of the community, year-in, year-out. The generosities of the family, however weakened by extension, now suffuse one's fellows, and are suggested and given emblems by the simple courtesies which most men grant and expect.

But once a community has arisen, then war can take the weak cohesion and make it strong. This is not wholly because war brings the strong man into office and gives him uncommon powers. Rather it is because war is an absorbing enterprise even for men not in office. It appeals to the huntsman and the adventurer and the avenger that exists in each of us. A single object now towers there for all men to fix their minds upon, while private and divisive interests shrink and disappear. And from some practice in the common work of war, there is begun and carried forward a habit of united effort which lasts, though weakened, into the brief intervals of peace. The group becomes welded, becomes definite and forceful, by reason of facing its enemies.

In time, however, this defining force of an outward enmity breaks through its own barriers into still wider forms of coöperation, and in more than a single way. By conquest the foe may be incorporated with the conqueror into a larger union. Started by compulsion, the union may grow into something vital by the quiet force of habit and consent. And this union is farther strengthened by participation in still larger wars.

But apart from conquest, one finds even among savages that the promise or the threat of war is an occasion not wholly for tightening the line about the tribe and excluding rigorously all who do not at once give proof of friendship. It is also an occasion for extending the circle of one's friends. The tribe becomes of a sudden all alive to the need of wider friendship; it seeks alliances with neighbors who before were neglected or despised or even hated; and if alliance is refused, they seek at least their neutrality.[1] The Great War illustrated on a stupendous scale what has been a custom from savage times. The German, expecting war, was in league with Austria and with Italy. This menace, which drew into the circle of its influence both Turk and Bulgar, made France look far across with wistful eye to Russia, and both of these to England. And when the war actually burst forth, even more distant nations suddenly became objects of tender regard which peace-times never knew. The Germans who had fairly spat upon us in Manila Bay and who had thought of us only as dollar-chasers, inventors of washing-machines, discovered us to be their brothers, fellow-worshippers of the Ideal, joined by the ties which ran through Goethe and Von Steuben. In his distress the German loved the Dutch, the Swede, the Spaniard, the Mexican, the South American, whoever and whatever of the world was not in oath against him. Under the stimulus of war he became for a brief moment of an international mind; he saw and repented that he had lived to himself and had made no lasting friends. And in a less degree the same was true of France and England, who now sought earnestly the good-will of others. Between us and England blood became thicker than the Revolutionary War; between us and France, the Revolutionary War became thicker than blood. And

[1] Cf. e.g., Waitz, *Anthropologie*, III, 152, VI, 664.

when we finally entered the war, not only their sympathy with us, but our sympathy with our comrades in arms knew no bounds. All the virtues were in them, all the vices were in our enemy.

Although these emotional reversals of judgment will lend themselves readily to satire, yet out of them comes a permanently widened attachment. It will hereafter be more difficult to trample on the interests of others, less difficult to enter with them into some large undertaking. Before the war, a leaguing of many nations, not to wage war but to prevent war, would have exceeded the imagining of any foreign office from China to Peru; to-day it is at least a possibility in every one of them; it has come within the sphere of practical politics. With all its bitterness, all its disintegration, with all its power to kindle as well as quench the wild-fire of international hate, the World War was an unequalled spur to organization, to a breadth of joint enterprise which before had a place only in the world of dreams. And after this fashion war has worked even from the dimmest past. Out of the eater comes forth meat.

But we must not think of this enlargement of organization as the only salvage from its horrid waste. Beside war's discipline in habits of coöperation, we must see its power to stimulate a conscious valuing. For the two are not the same: a man may have a habit of thrusting his hands into his trousers' pockets, and yet take no delight in the act. But what one fights for he usually values, and values more emotionally than before the fight. War in defense of the tribe and of the tribal lands and of tribal rights raises these in the eyes of the tribesman. Patriotism urges us to war, but in its turn it is intensified by war. The graves of their ancestors for which our American Indians fought became more endeared by the struggle. And not the mere ancestry but the great examples of conduct which ancestry usually offers thus become the more prized. The very war-honors of the individual brave, so coveted, so celebrated among our Indians after a war, have hastened that great movement of personal self-respect and of respect in the eyes of others. The qualities of character which the community can best use have thus through war come to a readier recognition. Not only has the ruler been so often forced into war that by prudence he had, in the past, come to train himself for war; but in war the qualities of leadership have been discovered and then applied, amid great praise, to civil life.

But one can hardly catalogue our debts to organized pugnacity without speaking of its selective power. McDougall has given much that is of value,[1] and that agrees with the judgment of others on this topic. I should doubt, however, that war is the prime, still less the sole, selector among rival tribes and peoples, the eliminator of the unfit. It is true that war has upon occasion worked for elimination, since we find victors who destroyed their vanquished, root and branch.[2] But this is by no means the invariable, indeed it is hardly the common, course. Often the conflict has brought weakening to both sides, only a little less to the victors than to the vanquished; and there follows some kind of accommodation of each to the other. Often the conquered are made dependent on the conquerors, and continue to live. If the victors' sway is extended to cover them completely, what is lost is their old governmental life, their independence, and far less their physical life. It is especially clear that the stocks which people the different parts of the world to-day differ vastly in strength of war. The African stocks still persist in teeming numbers in spite of their military inferiority to the Caucasian, and of their great differences in fighting ability among themselves.

[1] *Introduction to Social Psychology*, 1914, Ch. XI.
[2] Cf., e.g., Ellis: *Polynesian Researches*, I, 304; II, 57; Waitz: *Anthropologie*, VI, 151, 435; Fletcher: *Bulletin 30, Bureau Amer. Ethnol.*, 1910, 914 f.

And where warfare has been least checked; indeed where it has been well-nigh perpetual; where, accordingly, its selective power has had freest play and should (if war-selection is the prime factor in progress) come to ripest fruitage—as in aboriginal America, in the Philippines before the coming of the Spaniard, and in the islands of the South Pacific—we do not find stocks that surpass all others in the world. Too much talent and energy have gone into war, and too little into the great arts of peace and especially of accommodation and political organization which are the basis of effective defense. Where war is the main and more immediate interest, it prevents the rise of strong government, and leaves an enfeebled and disintegrated population. But where it works less destructively it is not so much the eliminator of weak peoples as of weak governments, leaving the mass of the conquered people, especially the women, to come into the new order and thrive.

While then we must give a place to the selective power of war, we must not magnify war's office. Otherwise we shall be contradicted by the history of the Jews, and of the Chinese. These peoples of venerable civilization, still in the green leaf of their physical and family life and institutions, have from of old been harried by more warlike neighbors. If war be the great eliminator of the weak, one could from these great stocks almost prove the thesis that it is the victor who is always weak. The Jew conquered by every new-comer still lives and thrives, while Egyptian and Persian, Assyrian and Roman, weaken and die. These victorious Semites have renounced the pride of political success, yielding in this and unyielding in all else. The old fable might have been written with them in mind, of the reed unharmed while the oak is uprooted by the storm.

There are, then, other elements than pugnacity that maintain races. Peoples live on because not only of the power to wage war, but of the power to resist disease, the power to adapt their mental and physical life to adversities of many kinds, to be constant in loyalty especially to the great institution of the family, and not to be so dazzled by the idea of wide political sway, that they are ready to sacrifice the substance of life for this relatively empty thing. Disease and infertility and a failing interest in social institutions therefore are also great eliminators, for these bring death to the tribe and to the nation. Death by violence is more dramatic, and tempts the imagination to the belief that it is the only way in which peoples die. But under scrutiny war is seen to be but one among many forces to select and to eliminate. Indeed when weakness in war is followed by death, the war-failure is usually but the symptom of a deeper sickness that would later have brought death of itself, without war.

War then is a special display of pugnacity offering itself chiefly to the support of one particular institution, that of government, and to whatever a government may have at heart—self-preservation, or plunder, or the aggrandizement of some man or family. *Thus anger, by taking the systematic and coöperative form of warfare, has been of great assistance in uniting men into large political bodies. It has been a prime means of selecting, not so much from among rival human stocks or lesser groups as from among rival political organizations. And it has enlivened men's appreciation of the qualities valued by the state.*

II

Leaving for a while this special and military form in which anger clothes itself, let us look to the service which anger and pugnacity render to the interests that are not political. For these, too, will be found to make what use they can of jealousy and angry retaliation and settled hate.

44   ANGER: ITS RELIGIOUS AND MORAL SIGNIFICANCE

And first of the family, which is the germ and for a time almost the sum of the social life. Like the state, it has been an anger-using and an anger-breeding organization. But here again one must, I believe, take issue with those who put pugnacity at the very center and foundation of the ancient family life. McDougall,[1] for example, adopts "provisionally" the picture of primitive society in which overt and actual fighting decides who shall marry and who shall not. According to the outline which he presents, this early society consisted of a polygamous family at whose head was a patriarch who would permit no one of the male offspring of his many wives to enjoy wedlock until there arose one of them who could conquer the head of the house, and victorious take his place. There was thus selected in each generation and to be father to the next, the one who could excel his fellows in love-energy, in prudence, and, above all, in fighting power. The fighter alone marries, and only by his fighting can he transmit his character to his children.[2]

The picture would be more impressive were it probably true. For unless the prime importance of fighting, in the

[1] *Introduction to Social Psychology*, 1914, 282 ff.

[2] The picture which McDougall gives is presented by him as the work of Atkinson and Lang in "The Primal Law." His reproduction differs from their original, however, in a very important respect. In "The Primal Law," instead of some *one young male* conquering and supplanting his father and ruling in his stead, as McDougall would have it, the father is conquered and deposed by the combined and repeated attacks of the *young males together*, whereupon the original group is soon broken up, each male survivor of the conflict taking away with him a part and "relapsing into lonely sovereignty" (Andrew Lang: *Social Origins;* Atkinson: *Primal Law*, 1903, 219 ff., esp. p. 221).

This difference is important because in Atkinson's account virtually *all* the males marry and there is no such rigorous selection of the one chief fighter to be the father of the next generation. Fighting here plays an important part, but there is no attempt to limit paternity to the one of the many brothers who could conquer all his own kin. Nor with Darwin, who likewise gives an important place to male jealousy and combat, is there an exclusion of the other brothers from marriage. (See *The Descent of Man*, 2nd ed., 1888, II, 395.)

selective process, is surrendered, there is no provision for the marriage of more than one of the many male children of this large family society. It does not provide for the establishment of new families. We may, before evidence, well doubt that a large group of lusty young men could in a primitive life be permanently bound in their most insistent impulse, first by the father and then by the successful one of their own number, all his brothers upon his success consenting to remain forever celibates. And against it is the evidence of fact. For as more is known of the least advanced forms of human life, such as is found among the Negritos of the Philippines and Central Asia, the Semangs and Senoi of the Malay Peninsula, and the Veddahs of Ceylon, society is found to rest not on polygamy but on monogamy.[1] The possession of many wives appears to be a departure from the early and dominant custom. If we are to draw our picture from evidence like this, it means that there will in any early normal community be almost as many marriages as there are pairs of men and women. There will not be a battle with one's aged father as the only door to wedlock. Fighting then ceases to be the sole selector of the few who will enter married life.

But this does not mean the elimination of anger as a bulwark and weapon of the family. The family, when once it has been founded by some attachment stronger than all mutual repulsion, presents an unbroken front to others, to resent wrong to its members, or even to support their unjust claims. Without the jealousy of the husband toward the wife, with its quality of vigilant anger, marriage could hardly have had the strength to maintain itself in the face of all its threateners. Among the Veddahs in the jungle of Ceylon, already mentioned as having a primitive life of monogamy, the man will kill from ambush any who menaces his marriage right. And we know that in due time jealousy and revenge are found

[1] Wundt: *Elements of Folk Psychology*, Eng. tr., 1916, 48 f.

also in the wife. Lacking the degree of physical strength and of self-assertion which marks the male, the women have shown their resentment not precisely after his manner. Because of the general mobility of their mind and especially of their emotion when the interest of the child is menaced, it seems probable that jealous anger with them too has strengthened the family tie.

And so it has been with the family when menaced in other ways than these which excite love-jealousy. Its solidarity has grown by angry rivalry with other families, ready to repel any encroachments upon its property or prestige,—a manner of action represented by those incessant feuds in the Italian cities, when the Orsini, for example, fought the Colonnesi;[1] and not unknown more lately in our Southern States.

Marriage, then, is not created and sustained primarily by mutual pugnacity. Except in the realm of humor, this is not the basis of marital bliss. The family exists because of a common affection, a common love, even though this love be reduced to its simplest terms. But once in existence, the family discovers both its capacity and its need for a united hatred toward some definite external point of threat. And this common passion and the common effort into which it flows is able to give an almost unbreakable strength to the family bond.

Imagine that, upon menace to wife or child or brother, fear had been the great and sole emotion, and never anger. The strengthened organization which now comes from a common defense or a common onslaught would have had in its stead a disintegration with fatal consequence. But an *initial and passing* fear is useful and leads to heightened anger; fear is a good prelude, but bad as a dominant theme. Enmity kept the outline sharp between families or tribes; it prevented intermingling and cankerous disorganization eating from edge to center. A mutual at-

[1] Machiavelli: *The Prince*, Ch. VII.

traction, then, creates the communal life; but its creative power is augmented by a common hate.

But besides the family, commerce has had the support of the pugnacious impulse. Marco Polo and his fellows on the trade-route from Europe to the Orient had to fight the Tartar. The solitary trader, the group of traders, the caravan, the rich merchantman on pirate-infested seas, the mediaeval guilds, the great commercial companies in India and early America, have asserted themselves vehemently against their enemies. If, in our day, trade of itself is less given to physical violence,—although in the eyes of many it has, in union with governments, been a prime mover toward war,—there is still in it ample suspicion, jealousy, anger, hate, perhaps a little less deep because checked in its outward expression of bodily assault. Open killing has in wide regions within the state yielded to competition, but the old passions still drive. And this will still be true even when hot competition is tempered into emulation. Under it, although covered and concealed with appreciation and some generous sympathy with the rival, there will be the motive force of the old pugnacious instinct as still found in friendly-contentious games.

This impulse, further, has helped to create and maintain the distinction of class and class. Whatever of help and of harm has lain in class solidarity, this we owe in part to the group-consciousness heightened by the passion that goes with attack and defense. Anger has been in the age-old struggle between plebeian and aristocrat, between those who hold and enjoy and those who suffer social privilege. It is found in India, where an outraged emotion has helped to keep sharp the distinctions of caste; even as in our southern states animosity is always smouldering, when not ablaze, between white and black. It bound together the militarists of Germany who resented the growing power of the Social Democrats, even as these roundly cursed the swaggering *Offizier*. It supports the rich manufacturer fattening behind our tariff walls, who with difficulty restrains his indignation toward one who would so much as question the justice of his system. And while the bitterness with which laborers and employers face each other is not the sole emotion in their clash, yet without it the clash would surely weaken and wane. Those who find in our modern life little pugnacity, who find that rage is no longer of any advantage to civilized man, as does Warren,[1] must regard in a mysterious way these and all the other active displays of the contentious spirit.

In a like manner the religious interests of the community—the manner of worship, the priesthood, the sacred precincts, the integrity of the membership—have angrily been defended, and angrily men have urged forward their claims. But anger has been steadily active in no interest, not even that of war, as it has been for elemental morals. The passionate anger directed against cheating and theft and murder, for example, is perhaps impossible to separate wholly from the interest in the family and the class and the state, but it finally loosens its close connection with these allies, and becomes more general, becomes a demand,—indeed an indignant demand,—that each shall render a certain simple due, a certain right to every man regardless of his special family or group-connection. Law reflects this interest in conduct widened beyond the special confines which had earlier held it in; and this interest would have been well-nigh powerless if it had not had anger at its right hand. Impartial justice, holding the scales, holds also the sword of wrath. Law and court and police are thus the creature, in part at least, of the resentment felt at first in one's own behalf and in behalf of one's children and brothers and parents, but at last becoming free from these limits

[1] *Human Psychology*, 1919, 104.

and ready to arise at sight of injury to the plain man though a stranger.

Anger it must now be clear is not a purely negative, a destructive, energy. It joins in the great work of upbuilding. *Apart from war, which faces usually outward and is political, we owe much of our social life within the state to indignation, resentment, jealousy, and revenge.* These have come to the help of the family and commerce and class and the institutions of law. They have been strength and defense to the whole fabric of rights and duties. The moral and social service of anger has thus to be acknowledged.

CHAPTER III

ANGER IN CONSCIENCE

The benefits of anger will not all have been recounted unless we now look more intently to the individual life. Anger we have seen in the public support of rights, coming also to the support of the great institutions by which rights are given their form and are encouraged. But the moral course of this passion takes also a direction less outward, my anger now aimed not to compel my neighbor or my enemy but to compel myself, urging me to fulfill what is another's due and right. In this we shall see hostility in the unfolding of conscience, without which there is no flowering of the moral life.

I

But let us first look to the facts, asking whether there is anger turned inward, anger against oneself. For unless we find it clear and fairly common, we shall hardly expect it to play a part in moral self-control.

In questioning healthy-minded students, it is surprising to find how often they experience some form or degree of impatience with themselves. Indeed the evidence seems to indicate that, instead of being the exception, it is the rule. The emotion here felt has many shades. It may move toward a purely intellectual disapproval; or in a different direction, it may pass into an unangry, while yet emotional, chagrin or depression at one's shortcomings—one is disappointed, discouraged with oneself. But somewhere between these comes an emotion certainly of anger, of which the following may serve as illustrations— illustrations which move, without order, between grave and gay, between the trivial and the important. "I often find myself very angry with myself," says one of my witnesses. "This anger seems to spring from various causes. There is a quick rush of angry feeling whenever I become aware of the fact that I have made a social error of some sort. For instance, if in a gathering I forget to introduce one who should be introduced, then on realizing the omission I feel embarrassed; but more than that, I am angry with myself."

"I was angry at myself the other day," writes another, an alien trying to accommodate himself to our country from a tropic isle, "because I broke a window while playing tennis. I was indignant at myself because I acted very poorly at a certain meeting; people there laughed at me for having been so ridiculous. I was indignant at myself because I was almost run over by a street car. I was very reckless and stumbled in front of a passing car."

"I have felt thoroughly angry with myself," still another tells me, "for an act of impoliteness, or the accidental dropping of a fork to the floor in a public dining-room; I have experienced the same emotion when I realized that I had done something of which my family or my church would not approve; and I have felt anger because I had not attained to a certain moral standard which I had set for myself." And another experiences the intensest moments of anger toward himself when on seeing some beautiful woman he thinks evil of her. He knows the wrong of it, and yet feels unable to prevent the malicious thought. Whereupon he turns upon himself in indignation.

Our final instance will be the following, which is clear and full: "My first recollection of an incident of self-directed anger was when I was about fourteen years old. I had got into the habit of telling falsehoods about all sorts of little things. For quite a while my parents had

urged and persuaded and punished me for this fault, and
I had begun to realize that it was a fault that must be
eradicated. I had tried to be very careful not to permit
myself to lie. Unfortunately the habit had become very
strong.

"I remember this incident especially. Something came
up and Mother asked me if I had done it. Involuntarily,
and not from fear of punishment, I said that I had not,
though in fact I had. Mother said nothing further, and
for all I ever knew she believed me. I sat down and began
to feel uncomfortable. I went outside and down the
ravine to the place where I usually made my headquarters
in play. At first as I remember, the feeling was of re-
morse. Then I seemed to see myself telling a falsehood
to my Mother. I became intensely angry and remained
so for a long time. The anger of that time made such
an impression that always now when I do something
that is not in accord with my moral ideas I clearly see
this picture, especially if I become angry with myself."

The occasions of self-enmity thus extend from airiest
trifles, through lapses from intelligence, into a region
clearly moral, where one is aware of wasted opportunity,
of neglect to help another in his need, of having with
haste or deliberation caused him pain, and on until we
include the gravest violations of one's principles of right.
This range, and the resemblance of behavior as we pass
to what is moral from what clearly is not, will, I believe,
be found important when conscience itself is well in
view.

*Among the many kinds of emotion directed selfward,
there is, accordingly, no lack of indignation against oneself, although persons differ in their readiness to be
aroused after this manner.* Over against those apt to
lose patience with themselves are those whose patience
is inexhaustible. The impulse to find another than myself responsible for every ill wind that blows, with many
is checked and with some seems absent. Such persons

may be toward themselves stern, if not despairing; while toward others they are of unfailing charity. It amounts almost to a contrast of temperament rather than of training,—the self-condemnatory persons set off against those given to self-praise.

II

But with this glimpse convincing us of the reality of anger turned against oneself, we should next perhaps look to its beginnings and its growth. There we shall find, I believe, that it is not an original mode of the mind's behavior, but is derived, coming secondary to anger with an outward look.

For the two great emotions that are of such contrast in their intrinsic quality,—namely love and anger,—are also opposite in their direction of movement as they enlarge the field of their objects: love at first having its objects near by, in parent, mate and child and self, and from these moves outward to those less close of kin and to neighbor and distant friends; while anger and hate are readiest toward those we fear, men little known and afar, and from them passes inward toward the center. And although anger does flash early against parent and brother and playmate, it approaches the self only with leaden feet. For in the life of the savage, self-appreciation and its connected confidence are of high value; his struggle for food and mate and shelter brings less need of cold attention to himself, with condemnation. Later comes the opportunity and need of scrutiny and check of one's own impulsions.[1]

Indeed in the earlier forms of mind there is little of self-review either before or after action. There is no

[1] In making self-review, and especially moral self-review, come later than an active attitude toward others' acts, the position here agrees with that of Westermarck: *Origin and Development of Moral Ideas*, 1906, I, 123, where conscience is not the original form of the moral consciousness.

pause before the deed's launching; it runs smoking down the ways without care whether wind and tide are right. Animals, children, savages, the undisciplined and irresponsible, and all of us when dealing with things of little moment, act in this unreflective way.

But even while this impulsive conduct continues we are beginning to gather memories of our own and others' anger which serve as material for the imagination to apply to our own anticipated acts, and make for a wider economy. We are thus enabled to experience before the fact, and without the hurt or the wasted effort to protect us against the hurt, the passion which others would feel were our purpose to be fulfilled. We are beginning to have emotions, also, in which one is intensely and painfully aware of himself,—when we are bashful or ashamed, for example,—and these may mingle with other emotions, with some tinge of anger or sympathy as I catch sight of myself in mid-career of action.

But now, with growing complexity of mind, there comes conflict and hesitation, and in any act that is not mere humdrum and habit there is a moment of review, when I and my conduct are seen in something of the detachment with which I appraise another's deed. Often this appraisal is made before the fact; the fiat is for an instant censored before it is allowed to pass into overt act. But again, and particularly with impulsive conduct, the examination cannot occur till later, like as we sit in judgment upon a general's order after the battle has long been lost or won. Yet whether the appraisal be before or after the fact, one comes in some degree to feel toward oneself the emotions prepared for others. In so far as anger or admiration or sympathy would be our response to a like act by another, so do we feel, even though in mildest strength, toward ourselves and our own act.

This of course does not mean that in time the current of emotion may not flow the more vigorously outward because of its temporary reflection toward the self. The angry regard of fault, sensitized by the inward look, may now be readier than before to detect and hate the fault of others. I emotionally appraise their conduct by what I have come to expect of myself, even as earlier I had adjudged my conduct by what I had demanded of them. The commerce thus comes in time to be in both directions and to be increasing.

But beside its late coming, we recognize, without wonder, that most of us remain to the end far more awake to others' than to our own shortcoming. Even those we love—our parents, our wives, our children, for example—do not escape our irate glance. What a changed world it would be, and not clearly for the better, if our own faults irritated us beyond measure, arousing our contempt and hostility as no others' could! Instead we find ourselves in triple bronze of self-appreciation,—though with a few open joints, or a heel uncovered. Indeed with all our protective passions joined with the self-assertive, it may well surprise us that we ever come to any degree of detachment and self-rebuke. This when attained may well be counted a great achievement of our inner life.

Anger toward oneself is therefore not an original experience: the individual does not begin by condemning in himself the deed which later he comes to abhor and resent in others. There must first be the anger toward the deed when done by another. We are natively of outward and not of inward interest, conscious of externals and of their irritation, menace, or delight. *And so our emotions and especially our hostile emotions are never at first aimed inward. Anger against others is the schoolmaster that brings us to anger against ourselves, only to lead us back with a more sensitive indignation again outward;* even as the love for parent and brother prepares us to extend these affections to a wider zone, from which they come home again enriched.

III

Now does this anger aimed at the self for its misdeeds, and having a source and varied history here but suggested, help toward an understanding of the inner life of morals?

There can hardly be doubt, I believe, of the light it brings. With its aid we may trace in new security that progress by which our morals cease to be an external constraint and become spontaneous, now urged from within by conscience.

It had been my own habit to think of conscience as a voice approving or condemning, condemning sternly or in fear or sorrow, but hardly if at all in wrath. Yet the evidence already offered has convinced me of mistake.[1]

The emotions that arise in moral self-review are not the same with all persons; not all feel anger, and some who feel anger at one kind of misstep may feel some different emotion at another. A friend tells me that she becomes enraged at herself for some stupid act, but for an act morally wrong she feels sorrow, rather, or regret, a chastened condemnation.

But with others the indignation is alive for moral things. Yet, as we have already seen, it seems never to be confined to morals. Anger when it is aroused against oneself is ready to support whatever interest is at the moment upmost; it freely enters or leaves the moral sphere. The examples earlier offered show that self-hostility is not reserved for moral transgression nor excluded from this type of offense.

---

[1] A similar error is long standing and seemingly of good repute. Bain, for example (*Emotions and Will*, 4th ed., 1899, pp. 285 ff.), speaks repeatedly of the *fear*, the *dread* of others' condemnation or punishment, a fear modified in time by love of others, as though these feelings alone were at the emotional core of conscience. He appears to have slighted the indignation, the anger, which one feels not toward another but toward oneself.

This indicates, I believe, that the powers within, which become conscience, are at first untroubled by the divisions we later make from an interest in morals. In our psychic nature, the offenses in our own conduct which upon later reflection and with farther discipline strike us as belonging to a class apart and as violating a peculiarly sacred principle, that of duty, are in their earlier occurrence irregularly commingled with those that lack all moral hue.

Or, to see the same fact from a slightly different point, the moral offenses do not appear to select and strike upon some special organ of the soul that is untouched by the shortcomings indifferent to morals. The same general psychic organization—intricately wrought of activities which we group under senses, intellect, emotion, and will—operates in all cases. What is alive in me to some display of my ignorance or bad taste must, in a broad way, also be depended on to awaken at my failure to give to another his due. The difference is mainly in the situations, in the objects, rather than in the powers or organs of notice and response,—even as the shocking contrasts of noise as well as the slight variations of harmony are reported by one and the same ear.

But the difference within us must not be slighted. The moral interest is not identical with the interest, for example, which supports avarice or makes us preen ourselves in vanity. When my anger is aroused because I have violated the well-ordered suggestions of friendliness, the total action of my mind is not the same as when my anger flares at some failure of mine in self-display. In both cases there is employed the same mechanism of self-observation, self-criticism, and of selfward anger and striving; but the motive, the dominant interest and something of the emotional reverberation from this source in the two cases is greatly different. Conscience[1] then is

---

[1] Those familiar with the variety of meanings attached to the word "conscience" by moralists during centuries of discussion—see, e.g., W. G. Sorley in Baldwin's *Dictionary of Philosophy and Psychology*,

not to be wholly merged with the other forms of self-review and self-sanction, nor is it to be wholly set apart from them.

Such a view of conscience, in which anger and other emotions are seen to be at work, leads us away from a prejudice held by some that this great power is purely of the intellect, busied only with the application of moral ideas. The emotional strain in the earlier moral responses will be recognized though we remain convinced that the core of conscience, all warm and ruddy as it is, includes an act of judgment. The intellectual process in this self-appraisal is not cool and detached until late, when the fires of life grow ashen and there comes casuistry and sedentary criticism. Early the moral judgment is but one aspect of a passionate attitude, as in children. In these more glowing days nearly the whole self is thrown into every situation: there is delight in what is offered, or there is fear or resentment, or perhaps all of these and others mingled. Conscience is neither a purely intellectual power nor a "sense" nor a sentiment,—

I, 215 f.—will already have become aware that I am using it more broadly and again more narrowly than have some of these writers. If I were to set the matter down with some attempt at precision, there would be included in the term any or all of the following, according to the degree of elaboration the mental state might have:
  (a) the cognition of general rules of conduct as having reference directed against myself,
  (b) the cognition of the relation of some particular thought or intent or overt act of mine to one or more of these rules,
  (c) the judgment of moral self-approval or of self-condemnation, whether because or independent of this cognition; and
  (d) in addition to the bare intellectual judgment, whatever of emotional and volitional activity, possessed of moral quality, is directed against myself.
Conscience I am consequently taking—in contrast, e.g., to Rée (*Entstehung des Gewissens*, 1885, 211 ff.) who would identify it with virtually all moral judgment, of others' conduct as well as of my own —to be far more than mere judgment, and far less than a judgment of everybody's action. Conscience, as I conceive it, is *my entire moral attitude toward myself and my own act*, whether this attitude come before, during, or after the act's completion.

a view that will offend all those who would have conscience simple and nicely within a particular and exclusive mental class. In its unsicklied state it is rather an impassioned confronting of one's intention or completed act, an impassioned confronting in which may be discerned representatives of every great class of activity of which the mind is capable, from sensation through intellect and emotion, into will.

Without taking from the honor due to conscience, we thus take away something of its special mystery. Even as self-consciousness, which has had a peculiar glamour with both poet and professor, is of no more mystical quality than is the consciousness of others—which already has enough mystery and to spare,—but is the common act of recognizing persons, now singling out for clear and ample reasons myself among these others; so conscience is my general moral attitude toward persons, now come to the point where it cannot leave out myself. It is not a power in addition to that by which I rejoice or am enraged or depressed at what they do; it is but an inevitable extension of its use, so that I come to apply it to the one person who so often looms largest in this field of critical and excited interest.

But we shall not have traced even the main connections of conscience if we do not see that its self-appraisal and self-urging involve a measure of that dissociation which is of such interest in the newer studies of mind. The following account given me by a friend will illustrate this, and will illustrate here again the closeness of moral self-review to what is not of morals.

"It seems as though I could look at a certain part of me and see that that part had failed. Because of this failure I am angry. This ability to feel that I am made up of two selves doesn't seem to be present all the time. It is called to my attention only when something happens to give my whole system a shock. After thinking it over, it seems that there are only two occasions that cause me to be aware of a multiple self—first, when there is a shock to my pride, and second, when I have made myself particularly gracious or shown especial intelligence or made some moral stand that I thought a very good one. This feeling of self-satisfaction, though, is much rarer than that of anger against myself."

This dissociation, which conscience illustrates, is clearly a normal and beneficent form of what often has seemed only hindering and diseased. The strange display of multiple personality in the hysterical is the morbid excess of what in conscience belongs in the very treasury of our powers. Even without disease, it is true, we need be careful against all habitual dissociation, and especially against all excessive interest in the self, excessive introversion. But if we could practice to the full the maxim to look outward and not inward, we should lose conscience itself, surrendering our life to unreflection and impulse. My angry turning against me, which is usually deserved, and oftener deserved than occurring, would then have passed away. In this dissociation we approach an impartial examination of ourselves. Conscience thus is in part almost the very "giftie" for which Burns prayed. In the precise form which he wished, it is fortunately withheld: under its untempered ray many of us would shrivel as a scroll. But if not to see ourselves as others see us, at least to see ourselves somewhat as we see others, and to visit ourselves with like emotions although softened,—this is a power which conscience surely brings.

When one is aware of the passion with which one may face his own thought or deed, there seems some fault of measurement in conceiving this as invariably a still, small voice. It is still and small only as is all moral force in contrast with the blare of what is physical. No one without can hear it; there are visible no symbols of authority, no compulsion as of battle-ships and armies. But to the man himself conscience may speak with a power not exceeded by the mandate of princes. Its approval leaves no hesitation, its condemnation is of paralyzing, of crushing, force. It speaks imperiously, as of one above us, uttering a command in wrath.

Thus conscience, elevated and mysterious though it be, does not wholly elude our study. We can see something of its source and history, something of its structure and mode of action. *It appears as a peculiar kind of division or dissociation of the mind; the self, which looks with an eye to the widest good we know, now turning against the more restricted self.* And in this sane and hygienic dissociation, self-anger holds an important place. To the service which anger renders in politics, commerce, law and the many other fields where men visibly control one another, we must add anger's service confined within the individual, where there is indignant self-control.

CHAPTER IV

THE UNCREATIVE CHARACTER OF ANGER

Having been compelled to go a mile with anger, shall we go with it twain? Shall we agree that anger not only supports the moral life but is in truth its chiefest pillar? In doing so we should find ourselves in learned company. For even Kant almost reaches such a view when he says that, were it not for a spirit of opposition deep in our being, early man might have enjoyed an Arcadian existence, but would have been little better than the sheep he tended. "Thanks then be to Nature," Kant exclaims; "thanks then be to Nature for man's intolerance, for his envious rivalry and conceit, for his insatiable lust of property and of power! Without these, all the splendid native abilities of mankind would have remained asleep, forever undeveloped. Man wishes harmony; but Nature knows better what is good for such as he; she will have Discord."[1] Opposition is for Kant not the origin of virtue but the spur to urge it on. Nor with him is antagonism thought of only in the form of physical conflict, of mutual human slaughter.

It remained for a later writer, and one imbued with a more modern—or shall we say, more primitive—spirit to believe that all depends on actual fighting, on battle and war; that, save for these, man would never have risen above the brute; that if he would have true discipline, he must fight, not with rude nature nor with the beasts, but with his own kind. It is to war, he holds, that humanity owes an intense and broader sympathy.[2]

[1] *Werke*, ed. Hartenstein, 1867, IV, 146 f.
[2] Steinmetz: *Die Philosophie des Krieges*, 1907, 16 ff.

His doctrine, to use in summary another's paraphrase, is that "the warlike spirit of early man was the source of all his early virtues, including his kindliness and his disposition to help his comrades in war and his dependents at home." [1]

I

Let us examine this doctrine, and it will appear, I believe, less than half the truth. For even before we reach the human level, in those marvelous communities of insects—bees, wasps, and ants—as well as among many species of animals on the higher levels, pugnacity is there in plenty and yet is not the central fact of their life. Fighting and anger are even here auxiliary to a great group of impulses that are of themselves wholly unangry—I mean mating and its passionate eagerness; effort on behalf of the young; food-getting for oneself and mate and offspring; leadership and the acceptance of the leader; behavior that aids concealment and more active escape; the discovery and use of materials for food that others cannot use or obtain; migrations toward more suitable places with changing times of the year. It is to these and a thousand other devices of their mental and physical constitution, in addition to the impulse to be angry and to fight, that animals owe their continued existence and advance. It is not, as some would have us believe, as though from birth to death, daily between waking and sleep, theirs was an almost unbroken course of bitter animosity.

And it is significant that their advance, their position in the scale of ascent, is not proportioned to the amount of their pugnacity. Pugnacity does not steadily increase as we come nearer and nearer to man. Anger and pugnacity come to their perfect flowering not at the top but upon certain side-branches of the great tree—down

[1] Royce: *War and Insurance*, 1914, 84.

where we find the social insects just mentioned, and higher with the predatory birds—the hawks and shrikes, for example,—and still higher, with the wolves and hyenas, lions, tigers and all the other flesh-eaters that catch and down their living prey.

But the animals that are most intelligent and in other traits are nearest to man—for example the elephant, the horse, the monkey,—show an unmistakable softening of their contentiousness. The unpredatory means of success have here been made still more eminent. Less suspicious and guarded, displaying more curiosity; better able to discern, to examine, to remember, what will serve their purpose; less easily thrown into ungovernable fury; more affectionate, readier to get along with others—these are qualities which have helped the elephant and the ape to defeat their ferocious foe, finding in themselves an unusual place for peaceful effort, fighting rather by exception, more formidable in defense than in attack. Anger and attack and slaughter have with these animals nearest to man ceased to be the very pivot of their effort.

And now, if instead of to animals, we look to man and ask whether the warlike spirit is indeed the source of all his virtues, have we not already seen that anger and pugnacity never created either the family or the state, but merely gave greater vigor and effect to other impulses that truly originate these great moral institutions?

Further, in estimating our obligation to these bellicose passions, it is at once clear that they are not untainted agents of morality. They fight for vice as readily as for virtue. Anger supports self-interest against the interests of the community; it exaggerates offenses when they come; it opposes the large and stable ordering of society. It makes me defend with heat and stubbornness a possession that rightly belongs to another. And when anger is on the side of right and sets out to punish injury, it often drives the avenging hand with excess of violence;

THE UNCREATIVE CHARACTER OF ANGER

the loss of one son is answered by destroying four. We say that the state could not be sustained without pugnacity in its citizens; and yet the chief danger which is thus averted lies in the very pugnacity of its own citizens and of foreign neighbors. Anger thus leads in the attack as well as in the defense of states; and for every government that stands because of this impulse, a hundred have fallen because of it. If it is a moral gain that the political organization of men should enlarge from clan to tribe and from tribe to nation and from small nation to large nation, and through war this gain has been accomplished, we must recognize that war has been the chief barrier to the enlargement. The mutual jealousy of the nations is now the great obstacle to an expression of international common-sense and mutual protection.

One can justly bring these charges against anger even though he withhold his hand from painting its character black. For it is clear that we cannot attribute chiefly to this passion the great mass of infractions of civil law to-day. It is not solely because of wrath that in times of high cost this man may fail to pay his shoemaker, or that man may join with others to profiteer in shoes. These acts may arouse anger, but need not arise from it. And while acts that are criminal are sometimes done in red passion, it is only the smaller number that are so done. And even in these cases the anger itself is due to some other impulsion and emotion,—sometimes dark and excessive, like lust and cupidity, but more often from an interest that is wholly moderate and right, the interest in property or in personal dignity or in wife and child. One of these deep instincts being thwarted has summoned anger to its aid. The proportion of crimes in which anger plays an important rôle is impossible as yet to state, but an indication is perhaps given when it is found that in England and Wales only about fifteen in a hundred crimes are ascribed to malice.[1] The breaking of law is

[1] Griffiths: "Crime," *Encycl. Brit.*, 11th ed., VII, 448.

therefore not wholly due to anger; this we may believe while yet seeing how large is the part which anger plays in crime.

II

But we shall hardly know whether the virtues find their one source in the warlike spirit unless we examine justice and ask whether anger which we have already found so important is in truth the central and mastering force in justice. For here, it might seem, the praise of anger might be sung without restraint.

And yet we soon see, when looking with judicial eye, that the substance of justice is not created by anger and its kindred impulses. The anger which is felt upon seeing a strong man strike a child is not the fount and origin of my sense of what is due the child. If it were not for a certain feeling of good-will perhaps dormant but ready to be awakened, I should not feel indignant at the blow. The anger here comes from an interest of mine that is being violated. Some positive interest in a fellow human being, or in an animal or in some admirable though inanimate thing summons anger in me when this interest is not respected by some other person. *This interest and not the anger* suggests what is due; the anger merely lends its aid to the interest. It is these interests that determine whether I shall be angry and in what direction my anger shall move. The positive contents of the idea of justice are thus supplied by emotions and impulses at whose center is both instinctive self-interest and an equally instinctive interest in other men. Only because I can count upon a certain favoring feeling toward me in men whom I have not offended, can my indignation at the taking of my property be fortified by their indignation at this same act. Only through this conspiracy of feeling does it become a part of justice that such an act shall not occur. In all strictness, then, we must say that justice,

THE UNCREATIVE CHARACTER OF ANGER   67

the sense of what is the right of each, springs neither from self-interest and friendliness together nor from anger acting alone, but from these three peculiarly combined, whereby anger responds to these other promptings, and warms into deed the sluggish judgment and inclination. The sanctions of the law are the organized communal expression of these constant tendencies to emotional response arising originally in individual persons.

But these emotions, intensified by anger, do not rest when once they have stimulated a certain conception of justice; they act also to modify what they have helped to produce. For there is in every vital community an unceasing change in the idea of rights, however slow the change. Even when punishment is meted out by a representative of the common will, his official act is apt to arouse in me emotions not wholly unlike those felt when I see one private individual punishing another. At first it may be indignation directed at the man who has broken the law. But later there may be sympathy with the punished, and anger against those who chastise. Or my feelings may run a still different course, becoming severe now against the *un*punished, demanding his chastisement although as yet there has been no organized sentiment against the kind of act that he has done. In so far as this new feeling of mine is shared by others, it comes in time to change the conviction of what is just. In this way we see the punishment of debtors, for example, gradually made less severe, while there is an increasing severity in the public condemnation of certain acts against children and women. Under the influence of new movements in sympathy and indignation, justice not only becomes more merciful but more rigorous. The weights of her scale are not constant, but are answerable to the fluctuations of love and hate.

If this be true, there is ample reason at first both for affirming that justice is a deeper conception than goodwill or love and for denying this. The poor, it is often said, need justice and not charity. But this should not mean that they can forego the communal good-will which is the very life-blood of the justice they seek. It means, rather, that the systematic,—we might almost say automatic—expression of good-will, regularly and impartially administered, is vastly more effective than impulsive or private or occasional benefaction, which requires some special stimulation of pity and indignation for each particular case. The results here are too uncertain, being now excessive, now niggardly. Better a steady pressure of good-will and anger to start the machinery that will thereafter work dispassionately a thousand or a million times. But the good-will and the indignation are needed to rear the machinery and to give it motion, and to keep it in repair. Woe to the community that ceases to value good-will in individual men, where indeed if it does not exist, it does not exist at all.

I see no reason, then, for holding as though it were the last word, that justice is greater than good-will because it is greater than disorganized and scattered and fickle good-will. Justice depends on friendly impulses and upon the indignation to which these lead; it is the product and instrument of good-will. The praise of governmental justice to the disparagement of sympathy, springs from an excess of confidence in mechanism, in contrast to whatever partakes of personal impulse and especially of emotion. There is a fine rigor in the idea of justice, since it is indeed controlled by intellect and will, and yet cannot long be without the very feeling of friendliness to which in reality it in part owes its life. An understanding of the way in which the emotions act thus corrects our partial view.

We must then refuse assent to the thesis that all the primitive virtues,—even that of kindliness,—spring from the warlike spirit. Anger and pugnacity are not of themselves creators; they do not set the task, they do not dis-

THE UNCREATIVE CHARACTER OF ANGER

cover the goal. But once the goal has been given by desires that are positive and constructive—the desire of property, for example, or wife, or personal eminence—then comes anger to destroy or break through whatever blocks the way. *Anger then is secondary. The affections, the appreciations—of one's self as well as of others—are the primal forces of life.* Not even pure intelligence, if one could have it free from all affections, could supply their motive power and leadership. Intelligence reveals more fully the object which awakens love, and the way by which the love can reach its object. But intelligence cannot take the place of love itself. Neither can hate. There would be no one of the kindly virtues if they had to arise from anger only. The desire to help one's comrades in war does not originate in the warlike spirit of early man. The causal current runs the other way. The warlike spirit, the hatred of the enemy, springs normally from some barrier real or imagined which the enemy raises to an active liking. Virtue springs from positive desire.

III

If we were to define with more precision, then, the relation of anger to the motive forces of appreciation, it would be well to say that anger is a sign and intensifier of appraisal but not the *source* of the appraisal. Other desires go deeper. *For there are four great emotional impulsions: two that are originative and leading, namely love and self-interest; and two that are ancillary and supporting, namely anger and fear.* Each of these has its distinctive quality, yet they have in common the power to give value to an object or the power to change its value. Whatever inspires one or another of these feelings in me, at once attains *importance;* without them the world would be flat, lacking all light and shade. Anger that seems to deny value, does this in seeming only: the man

I hate is one who can thwart my interests. He must show power over things dear to me, before I can feel this bitterness. I cannot hate an inhabitant of Mars, since he, so far as I know, does not menace the fabric of my desires. One must indeed be lowly or remote to be beneath my anger. Anyone who enrages me has already drawn from me a sincere expression of regard. In anger and fear and self-regard and friendliness, then, we have a foundation four-square of that superstructure in which our moral life is passed, the superstructure of appreciation.

These passions then work together and are not inconsistent. For it is only within special bounds that love casts our fear or anger. It is true that we cannot hate, neither can we fear, the man we perfectly love. But we can, and perhaps must, hate others for his sake. When we speak widely and according to our science, love does not merely cast out fear and anger; it invites them in. Not until something attracts us, until something is desired by us, are we afraid. It is because we love, that we become outraged at the despite done to what we love. *Take love away,—the love of one's self, I mean, along with the love of others and the love of possessions,—and there would be nothing to give motive to our fear and anger.* Far down in the animal scale and in the earliest period of our personal life, and in some forms of mental and nervous disease, it may well be that there is an immediate fear, an immediate anger, without awareness that some positive interest is threatened. Nature perhaps in exceptional cases provides the fear, the anger, before the creature is quite conscious of its use for positive interests. But in our human and healthy life this form of reaction takes an unimportant place, and our fear and anger become clearly motivated by our conscious and positive attachments.

In this part of our discussion which now must not be extended, we have seen anger coming as a gift to the

THE UNCREATIVE CHARACTER OF ANGER 71

higher forms of mind. And when it comes it is soon a servant of the moral life, lending its ardor against the enemies of the family and of justice and government. It lends strength to the union between husband and wife, it protects the child, it defends home and possessions, it maintains the rights of the citizen, it jealously favors justice, it wards off the foreign foe. Whatever a man values has become of more splendid value through its defense, through a fear changing into anger whenever its possession is threatened.

But it is also seen to be an enemy of morals, destroying government, disrupting the family, supporting injustice, coming to the help of greed and lust and selfish ambition. We have found anger unproductive save only when it became subject to some positive creative impulse.

But where there is so much to be said on both sides it is difficult to hold all in even balance. It is therefore not strange that anger is difficult to appraise with an impartial hand; and that wherever morals come to high development, anger should be viewed askance. A hundred strands of evidence reveal the deep distrust with which anger comes to be viewed. There can be no doubt of an effort in morals to have good-will wholly displace anger and hate. Yet are morals to be the better if this effort is crowned with success? Can morality dispense with so powerful an agent? And yet can she afford to use such doubtful means? Shall we find good-will strengthened if freed from this embarrassing retainer?—who is helpful, no doubt, but with a troublesome help such as was rendered to those Italian noblemen of old by their hired bravoes. To deal justly with anger and hate and pugnacity is a moral problem of deep concern. And it is to religion that men have long looked for guidance in making their decision. And perhaps nowhere has religion seemed in more perplexity. It has used and again condemned all anger. According to its time and place, religion has anxiously taken now one and now another horn of the dilemma. It will be of interest to observe the gradual growth of religion's attitude, and to notice a few great religions in their difficulty, seeing the changes of Christianity itself as it grows older in its experience of fiery temper. Into this farther field, if the reader is of favoring mind, we shall enter in the sections that now follow.

PART II

THE DILEMMA OF RELIGION: ANGER IN THE GREAT FAITHS

CHAPTER V

THE IRATE AND MARTIAL RELIGIONS

Judaism, Zoroastrism, Islam

Anger, we have seen, is at once an ally and a foe of the moral life. It strengthens and defends the family; and yet turns husband against wife, brother against brother, parent against child. It supports the law, and the law-breaker. It assists at the building of the State, and resists its building, and attacks and destroys it when built.

Facing such a turncoat, what wonder that religion should be found in a quandary! Can the very sponsor of morals accept with whole heart this impulse that opposes and chills the love not yet warm among men? And yet can it reject a passion that rushes to the help of love endangered, so that without it love seems unable to shelter and protect her own? It is a situation as in a drama: a fatality seems to lie in either course; religion, it would appear, must choose and, whatever her choice, regret it. Let us watch in the strange deliberations of history some of the ways in which advanced religion has made its great election.

I

And first of the religions that make free use of anger: the religion of the ancient Jew, of Zoroaster, and of Mohammed. Of Judaism I shall attempt no full account; its aggressive and defensive spirit, its armies fighting the foes of Israel, Jehovah breathing courage into those armies, showing his wrath also against his own people in their disobedience—of all this and more the reader's memory will offer illustration; and should it hesitate, something of the lack will be supplied when, upon one aspect, I shall venture a detailed discussion at a later page.[1]

Yet to avoid mistake it should be said that both of the great forces, love and hate, are present in the Jew's scripture, but in a proportion different from that found later. The new proportion of these in Christianity helped toward the rejection of the new faith by the very people to whom it owed its birth. In the new faith is the flowering of that of which the Jew could give the seed but which he could not cultivate with all his heart. Wide antipathies were too powerful in his spirit. For to this day has the Jew been marked by the limit of his sympathies, finding himself not at ease nor of homely intercourse with those of another blood and culture. This checks in others the normal responses awakened by men less richly endowed and perhaps less desirous of showing and receiving good-will.

Some emotional inhibition has thus prevented the Jew from recommending to the alien, deep from his heart, his own dream of a spiritual union of all men, independent of blood and tribe, bound together in a common loyalty toward a God, himself passionate in his love of all. Others took the Jew's dream, and with tragic failure are still struggling to make it true. In the Hebrew scriptures there is dominant a national temper which could well occasion, even though it could not fully justify, that estimate of the Jews made in the ancient world: "Compassionate and unflinchingly loyal to each other," is the Roman description of them, "they hate all other men with a deadly hatred." [2]

[1] See pp. 209 ff.
[2] Histories of Tacitus, V, 5, tr. Ramsay, 1915.

II

Hastening then from Judaism, let us look to the religion of one of the foes of Israel, to the religion of the Parsee.

The ancient Persian, himself a conquering warrior, sees armed conflict at the very center of the universe. There has from of old been warfare between Ahura Mazda, the divinity of light and goodness, and Angra Mainyu, the spirit of darkness and evil.[1] It will be well to see the great spirits upon the one side and upon the other, and something of the manner of their struggle. Thereafter we can better understand the temper shown by the men of the faith.

Ahura Mazda, the Creator, is bountiful, bringing good to the good, and evil to the evil; he gives gladness and abounding grace; his is the sovereign power, and righteousness is maintained by him;[2] he prays and his prayer is granted, that he may smite the creation of Angra Mainyu, and that none may smite the creation of the Good Spirit.[3] Yet Ahura Mazda is not seen in anger, as is Jehovah: he appears rather as the active leader of an invisible war, himself fighting dispassionately, as befits a great general. Without malice he crushes by his warrior-power his foes. And he is singularly without jealousy, generous to his subordinates; whoever offers sacrifice to the Sun, offers it to Ahura Mazda;[4] Mithra and the star Sirius, Tistrya, are declared by Ahura Mazda to be as worthy of worship as himself.[5]

[1] Gathas, Yasna XXX, 1 ff. (XXXI, 28 ff.). My account throughout is drawn wholly from the Zend-Avesta; no attempt has been made to follow the farther development appearing in the Pahlavi texts.
[2] Gathas, Yansna XLIII, 1 ff. (XXXI, 98 ff.).
[3] Yast XV, 3 f. (XXIII, 250).
[4] Yast VI, 4 (XXIII, 86).
[5] Yast VIII, 50; Yast X, 1 (XXIII, 93, 119 f.).

78 ANGER: ITS RELIGIOUS AND MORAL SIGNIFICANCE

And with the friends of righteousness is Vohu-Mano, the Good Mind, a creature of Ahura Mazda,[1] and possessed of vigorous might.[2] And this Good Mind smites Akem-Mano, the Evil Mind;[3] with Atar he destroys the malice of the fiend Angra Mainyu;[4] Vohu-Mano with Asha-Vahista and Atar, the son of Ahura Mazda, hurl darts against the Evil One.[5]

On their side, too, are Mithra, the Lord of Nations; the good and holy Sraosha; and Rashnu, tall and strong; with whom are arrayed the waters, the plants, and the souls of all the faithful.[6] Mithra is terrible in his anger; he is the strongest, the most valiant, the most energetic, the swiftest, the most fiend-smiting of all the gods;[7] at night he goes over all the earth, swinging in his hands a club of red brass, a club with a hundred knots, a hundred edges; he goes forth in his chariot, with him goes the cursing thought of the Law and the wise men; with him go a thousand spears, a thousand steel hammers, a thousand two-edged swords, which fall upon the skulls of the demons; from him Angra Mainyu and all the fiends flee away;[8] to him do the chiefs of nations sacrifice as they go forth to war.[9]

Sraosha, the Divine Obedience, is of manly courage, a warrior of strong arms, who smites with heavy blows, breaking the skulls of the fiends;[10] his knife-like battle-axe cleaves the demons' skulls, hewing down Angra Mainyu and Rapine of the bloody spear.[11]

Rashnu, the Spirit of Truth, holy and beneficent, is

[1] Yast I, 25 (XXIII, 31).
[2] Gathas, Yasna XXXI, 21 (XXXI, 52).
[3] Yast XIX, 96 (XXIII, 308).
[4] Yast XIII, 77 f. (XXIII, 198).
[5] Yast XIX, 46 (XXIII, 297).
[6] Yast X, 99 ff. (XXIII, 145).
[7] Yast X, 98 (XXIII, 144).
[8] Yast X, 93 f., 123 ff. (XXIII, 143 f., 152 ff.; cf. also 126, 136).
[9] Yast X, 8 (XXIII, 122).
[10] Yast XI, 19 (XXIII, 165).
[11] Yasna LVII, 13 ff., 30 f. (XXXI, 301 ff., 305).

THE IRATE AND MARTIAL RELIGIONS 79

tall and strong, far-seeing, the best doer of justice, the best smiter and destroyer of thieves.[1] And there is worshipped Manly Courage, firm of foot, unsleeping, quick to rise;[2] and with Mithra and Rashnu fight also the awful souls of the faithful, fight in armor of brass and with weapons of brass, in battle array; they kill thousands of demons; without them the Fiend would everywhere prevail, and never afterward would Angra Mainyu give way to the blows of Spenta Mainyu.[3]

Chief of the hosts of evil is Angra Mainyu, "that fiend who is all death,"[4] the "ruffian Angra Mainyu, the deadly," who "wrought by his witchcraft nine diseases, and ninety, and nine hundred, and nine thousand, and nine times ten thousand diseases."[5] The Evil Spirit rushes up from dreary Hell.[6] A most frightful spirit, Azi Dahaka—three mouthed, three headed, six-eyed, with a thousand senses, most fiendish, a demon baleful to the world, the strongest "Drug" that Angra Mainyu created,—begs to be allowed to destroy all men.[7] From the hour when the sun goes down the material world is threatened by fiends.[8] There is the Wrath-demon of rapine, the Demon of Envy,[9] the Demon of the Lie,[10] Dahakas, Murakas,[11] "Rapine of the bloody spear, the Daevas of Mazendran, and every Demon-god."[12] The demon Buiti, the unseen death, hell-born, attacks Zarathustra.[13] Many are the particular fiends that must be

[1] Yast XII, 7 ff. (XXIII, 170 ff.).
[2] Yast XIX, 36 ff. (XXIII, 294 ff.).
[3] Yast XIII, 12 f., 45 (XXIII, 183, 191).
[4] Yast I, 19 (XXIII, 29).
[5] Vendidad, Fargard XXII, 9 (IV, 232).
[6] Yast XIX, 44 (XXIII, 296).
[7] Yast V, 29 f. (XXIII, 60 f.); Yast IX, 14 (XXIII, 113); Yast XIX, 37, 46 (XXIII, 294, 297 f.).
[8] Yast XI, 11 f. (XXIII, 163).
[9] Gathas, Yashna XLVIII, 7 (XXXI, 156).
[10] Gathas, Yasna XLIX, 3 (XXXI, 163).
[11] Yasna XI, 6 (XXXI, 245).
[12] Yasna LVII, 30 (XXXI, 305).
[13] Vendidad, Fargard XIX, 1 (IV, 204).

driven away.[1] And there are demoniac monsters that threaten men: an "aroused and fearful Dragon, green and belching forth his poison";[2] the snake Srvara, horse-devouring, man-devouring, yellow, poisonous; "the golden-heeled Gandarewa, that was rushing with open jaws, eager to destroy the living world of the good principle"; "the brood of Pathana, all the nine; and the brood of Niviki, and the brood of Dastayana."[3] It is from the hate of the fiend, and of the brood of the fiend that sickness comes to men; Sickness and Death and Pain and Fever and Disease are personal and hateful powers against which the holy protection of Thrita must be sought.[4] The Daeva Apaosha, the demon of drought, "stamped with brands of terror," fights terribly until overcome by Sirius, "the bright and glorious Tistrya, the leader of the stars, the Star of Rain."[5] The great company of the fiends is constantly enlarged by there coming to it the souls of wicked men,[6] and by wicked acts which cause the birth of fiends. The demons have their habitation, where also sinners dwell with them; the wicked, evil-doing demons rush away into the depths of the dark, horrid world of hell,[7]—the dismal realm, the world of woe.[8] And there are places, even in this present and visible world, where troops of fiends "rush together to kill their fifties and their hundreds, their hundreds and their thousands, their thousands and their tens of thousands, their tens of thousands and their myriads of myriads."[9] The demons, the seed of the Evil Mind, would beguile mankind of happy

[1] Vendidad, Fargard XI, 9 ff. (IV, 141 f.).
[2] Yasna IX, 30 (XXXI, 239).
[3] Yast XIX, 40 ff. (XXIII, 295 f.).
[4] Vendidad, Fargard XX (IV, 220 ff.).
[5] Yast VIII, 26 ff. (XXIII, 100). For the individual names of many other fiends, see Vendidad, Fargard XIX, 43 (IV, 217 f.).
[6] Vendidad, Fargard VIII, 31 (IV, 102).
[7] Vendidad, Fargard VIII, 107; Fargard XIX, 47; (IV, 119, 218).
[8] Vendidad, Fargard III, 35 (IV, 31).
[9] Vendidad, Fargard VII, 55 f. (IV, 88).

life upon earth and afterwards of immortality.[1] The fiend not only afflicts men; he *hates* them. Men pray to God to keep them from their hater, and that he may be driven off to his own place into the regions of the North.[2]

But this ancient conflict,[3] of which we have seen some of the warring hosts, was not to last forever. A blow of destruction, it is known, will fall upon the Demon of Falsehood.[4] A Savior, the victorious Saoshyant, bodily and living, will withstand the Fiend;[5] he will smite the Fiend; Angra Mainyu becomes powerless; and the Beneficent One, with the eye of intelligence, will look down on all the creatures of the Fiend, her of the evil deed: "he shall look upon the whole living world with the eye of plenty, and his look shall deliver to immortality the whole of the living creatures." [6]

With this foreseeing by faith the victory of Goodness over Evil there was joined far more distinctly than in the mind of the ancient Hebrew, the thought of reward and punishment after death. The good deeds of this world are recompensed in another life,[7] a place of blessed abode.[8] One can escape the pangs of hell and have, now and forever, a seat in the bright, all-happy, blissful abode of the holy ones.[9] After death, when the third night has

[1] Yasna XXXII, 3 ff. (XXXI, 58 f.).
[2] Vendidad, Fargard XX, 13; XXII, 25 (IV, 223, 235).
[3] Along with the thought that the warfare between the Good and the Evil Mind had been from the beginning, was the thought of a Golden Age, a time of peace and perfect happiness on earth, in the reign of Yima, the good shepherd, who ruled even the fiends. In that happy time there was no heat or cold, famine, old-age, death, or envy; see Yast XIX, 31 ff. (XXIII, 293). And even when this age passed, there was created by Yima, at the command of Ahura Mazda, a happy land where was no deformity, poverty, meanness, lying, or jealousy; see Vendidad, Fargard II, 25 ff. (IV, 16 ff.).
[4] Gathas, Yasna XXX, 10 (XXXI, 34).
[5] Yast XIII, 129 (XXIII, 220).
[6] Yast XIX, 92 ff. (XXIII, 307 f.).
[7] Vendidad, Fargard VIII, 81 ff. (IV, 112 ff.).
[8] Vendidad, Fargard IX, 44 (IV, 130).
[9] Atas Nyayis, 11 f. (XXIII, 360).

ended, the soul of the faithful seems to be inhaling an air sweeter scented than any ever breathed, and he sees coming to him his own conscience as a maiden, white-armed and tall, as fair as the fairest things in the world, telling him, "I was lovely and thou madest me still lovelier." And he, passing through the three Paradises,—of Good Thought, Good Word, and Good Deed,—comes into Endless Light.[1] To him who in spirit and in deed is a friend of Ahura Mazda, and in faith fulfills his vows, there is given Universal Weal and Immortality.[2]

For the wicked, however, there is dire distress. He who deceives the saints shall suffer destruction: "long life shall be his lot in the darkness; foul shall be his food; his speech shall be of the lowest."[3] The wicked man's spirit will be crushed by the righteous man's conscience, while his soul rages fiercely on the open Kinvat Bridge, from which he falls into hell.[4] The souls of the evil dead shall have to live with evil men, men of evil conscience; in hell such souls will come to greet them, bringing evil food;[5] there will be crying and wailing there.[6] On the night of death, and again on the next night and on the third, the soul of the wicked man tastes as much of suffering as the whole of the living world can taste"; then it passes through snow and stench, through the three hells,—of Evil Thought, of Evil Word, of Evil Deed,—into Endless Darkness.[7] Beyond this, there is the least of interest in setting forth in horrible detail the punishment of the wicked. The suffering which is their penalty appears to be less a physical than a mental torture: something in one's own spirit leads to the retribu-

---

[1] Yast XXIV, 53 ff. (XXIII, 342 ff.). Cf. Yast XXII, 1 ff. (XXIII, 314 ff.).
[2] Yasna XXXI, 21 (XXXI, 52).
[3] Gathas, Yasna XXXI, 20 (XXXI, 52).
[4] Gathas, Yasna LI, 13 (XXXI, 183).
[5] Gathas, Yasna XLIX, 11 (XXXI, 167).
[6] Vendidad, Fargard V, 4 (IV, 49 f.).
[7] Yast XXII, 20 ff. (XXIII, 318 ff.).

THE IRATE AND MARTIAL RELIGIONS   83

tion, whose core and center is a continuance of the foul
thought and action of this present life. The punishment
is less from divine wrath than from an intuition, since
the sinner at last perceives the stench of his own foul
inner and outer life.

And yet this religion is not without its intense disapproval, its hot indignation, toward human wrong. There is a curse upon the man of evil intent, of evil deeds; upon those who offend their friends, who harm workmen, who hate their kindred; for the thief, the bludgeon-bearing ruffian, the sorcerer, the jealous one, the niggard, the tyrant.[1] There is punishment for ritual offenses: for burying the dead, whether man or animal;[2] for throwing a garment over the dead;[3] for failing to wear the sacred girdle and the sacred shirt.[4] More elaborate and detailed is the condemnation of offenses apart from rite: unrepaid loans, broken contracts, assault, bodily injury, false oaths, and sexual immorality.[5]

Nor is the condemnation wholly of outer acts: the sin of pride, the sin of unbelief, the sin of utter unbelief, are creatures of Angra Mainyu.[6] Of some sins repentance brings remission, brings absolution; but for others there is no atonement.[7] And while the faithful will act justly toward the wicked, into his justice will be woven vengeance; for he who does evil to the wicked—not dallying but laboring with both hands—shows thereby his devotion to Ahura Mazda and his own conscience.[8]

Over against the condemnation of evil, is the praise of good. The Great Creator inspires good thoughts in

[1] Yasna LXV, 7 (XXXI, 318).
[2] Vendidad, Fargard III, 36 ff. (IV, 31 ff.).
[3] Vendidad, Fargard VIII, 23 ff. (IV, 99 f.).
[4] Vendidad, Fargard XVIII, 54 (IV, 199).
[5] Vendidad, Fargard IV; VIII, 26; XVIII, 62 ff. (IV, 33 ff., 100 ff., 200 ff.).
[6] Vendidad, Fargard I, 8, 11, 16 (IV, 6 ff.).
[7] Vendidad, Fargard III, 21, 39, 41; IX, 50 (IV, 28, 32 f., 131).
[8] Gathas, Yasna XXXIII, 2 (XXXI, 72).

the souls of men.¹ Righteousness and the Good Mind are where there is care of God's poor in their distress.² The earth rejoices with great joy over him who gives kindly and piously to the faithful.³ He who relieves the poor is using a divine power and is obeying the divine will; ⁴ he who refuses the entreaty of the faithful for even a slight gift from his riches makes the demon pregnant with other dmeons.⁵ Earnest is the support which this religion gives of charity and righteousness and goodwill; earnest the opposition to violations of the social and religious order.

Looking now to the attitude of this religion toward those not of its faith, we discover appreciation but still heartier intolerance. The sacred writers recognize that there are righteous men even in an alien race. Among the tribes of the Turanian will be found those who help the cause of piety; ⁶ the spirits of holy men and women in foreign lands are included among the beings worthy of worship.⁷ There is the thought of a world-wide extension of their own religion: there is prayer that Mazda may give such inspiration to men of the true faith that all the living may believe.⁸

Yet there is cordial hatred of unbelievers. The faithful should eat heartily in order the better to strive against the ungodly heretic who fasts.⁹ A live heretic defiles fire and water and does injury far beyond; a dead heretic is harmless—harmless as a dead frog.¹⁰ It is a sin to give the wicked ungodly heretics the sacred Haoma juice;

[1] Gathas, Yasna XLIV, 4 (XXXI, 113).
[2] Gathas, Yasna XXXIV, 5 (XXXI, 85).
[3] Vendidad, Fargard III, 34 (IV, 31).
[4] Vendidad, Fargard VIII, 19 (IV, 98).
[5] Vendidad, Fargard XVIII, 33 ff. (IV, 196).
[6] Gathas, Yasna XLVI, 12 (XXXI, 141).
[7] Yast XIII, 143 f. (XXIII, 226 f.).
[8] Gathas, Yasna XXXI, 3 (XXXI, 41).
[9] Vendidad, Fargard IV, 49 (IV, 47).
[10] Vendidad, Fargard V, 36 ff.; XIII, 21 ff. (IV, 59 f., 150 f.).

a blessing upon such may be a curse upon him who utters it.[1] If a heretic attempts in his ignorance to purify the unclean, the land cannot be restored to sweetness of plenty until the ungodly heretic is put to death.[2] Two-legged heretics are, in their malice, of a class with wolves, murderers, and demons,[3] with Sickness and Death and the brood of the Snake;[4] from them come persecution and insulting malice.[5] Parseeism thus is not merely lukewarm and charitable toward those who are not of the true faith. From sources outside the Zend-Avesta we know that there was persecution of the followers of Mani whose religion was of kin to that of Mazda;[6] while Jews and Christians, "and others of this sort," are declared to be "of a vile law."[7]

In a people historically so militant as were the Persians, it is not surprising to find a religion attentive to war, accepting it and knowing when to urge it on, in spite of some praise of peace. But the peace that is praised is of the muscular variety, doubtless acceptable to Persians of Rooseveltian temper,—a peace "more powerful to destroy than all other creatures," the "peace that smites,"[8] the "victorious and unprostrated peace."[9] On the other hand and in clear sympathy with war, it is prescribed that certain offenders shall, for atonement, "godly and piously give to godly men a set of all the war implements of which warriors make use,"—a javelin, knife, club, bow, a quiver with belt and thirty arrows, a sling with thirty sling-stones, a cuirass, hauberk, tunic,

[1] Vendidad, Fargard XVIII, 11 ff. (IV, 192).
[2] Vendidad, Fargard IX, 51 ff. (IV, 132 f.).
[3] Yast, I, 10 (XXIII, 26).
[4] Yast III, 76 (XXIII, 44).
[5] Yasna XVI, 8; LXVIII, 8 (XXXI, 257, 322).
[6] (IV, p. xxxviii).
[7] Shayast La-Shayast VI, 7 (V, 296).
[8] Sirozah I, 2; II, 2; Yast II, 1, 6; XI, 15; XV, 1 (XXIII, and n., 13, 35, 37, 164, 249).
[9] Vispard VII, 1; XI, 18 (XXXI, 345, 353).

86   ANGER: ITS RELIGIOUS AND MORAL SIGNIFICANCE

helmet, girdle, and greaves.[1] The Divine Glory brings Riches and Victory and Strength; attended by that Victory, one will conquer havocking hordes, will conquer all who hate him.[2] And the Divine Obedience is besought to "grant swiftness to our teams, soundness to our bodies, and abundant observation of our foes, and their smiting," and "their sudden death."[3] Finally, upon occasion, the believer is to close his ears and fly to arms and hew sinners all with halberd or sabre.[4]

The religion of the Parsees is thus a warrior religion, suited to a people of whose blood were Cyrus, Cambyses, and Darius. Its spiritual animosities are persistent and terrible. Of its great spirits, their power to fight is named high among the marks of their greatness: Zarathustra is called the first Warrior and Priest and Plowman;[5] Karesna the incarnate Word is mighty-speared and lordly;[6] among the names of Ahura Mazda himself are He who conquers everything, He who conquers at once.[7]

Anger and hate are wholly acceptable to it. Vengeance is proper to the spirit of piety: the sacred Fire delights in taking vengeance on one who has harmed him.[8] Indeed the high use of aggression and hatred appears in the very profession of the faith. The worshipper declares: "Here I take as lord and master the greatest of all, Ahura Mazda; to smite the fiend Angra Mainyu; to smite Aesma of the wounding spear; to smite the Mazainya fiends; to

---

[1] Vendidad, Fargard XIV, 9 (IV, 169).
[2] Yast XIX, 53 f. (XXIII, 299).
[3] Yasna LVII, 25 f. (XXXI, 303 f.).
[4] Gathas, Yasna XXXI, 18 (XXXI, 50). In other sacred books of the Parsees, minute directions are given for the conduct of war as well as of private quarrels; see Dinkard, Book VIII (XXXVII, 52, 69, 86 ff., 107). Even the stars were regarded as organized as an army ready for battle; see Bundahis, II, 5 (V, 12).
[5] Yast XIII, 88 f. (XXIII, 201).
[6] Yast XIII, 106 (XXIII, 209).
[7] Yast I, 14 f. (XXIII, 28).
[8] Atas Nyayis, 18 (XXIII, 361).

smite all the Daevas and Varenya fiends; to increase
Ahura Mazda, bright and glorious." [1] And in that
declaration which corresponds to Islam's "There is no
god but Allah, and Mohammed is his Prophet," the Parsee goes farther and pledges himself not only to loyalty
to God, but to active hatred of the spirits of evil: "I confess myself a worshipper of Mazda, a follower of Zarathustra, one who hates the Daevas, and obeys the laws of
Ahura." [2] Hatred of the demons thus recurs as the
counterpart of fealty to the good. And in that part of
the scriptures called the Gathas,—containing passages
singularly noble, setting forth the benefits of Ahura's law,
and the way to advance his kingdom,—linked with this
kingdom are warfare and victory and vengeance upon the
foe.[3]

There is a high valuing of worldly welfare, counting
this even worth defense by fighting; but the warfare which
Zarathustra has at heart is a spiritual warfare in which
God needs man's active help, man's hatred of God's
enemies. Ahura is an untiring warrior, summoning all
good men to come as recruits beneath his banner. Zoroastrianism is clearly one of the great religions of battle
and wrath.

III

Our next and final example within this group shall be
Islam—Islam that calls itself "the resignation," but shows
no moment of hesitation in receiving anger into the company of passions suited to the righteous. But lest we
misjudge, seeing nothing except the anger, we must look
first to its gentler emotions, amongst which hate is finally
to find its place. It will then be clear that a religion
which takes anger into its service does not dismiss all else.

[1] Yast I, 32 (XXIII, 33).
[2] Yast I, o, and in the introduction to each and all of the Yasts (XXIII, 22).
[3] Yasna XXX, 8; XXXII, 3, 10 ff. (XXXI, 33, 58, 62 ff.).

88 ANGER: ITS RELIGIOUS AND MORAL SIGNIFICANCE

The fiercest faith, if it would dominate the human spirit, must temper its wrath with love.

In private affairs rage is to be repressed, and men are to be patient and forgiving.[1] Evil is to be repelled, not with evil but with good.[2] God loves those who are patient and kind.[3] Men are to give alms, and not for appearance before men;[4] part of the spoils of war must be given to the poor;[5] but no alms may be accepted from unbelievers.[6] Especially is there to be no quarreling amongst those on pilgrimage.[7] There is to be no killing of believers unless by mistake;[8] there must be no slaying save for just cause.[9]

For a religion so fierce, there is at times a surprising hesitation in its intolerance of other faiths. There is no unvarying hostility toward those who refuse to acknowledge Mohammed as the Prophet of the Lord. Now and again there is something like kindly invitation of those who belong to another faith. Allah accepts Moses and Jesus, without distinction;[10] he has inspired them.[11] The Jews, the Sabæans, the Christians shall not be made to suffer the grief of the misbelievers;[12]—indeed every nation has its messenger, its prophet of the Lord.[13] Again, the Jews are set down as the strongest foes of the faith, while the Christians are nearest to believers in their love.[14]

---

[1] VI, 62; IX, 209. The references throughout this account are to Palmer's translation of the Koran, in the *Sacred Books of the East*, edited by Max Müller, vols. VI and IX.
[2] VI, 235; IX, 202.
[3] VI, 64.
[4] VI, 78.
[5] VI, 168.
[6] VI, 180.
[7] VI, 28.
[8] VI, 85.
[9] IX, 5, 7.
[10] VI, 19.
[11] IX, 68, 206.
[12] VI, 8, 107.
[13] VI, 198.
[14] VI, 109.

THE IRATE AND MARTIAL RELIGIONS 89

And yet again both Jews and Christians are alike denounced: "God fight them, how they lie!"[1]

There is also wavering in regard to sects within the faith. A certain freedom seems permitted to believers, because of a sign from heaven;[2] and again a sect is mentioned without being condemned.[3] Yet the doctrine of the sect holding that God's punishment is not eternal is declared to be untrue,[4] and all sectarianism within the faith is condemned;[5] those in every sect who have been most bold against Allah will be dragged off to hell and broiled.[6]

Nearly every chapter of the entire Koran opens with the words, like a herald's summons to give ear, "In the name of the merciful and compassionate God." And the ways in which God makes himself known are not always fierce and blinding: among the signs of his presence and favor are feelings tender and noble in the heart—the craving for his grace, the incoming of affection and pity between husbands and wives.[7] He answers the prayer of those who believe and do right; he pardons the offenses of his penitent servants,[8] especially of those whose evil was done in ignorance.[9] He pardons anything but the one great transgression, of "associating aught with Him."[10] Numberless are his favors.[11] Earth, sea and sky declare his kindness, his knowledge:[12] he is clement and forgiving.[13] He bestows delights upon those who be-

[1] VI, 177.
[2] IX, 338.
[3] VI, 58.
[4] VI, 10, 49.
[5] VI, 59; IX, 206.
[6] IX, 32.
[7] IX, 126 f.
[8] IX, 208.
[9] VI, 263.
[10] VI, 79, 88 f.
[11] VI, 242, 252.
[12] IX, 63.
[13] IX, 6.

lieve,—a Paradise as broad as the heaven and the earth,[1] where are gardens watered with rivers of water,[2] and shade that is shade indeed.[3] Rich garments and jewels await the blessed,—bracelets and pearls and silk,[4] robes of green silk and brocade;[5] rich couches and fruit[6] and drink. With the rivers of water are rivers of milk, and (of especial interest to those who for centuries had abstained) rivers of wine[7] of which they may drink without harm.[8] All their wants shall be cared for by beautiful maidens, modest of glance, and of their own age;[9] maidens untouched shall await them in tents;[10] pure wives they shall have forever.[11] There shall also be goodly speech[12] and friendship and all family happiness.[13] There will be no more grief, nor toil, nor weariness;[14] forgiveness shall flow by as a river,[15] malice will be stripped from them, and with their comrades they will live as brothers.[16]

Although as one reads the sacred book of Islam there is the feeling that God is more concerned with the outward submission of men than with their private conduct and the hidden righteousness of the heart, yet private aspiration, private conduct is not neglected: the meat offering does not reach God, but only the piety of those who offer it;[17] men are commanded to be kind to their

[1] VI, 62, 269.
[2] IX, 58.
[3] VI, 80.
[4] IX, 58.
[5] IX, 17 f.
[6] IX, 180.
[7] IX, 230, 263.
[8] IX, 249.
[9] IX, 180.
[10] IX, 261 f.
[11] VI, 4, 11, 48.
[12] IX, 58.
[13] VI, 235; IX, 249.
[14] IX, 160.
[15] IX, 230.
[16] VI, 247.
[17] IX, 60.

parents, to give to the poor, to walk not proudly, to pursue not that of which they have no knowledge.[1] And doubtless something higher is required than in the tribal religions which Mohammed swept away. But although men are summoned to fight the friends of Satan,[2] the good fight is not a purely spiritual fight; it is with carnal weapons and for the church and state. On the side of the faith is the sword of government. Politics and religion here greet each other; the desire to unite the tribes that warred on one another joins with the longing for a common worship. Mohammed is a political as well as a religious reformer, relentless, clement only upon full surrender and when the blood-lust has been appeased.

Although Allah commands that his followers fight for his faith, he is not pictured as himself a leader of armies; he seems not to be engaged in person in the wars on earth. Nor is he in angry conflict in the mysterious realm of spirits. Iblis, the Mohammedan Satan, is no antagonist that imperils the very throne of God; there is no call upon men and spirits to the help of a God whose every nerve is in the struggle, as in the religion of the Persians. Satan seems bent not so much on warring direct with God as in creating ill-will among men; he is an open foe of men.[3] Iblis is a proud angel who refused to humble himself and adore Adam at God's command. God, it would appear, could then and there have sealed his doom, but Iblis pleaded for respite, and the prayer was granted.[4] Iblis's tricks are weak,[5] his power is from the Lord, that there might be a tempter and that God might know who believed in the hereafter and who was still in doubt.[6] Yet Iblis also harms men [7]—but he has no power over

[1] IX, 5-7.
[2] VI, 82.
[3] IX, 6, 166.
[4] VI, 5, 138, 246 f.; IX, 8, 181.
[5] VI, 82.
[6] IX, 153.
[7] VI, 138.

those who believe and rely upon the Lord;[1] the harm of his temptation is possible only if God permits [2]—and Iblis introduces into the work of every apostle or prophet something of untruth, or evil, which God must annul.[3]

For Islam, then, the universe is not torn with the conflict between good and evil; men are not beset at every moment by the hidden forces of insurrection. God is a grand monarch, within whose empire are petty disloyalties known to him and permitted. Evil is clearly defined and unmystical: it is a plain and patent refusal to submit to Allah. Man, created of a clod, has dared to set his will in open opposition to God.[4]

So much, lest we see the emotions of Mohammedanism in disproportion; and now for its clear side of wrath.

God is the Lord of vengeance,[5] terrible in his smiting;[6] he curses Iblis;[7] he curses those who depart from the faith and do not again return;[8] his curse and wrath, with everlasting hell, is the reward of one who intentionally kills a believer;[9] his curse is on those who die in misbelief—God's curse, with the curse of men and of angels.[10] He strikes dread into their hearts, he strikes off their heads, he strikes off their finger-tips.[11] In his attack upon untruth he is pictured like some primal and angry giant: he hurls truth against falsehood and it crashes into it, and it vanishes.[12] His sway is that of a despot: no one may share his power, no one is his companion; he has no

[1] VI, 261; IX, 8.
[2] VI, 14.
[3] IX, 62.
[4] IX, 167.
[5] VI, 46, 244.
[6] IX, 339 f.
[7] IX, 181.
[8] VI, 57.
[9] VI, 85.
[10] VI, 22.
[11] VI, 164.
[12] IX, 47.

THE IRATE AND MARTIAL RELIGIONS

daughters;[1] it is a monstrous falsehood that God has a Son; all are to him as servants.[2]

In no scripture are the torments of hell in so horrible detail. Nothing is withheld, nothing is left vague, nothing is unthought of. The misbelievers are driven into hell in troops,[3] by seven gates do they crowd in;[4] at a fixed time Iblis and all his followers will be cast into hell and will fill it.[5] Here broiling awaits them[6] in the flames[7] that are never quenched.[8] They shall have garments of fire, and boiling water shall be poured upon their heads; and whenever they wish to come forth from the agony, they are driven back with maces of iron.[9] They shall drink boiling water,[10] like thirsty camels they shall drink boiling water,[11] their faces shall be roasted;[12] when their skins are thoroughly broiled in the terrible heat, new skins will be given them[13] that the torment may last forever. They shall be fettered in the flames; fire shall cover their faces, and on their bodies will be shirts of pitch.[14] The faggots that broil the unbeliever shall be carried by his own wife;[15] so frightful will be his torment that the man would give for his ransom his sons, his mate, his brothers and kin and all who are on the earth.[16] In such tortures does God show his undying wrath.

[1] IX, 174, 212, 250.
[2] IX, 34; VI, 200.
[3] IX, 189.
[4] VI, 247.
[5] IX, 181.
[6] IX, 180, 195, 217.
[7] VI, 72, 242.
[8] VI, 6, 11.
[9] IX, 58.
[10] VI, 123; IX, 170, 230.
[11] IX, 264.
[12] IX, 1, 17.
[13] VI, 80.
[14] VI, 244.
[15] IX, 344.
[16] IX, 301.

And God, himself an angry God, commands fighting in men. No man shall escape hell's torments unless, submitting to God, he fights, and fights well.[1] Endless is the urging to fight the enemies of the Lord. Fighting, though it be hateful to the believer, is prescribed by God;[2] he knows best.[3] There must be vows to fight till death.[4]

Believers must believe *and fight*.[5] God loves those who fight in his cause, and fight in close battle-array, shoulder to shoulder with their fellows.[6] Strenuous and stern must be their fighting.[7] Against unbelievers, God and his Prophet proclaim war.[8] Unbelievers are to be killed;[9] after the sacred month is past, idolaters are to be killed wherever found.[10] Fighting in the sacred month is a great sin, but sedition is a greater sin.[11] Retaliation, even in the sacred month, is approved of God.[12] The believer is to fight in God's cause those who fight the faithful; to fight and kill; to stop only when the enemy stops.[13]

And in general there must be no taking of prisoners until there has been slaughter.[14] The heat even of Arabia is no excuse from marching to the fight;[15] the believer under arms is not to be careless, putting his trust foolishly in God; he must exercise care of his arms and baggage; sickness and rain are his only excuse for laying

[1] VI, 63.
[2] VI, 37, 167 ff.
[3] VI, 31.
[4] IX, 142.
[5] IX, 241.
[6] IX, 281.
[7] IX, 292.
[8] VI, 44.
[9] VI, 84 f.
[10] VI, 173.
[11] VI, 31.
[12] VI, 27 f.
[13] VI, 27.
[14] VI, 171.
[15] VI, 184.

aside his arms.[1] He must be alert; he must not allow even the rites of his religion to interfere with military prudence; the rather, fear of attack excuses the believer for neglect of his sacred rites.[2] Pardon and Paradise and return to God are granted to those who die in holy war.[3]

This, then, is the one answer to the question what is to be done with anger: Use anger freely in the service of God; feel it hot against the enemies of the faith; make religion merciless toward those who refuse submission. Allah himself is a God of anger and of awful retribution, unequalled in the horror of his eternal punishment, driving his servant-followers, in the dread of his wrath, to fight his relentless war, instructing them minutely in the method and time of their fighting, which their religion is not to hinder but is to make more passionate. Mohammed the Prophet is also a military general, a leader of armies. It is a religion surpassing all others of wide sway in its warlike temper that rises freely into ferocity. But whether the mood be for the moment fierce or mild, one never in its sacred writing is away from the sound of conquering armies and the avenging voice of God.

[1] VI, 87.
[2] VI, 86.
[3] VI, 65, 82; IX, 281 f.

CHAPTER VI

THE UNANGRY RELIGIONS

Taoism, Vishnuism, Buddhism, Jainism

Turning now to the faiths that reject anger, their chief examples are found in the far Orient, in Asia at its south and east. There our attention is at once caught by Taoism, Vishnuism, and the religions of the Jains and of the Buddhists.

I

The religion of Tao, the Way, one of the great native faiths of China, urges upon men not anger and struggle, but utter calm. A high spiritual indifference is commended to men: heaven, like earth and the sage, is without preference, even the preference to be benevolent.[1] Those who have found the true Way are without desire.[2] The sage in the exercise of his government will strive to keep others without knowledge and without desire.[3] Nor shall we find in this religion as in some others soon to be before us, a later half-turning from this indifference, by exhorting men to love their fellow men.

Looking more closely into the passivity, the quietness, of this religion's ideal, the sage is described as humble, free from self-assertion, free from striving;[4] he makes

[1] Tao teh King, I, 5, 1 (XXXIX, 50). The later references of this account, it will be understood unless otherwise stated, are to this ancient and chief scripture of Taoism.
[2] I, 1, 3 (XXXIX, 47).
[3] I, 3, 3 (XXXIX, 49).
[4] I, 22 (XXXIX, 65).

the mind of others *his* mind; he is indifferent to all, good to others, whether they are sincere or insincere to him;[1] the greatest fault is the wish to get;[2] the negative, the empty qualities are the most useful, the most valuable.[3] Failure awaits the one who would actively seek the kingdom; for it is spiritual and cannot be attained by active doing; he who would so win it destroys it; he who would grasp it loses it.[4] He who has in abundance the true qualities is like a babe; when things grow strong, then they grow false and old;[5] firmness and strength go with death; softness and weakness with life.[6] He who knows most of the truth is silent upon it,[7] he is not disputatious, he is ungrasping; the more he gives away, the more he has.[8]

As the world misses the truth, therefore, it begins to seek after virtue, seek benevolence and righteousness: with these come wisdom and shrewdness and hypocrisy.[9] Those who possess the truth in highest measure do not seek to keep it; they do nothing, and have no need to do anything.[10] The conquests of Tao are unmartial, without rage, by keeping away from the foe.[11] If Taoism has no heart for conflict, its heart delights in paradox in its zeal for quiet and non-resistance: the soft overcomes and breaks the hard, the best action is inaction; we weaken another by first strengthening him; we overthrow him by first raising him up.[12] Not the one who comes mightily to the help of the Lord, then, is a pattern of the follower of Tao, the Way; but,—as we have already seen,—the

[1] II, 49, 1 ff. (XXXIX, 91).
[2] II, 46, 2 (XXXIX, 89).
[3] I, 11 (XXXIX, 54 f.).
[4] I, 29 (XXXIX, 71 f.).
[5] II, 55 (XXXIX, 99).
[6] II, 76 (XXXIX, 118).
[7] II, 56 (XXXIX, 100).
[8] II, 81 (XXXIX, 123 f.).
[9] I, 18 (XXXIX, 61).
[10] II, 38 (XXXIX, 80).
[11] II, 68 (XXXIX, 111).
[12] I, 36, 38; II, 43 (XXXIX, 78, 80, 87).

little child.¹ It is indeed the most passive, the least pugnacious, the most consistently opposed to all striving, all effort, all preference, of any of the great religions.

It is therefore against war, and for non-resistance, yet with certain sad concessions to the needs of state. "Wherever a host is stationed, briars and thorns spring up." Bad years are in the train of great armies. A certain hard necessity of war is recognized; but a skillful commander strikes a decisive blow and stops; he aims at no complete mastery; he guards against vanity, boastfulness and arrogance. "Arms, however beautiful, are instruments of evil omen, hateful, it may be said, to all creatures;" the superior man "uses them only on the compulsion of necessity." To love victory is to delight in the slaughter of men.² The master of the art of war is wholly defensive; he acts the guest and not the host; he would yield a foot, rather than advance an inch.³ A State may be ruled by measures of correction; weapons of war may be used with crafty dexterity; but the true kingdom comes by inaction and want of purpose, by want of ambition; lowliness, condescension, stillness, make a state great; then smaller states are won to it and become its adherents; they flow into it as brooks flow into the great rivers below them.⁴

Indeed states and men should know that Heaven—which comes into being after Tao ⁵—does not strive, and yet it overcomes; it does not call to men, yet men come to it; nothing escapes its net; in poetic phrase, it may be said to smite in anger, but its ways are past finding out.⁶ Heaven alone should be left to inflict the penalty of death; Heaven is the great Carpenter; and he who would hew

¹ II, 55 (XXXIX, 99).
² I, 30 f. (XXXIX, 72 ff.).
³ II, 69 (XXXIX, 112).
⁴ II, 55-61 (XXXIX, 100 ff.).
⁵ I, 25 (XXXIX, 67).
⁶ II, 73 (XXXIX, 116).

in its place, seldom will avoid cutting his own hands.¹ Heaven's actions are not personal and intended, Heaven is without a feeling of kindness, says a far later scripture, though from Heaven the greatest kindness comes: "the crash of thunder and the blustering wind both come without design." ²

As for the future life and a spirit world, the view, as in Confucianism, is almost confined to the world of human experience: there is no wealth of imagination, no speculation directed to an unseen world.³ Especially have we no hint, as in Zoroastrianism, of terrible conflicts, of terrible armies contending in that realm. There is a quiet confidence that death cannot harm the man who has the Truth,⁴ that a man may die and yet may not perish; ⁵ that especially in a State that is ill-governed, the manes of departed men return to hurt the living.⁶

Taoism is thus both like and unlike the religion of the Quakers. It is a religion of mystic quietude; but it is far less absorbed in personal piety and in the conscious relation of the individual to a personal God than is the Christianity of the Friends. It has, indeed, a deep distrust not only of rites but of duties, of personal responsibility, of individuality, a distrust which comes into full flower only in the East. Confucius, as we shall see, urges a faith that is untroubled, but there is a spur to action, to the performance of rites, and under extreme provocation, even to revenge. But for the man who knows Tâo, there can be no such interest, no such passion, nothing but complete freedom from both hatred and love.

¹ II, 74 (XXXIX, 117).
² Yin Fu King, 3, 2 (XL, 261 f.).
³ In the later development of Taoism, this is not true. See e.g., the Zah Yung King, 2 f. (XL, 270 ff.), *The Stone Tablet to Lao-tsze*, 10 (XL, 319 and n.), The Thai-Shang, 2 (XL, 235); the Writings of Kwang-tsze, Book XVIII, pt. II, sect. 11, 4 (XL, 6).
⁴ II, 50 (XXXIX, 92 f.).
⁵ I, 33 (XXXIX, 75).
⁶ II, 60, 2 (XXXIX, 104).

II

Among far-Eastern faiths we have in the Bhagavadgita, the "Divine Song," the expression of another religion in which there is no final place for anger or even for any kindly feeling. Short of the goal, however, there is room for the martial virtues, and for active conflict.

For it is on the battle-field that Krishna appears to Arjuna and reveals to him the Truth, the truth that comforts the warrior troubled by his own scruples at human killing. There is, it is declared by the Divinity, no greater good for those of the warrior caste than righteous battle; the avoidance of such battle brings infamy and sin; its acceptance is the open door to heaven.[1] For another caste, the Brahmanas, there are other supreme duties, other highest virtues, including penance, purity, forgiveness, and faith; but the natural duty of the warrior caste holds within it valor, glory, courage, not slinking from battle, generous giving, and the exercise of lordly power.[2]

Men may thus rightly fight external foes. But the great enemy, the enemy that is utterly unmanageable, is desire, whose seat is in our senses, our mind, our understanding; desire, born of the quality of passion, is ravenous, sinful.[3] Desire is the constant foe of the man of knowledge;[4] with a firm resolve, joined with courage, all desire must be abandoned, must be actively suppressed.[5]

And everywhere anger is seen to be of the loathsome litter of desire. Lust, anger, and avarice are the threefold way to hell; men who have such passions pass into

---

[1] Bhagavadgita, II (VIII, 46). In this section the references hereafter, unless indicated otherwise, will be understood to be to this work.
[2] XVIII (VIII, 126 f.).
[3] III (VIII, 57 f.).
[4] III (VIII, 57).
[5] VI (VIII, 70).

demoniac wombs and never come to the Deity.[1] Anger, brute force, arrogance, the readiness to say "this foe I have killed, others too I will destroy," are among the marks of the demoniac person;[2] anger is in the chain of causes which lead from desire to utter ruin.[3] And on the other hand, freedom from anger is necessary if one is to be identified with Brahma;[4] he who is free from all attachment, who has no enmity toward any being, comes to the Deity;[5] the man of godlike endowment is free from anger, free from back-biting, is gentle, modest, compassionate, forgiving, courageous, without desire to injure others.[6]

This faith is of divided mind toward the kindly affections, now praising and now condemning them. The straight and consistent course, in accord with the purpose to be rid of all desire, leads not to love but to complete indifference. Such a course is indeed recognized and approved: the true warrior looks alike on pleasure and pain, gain and loss, victory and defeat; he knows that his weapons do not touch the very self; so he prepares for battle and incurs no sin.[7] The wise man feels neither joy nor aversion, he neither desires nor grieves, he is alike to friend and foe;[8] he sees no difference between a Brahmana, a cow, an elephant, and a man of low caste.[9] Affection itself, equally with anger, goes with what is banned: those come to the Deity from whom affection, fear and wrath have departed;[10] the desired tranquillity is to be had by freedom from both affection and

[1] XVI (VIII, 116 f.).
[2] XVI (VIII, 115 f.).
[3] II (VIII, 50 f.).
[4] XVIII (VIII, 128).
[5] XI (VIII, 99).
[6] XVI (VIII, 114 f.).
[7] II (VIII, 45, 47).
[8] XII, XIV (VIII, 101, 110).
[9] V (VIII, 65).
[10] IV (VIII, 59).

aversion;[1] he is highest to whom not only friends and enemies, but the good and the sinful are alike.[2]

Yet this indifference is not left without suspicion toward it, and the creeping in of its opposite, a lively concern for the distinction of right and wrong. Here the good is set opposite to the evil; godlike endowments are there, and also demoniac;[3] there are worshippers of gods, and worshippers of what is not divine;[4] there is a clear difference between what should, and what should not, be done.[5]

This wavering of mind—a stoic movement toward utter indifference, and yet an involuntary shrinking from it, and a drawing toward what is lovely—is reflected also in the portrayal of Krishna, of the Divinity, of great Vishnu, terrible in his splendors, fierce and awful in his true form.[6] The Divine Being produces, upholds, and destroys the unwise; is all and in all, is love and goodness, but also passion and darkness;[7] from him come good and evil, and to him none is hateful, none dear.[8] He is above the understanding of both gods and demons;[9] within his body are sages, demons, the gods, even the Lord Brahma, seated on his lotus throne.[10] Such a being can well be without jealousy: he knows that all who worship in faith worship him;[11] he grants the prayer, whoever be the god to whom the prayer is offered.[12]

Yet again, the Divinity is far from indifference in himself, or a ready accepter of indifference in others. He

[1] II, XVIII (VIII, 70, 127 f.).
[2] VI (VIII, 68).
[3] XVI (VIII, 114 f.).
[4] IX, XVII (VIII, 84 f., 118).
[5] XVI (VIII, 117).
[6] XI (VIII, 93 ff.).
[7] VII (VIII, 74 f.).
[8] IX, X (VIII, 85, 86).
[9] X (VIII, 87).
[10] XI (VIII, 93 f.).
[11] IX (VIII, 84).
[12] VII (VIII, 76).

praises, he condemns; according to their character, their thought, their knowledge, their illusion, men are to him abhorrent or dear. He hurls down the unholy for rebirth in demoniac wombs;[1] he destroys the evil-doer, and protects the good;[2] he has compassion on those devoted to him;[3] the one who has attained righteousness is dear, is very dear, to the Divinity;[4] Arjuna is dear to him, and will be set free from all sin;[5] the Lord is the friend of all beings,[6] but the man of knowledge is to him most dear, he is to the Deity as his very self.[7] Nor does he require indifference in his followers, but rather a positive kindliness: he prefers the man who is without hatred, who is friendly and compassionate;[8] the man of knowledge will hold the Lord dear above all things,[9] and the worship of the Deity which pleases him is not formal but is with love.[10] Doctrine is not all alike to him: those who hold that the universe is devoid of truth, devoid of principle, without a ruler, the product of mere lust,—these men are enemies of the world, are ruined selves.[11]

There is belief in life after death, but not (save for the inconsistencies just before us) of divine love or wrath. The enjoyment or suffering comes of an impersonal linkage between cause and effect; their source then is unemotional, without judgment wherein lies praise or blame. But interest in the future centers about rebirth, and escape from rebirth. Men who are caught in the net of delusion, who are attached to the objects of desire, are destined to

[1] XVI (VIII, 116).
[2] IV, XI (VIII, 59, 94).
[3] X (VIII, 87).
[4] XII (VIII, 101 f.).
[5] XVIII (VIII, 129).
[6] V (VIII, 67).
[7] VII (VIII, 75).
[8] XII (VIII, 101).
[9] VII (VIII, 75).
[10] X (VIII, 87).
[11] XVI (VIII, 115).

104 ANGER: ITS RELIGIOUS AND MORAL SIGNIFICANCE

hell; deluded in birth after birth, they go down to the vilest state, and never come to the Divinity.[1] In particular does death during passion make it certain that there will be rebirth and continued attachment to action.[2] If desire departs—desire and fear and wrath—there is eternal release from birth and death.[3] By devotion, however, one may "repair to that seat where there is no unhappiness;"[4] while for those whose course is between sin and piety, who perform meritorious action without true devotion, there is rebirth; but happy rebirth.[5] But the worlds of those who act meritoriously, and all other worlds, even the world of Brahma, are transitory; in them there is return and rebirth. Only the highest goal, unperceived, is eternal; attaining this, none returns;[6] by supreme knowledge one transcends the qualities by which bodies are produced, and attains immortality.[7] The devoted one attains a tranquility that brings final emancipation, and assimilation with the Deity,[8] brings one to Brahma-Nirvana, to the bliss of Brahma.[9] The supreme goal is thus an escape from the very conditions of right affection rather than preservation of it refined from all anger and ill-will.

Thus the religion of the Bhagavadgita—addressed, in its poetic expression, to a warrior and giving a high place to righteous warfare—is at heart in doubt if not in denial of the worth not only of all struggle, but of all affection, all attachment which gives motive and energy to conflict. There is no real battle, no real action, no responsibility for man; all is predestined; man himself does in truth

[1] XVI (VIII, 116).
[2] XIV (VIII, 108 f.).
[3] V (VIII, 67).
[4] II (VIII, 49).
[5] VI (VIII, 72 f.).
[6] VIII (VIII, 79 f.).
[7] XIV (VIII, 109).
[8] VI (VIII, 69).
[9] II (VIII, 52).

accomplish nothing; all is done by Krishna; and when Arjuna fears that fraternal killing is evil, since it will end the family and all family rites, and will send his ancestors down to hell, Krishna declares the indifference of all such deeds. Without human action those killed in battle would still be killed.[1] "Even without you," says Vishnu to the hesitant warrior, Arjuna, "the warriors standing in the adverse hosts, shall all cease to be. All these have been already killed by me. Whom I have killed, do you kill. Be not alarmed. Fight."[2] He who is without the delusion that he really is an agent, even though he kills, kills not, and is not fettered.[3]

Starting with loyalty and righteous warfare, with a preference for attachment and good-will to what is right, this lofty utterance of the human spirit attains to a spiritless ideal where worthy distinction and preference quite vanish, where of all the possible sides no one is ours, where friends and enemies, the good and the bad, are alike to the Highest Reality and to the man who has knowledge of this Highest. In the recognition of the delusion which clouds all process, inner and outer, at first wrath and all dark passions are put away, but in the end there go with these even affection and preference for goodness.

III

We shall now let Buddhism speak, and wholly in its canonical and early form.

Here the supreme goal is a quieting of all that troubles either the surface or the depths of the spirit. Tranquillity is to be attained; the true disciple has the stillness of a deep lake, a stillness that pervades his thought, his word,

---
[1] I (VIII, 41 ff.).
[2] XI (VIII, 96), with omissions.
[3] XVIII (VIII, 123).

his deed.¹ This calm has a sweetness, a joy, which even the gods do not know.²

He who has this stillness which is as the depths of the sea is without desire not merely for the things which are commonly counted evil, but for anything whatever.³ He cares no longer whether things are thus and so;⁴ he has cut the knot of attachment, he embraces nothing, he longs for nothing; utterly without preference, he desires neither this world nor the next.⁵ In turning from all desire, he knows the vanity not only of earthly pleasure, but even of pleasure that is heavenly.⁶ The steps are told by which there is an utter emptying of the mind of all perception, all thought, and, in consequence, all preference, all purpose.⁷

Fearlessly this great doctrine of renunciation follows its course and includes the gentler attachments in its refusal, along with the fierce and destructive passions. We should expect in it a fear of women: they are dangerous, every sentry must be up and alert when they are near; one is a bondsman if there remains in him the least remnant of love for them.⁸ But beyond this, one must be without every other affection: the affection not alone of husband, but of father, of friend, is a fetter on the mind; better is it to be unattached, to wander alone like a rhinoceros.⁹ Good and evil are alike ties and are to

¹ Akankheyya-Sutta, 14 ff. (XI, 215 f.); Dhammapada, 81, 93 (X (1) 24, 28).
² Akankheyya-Sutta, 3 ff. (XI, 210 ff.); Kullavagga, VII, 1, 6 (XX, 233); Dhammapada, 99, 205 (X (1) 30, 55); Sutta-Nipata, 256 (X (2) 43).
³ Sutta-Nipata, 920 (X (2) 175); Dhammapada, 153, 271 f., 305 (X (1) 43, 66, 73).
⁴ Kullavagga, VII, 1, 6 (XX, 233).
⁵ Sutta-Nipata, 634, 794 f., 849 (X (2) 114, 151 f., 163); Dhammapada, 410 (X (1) 92).
⁶ Dhammapada, 187 (X (1) 51).
⁷ Maha-parinibbana-Sutta, III, 33 ff.; VI, 11 (XI, 51 f., 114 f.); Maha-sudassana Sutta, II, 3 ff. (XI, 271 f.).
⁸ Maha-parinibbana-Sutta, V, 23 (XI, 91); Dhammapada, 284 (X (1) 69).
⁹ Sutta-Nipata, 34 ff., 368 (X (2) 6, 61).

be overcome; joy must be destroyed.[1] One who hates nothing and loves nothing, at last is free.[2]

In a religion of this temper there is inevitably no place for anger, for hate. The condemnation of it, without reserve, is explicit and repeated. The Blessed One is troubled by disciples who are "litigious, contentious, quarrelsome, disputatious."[3] Ill-will and hatred are named with lust, as passions to be checked.[4] Happy is he who does not hate those who hate him;[5] it is well to avoid hostility among the hostile, to be peaceful among the violent; to be rid of passion and hatred, arrogance and hypocrisy.[6] Anger and hatred are among the just reasons for regarding one as an outcast.[7] A man should beware of anger of the body, of the tongue, of the mind; he who can hold back rising anger like a rolling chariot, is a driver indeed; others but hold the reins;[8] anger is to be checked within one, like weeds in a field,[9] like the poison of a serpent.[10]

And if anger and hatred are alien to this faith, much more is all killing, all war. Deep is the purpose to cause no pain to any creature. And partly for this reason, as well as from the purpose to attain inner peace, is gentleness prescribed. All beings long for life and happiness, therefore one should not punish or kill; nor will he even speak harshly to anyone, for angry speech is painful.[11] The disciple will destroy no life;[12] he will not intention-

[1] Sutta-Nipata, 636 f. (X (2) 114).
[2] Dhammapada, 211 (X (1) 56).
[3] Mahavagga, X, 4, 6 (XVII, 312).
[4] Maha-sudassana Sutta, II, 3 (XI, 271).
[5] Dhammapada, 197 (X (1) 53).
[6] Sutta-Nipata, 630 f. (X (2) 114).
[7] Sutta-Nipata, 115 (X (2) 21).
[8] Dhammapada, 221-234 (X (1) 58 f.).
[9] Dhammapada, 356 ff. (X (1) 84).
[10] Sutta-Nipata, 1 (X (2) 1).
[11] Dhammapada, 129 ff. (X (1) 36 f.).
[12] Tevigga Sutta, II, 1 f. (XI, 189).

ally destroy a worm or an ant;[1] he will not knowingly drink water that has in it any living creature;[2] he will not injure even any herb or plant or vegetable or its seed.[3]

As for war,—perhaps because its inherent violation of all that Buddhism prized was so evident—we find surprisingly little in the canon in direct condemnation. The paths to it however are clearly blocked: the good man is "an encourager of those who are friends, a peace-maker, a lover of peace, impassioned for peace, a speaker of words that make for peace;" he refrains from maiming, killing, imprisoning, plundering;[4] he will not go to "combats between elephants, horses, buffaloes, bulls, goats, rams, cocks, and quails, cudgel playing, boxing, wrestling, fencing, musters, marching and review of troops;" he will refrain from tales of arms, war, and terror,[5] and from the art of foretelling the events of war.[6] And yet for all this avoidance of the hem of the garment of war, the imagery of combat—as in so many other religions—is felt to befit the spiritual endeavor of even this irenic faith: Buddha goes out to do battle with the tempter, Mara, who comes against him as with an army; against the tempter is used the weapon of knowledge;[7] and Buddha is conqueror.[8]

And that neighbor of warfare, religious persecution, was evidently so clearly repellant that its condemnation was not needed. Yet Buddhism, much as it praises indifference, is not indifferent to heresy: certain disciples are condemned for taking the vow of silence, as do heretics;[9]

[1] Mahavagga, I, 78, 4 (XIII, 235).
[2] Patimokka: Pakittiya Dhamma, 62, and cf. 20 (XIII, 46, 35).
[3] Tevigga Sutta, II (XI, 190, 192); Mahavagga, V, 7, 1 (XVII, 21 f.).
[4] Tevigga Sutta, II, Kula Silam, 5 and 11 (XI, 190 f.).
[5] Tevigga Sutta, II, Magghima Silam, 3 and 7 (XI, 192, 194).
[6] Tevigga Sutta, II, Maha Silam, 3 (XI, 197).
[7] Dhammapada, 40 (X (1) 14).
[8] Sutta-Nipata, 438, 563, 571 (X (2) 71 f., 103, 106).
[9] Mahavagga, IV, 1, 11 ff. (XIII, 327 f.).

the disputatious ways of heretics are condemned;[1] before ordination, four months of probation are specially prescribed for those who have belonged to certain heretical schools; and if one goes back to his old heresy, he shall not be received again.[2] There is no interdict, however, on common human kindliness toward those with whom one has been associated, though heretics they be.[3]

Thus we find that the logical severities of the faith begin early to be tempered. In its love of tranquility, of perfect spiritual calm, in its abhorrence of self-assertion, of desire, of attachment, we have seen this intrepid doctrine approve the thought not only that anger and hatred, but that all preference, all affection, all love, are wrong; and that there must be complete indifference. Not only is there indifference to learning,[4] but to action: the true Brahmana goes scatheless though he have killed father and mother, and have destroyed a kingdom and all its subjects.[5] But we can understand how there is revulsion from this idea even when it is received. For indifference kills the root of all morals and indeed all spiritual life: and love is at essence so winning that some place for it must be found. In truth Buddhism comes to be of divided mind, praising what it condemns. It no sooner says that there is to be perfect quietude, without desire or thought or preference, than it calls men to effort;[6] it calls them to desire,—to desire the Ineffable;[7] it calls them to

[1] Sutta-Nipata, 891 ff. (X (2) 170).
[2] Mahavagga, I, 38, 1 ff. (XIII, 186 f.); Kullavagga, X, 26 (XX, 366).
[3] Mahavagga, VI, 31, 11 (XVII, 115).
[4] Sutta-Nipata, 911 (X (2) 174).
[5] Dhammapada, 294 (X (1) 70), where will be found also Max Müller's discussion of this striking passage which seems to me but a fearless pursuit of the principle that action is indifferent, met frequently in the Buddhist canon. Yet the opposite is also asserted, as in Sutta-Nipata, 140 (X (2) 23), where a sinful Brahmana shall not escape hell or blame.
[6] Dhammapada, 276 (X (1) 67).
[7] Dhammapada, 218 (X (1) 57).

thoughts of love, to send forth thoughts of love, as a trumpeter,—thoughts of love and pity and sympathy—to all the four quarters of the world, north, south, east, and west.[1] One should cultivate friendliness toward all beings, toward all the world, a boundless unobstructed good-will.[2] The Buddha suffuses with a feeling of his love the one whom he would make his disciple;[3] he commends in another the love felt toward himself.[4]

Indeed love is the means of large accomplishment: it is the only means of overcoming hatred;[5] by love the venom of serpents, the anger of wild beasts, can be made harmless; by much love laid up in the heart is it possible to attain ripeness of years.[6]

In a faith which is thus wholly turned from anger, there can be no central place for the angry condemnation of wrong. Buddhism is too temperate even for passionate rejection. There is no poignant sense of personal responsibility for sin. Even if moral indignation were an acceptable passion, there would be here everything to quiet it, since evil is not, as Islam and Christianity see it, a choice; it is not a free act for which you and I can be held to answer; it is a fatality that is part of very life as an individual and from which we can escape only by escaping individual existence.

And while there is no hint of divine assistance, which would call forth man's gratitude for such escape, there is ample word of supernatural hindrance. Dangerous, and perhaps malicious beings, demons, were feared; a belief in their reality is ascribed to the Buddha himself.[7]

[1] Tevigga Sutta, III; Maha-sudassana Sutta, II (XI, 201, 272 ff.).
[2] Sutta-Nipata, 148 ff. (X (2) 25).
[3] Mahavagga, VI, 36, 4 (XVII, 136).
[4] Maha-parinibbana-Sutta, V, 35 (XI, 96 f.).
[5] Dhammapada, 5 (X (1) 5); Mahavagga, X, 3 (XVII, 307).
[6] Kulavagga, V, 6; VII, 3, 12; XII, 2, 5 (XX, 76, 248 f., 404 f.).
[7] Mahavagga, III, 9, 2 (XIII, 313), and other passages in the canon (cf. XIII, 261, 340; XVII, 188; XX, 312).

THE UNANGRY RELIGIONS

In particular there is conceived a personal Tempter, Mara, who strives to bring to naught the work of the Buddha. The Lord is tempted, not to attain wealth and power, as in the faith most Occidental, but to surrender all-too-early his individual existence. Mara knowing that at the heart of Buddha's purpose is the desire for release from life, cunningly assaults him there, urging him to pass away before his disciples have been fully instructed, or (when this proposal is rejected) before his teaching and theirs has won the victory.[1]

This Tempter is no mere tester of men's sincerity, as in the Book of Job; he is the Wicked One;[2] he deceives and overthrows men, and holds them in bondage;[3] he is king of Death,[4] he is Death itself;[5] he tries in vain to turn back "the supreme wheel of the Empire of Truth."[6] With evil so near, so powerful, and so personal, and with no sign of help from on high, it is not surprising to learn that few attain to heaven.[7]

Punishment is not wholly wanting. But the hells of Buddhism seem less a place of malignant retribution into which men are thrust by some supernatural power, than an inevitable continuance and increase of the natural passions which men have allowed to grow. Birth may follow birth, until their number for the same individual may reach a hundred, a thousand, a hundred thousand.[8] The evil-doer is reborn into some state of distress and punishment; liars, all evil-doers, go to hell.[9] for a re-

[1] Maha-parinibbana-Sutta, III, 7 ff., 43 ff. (XI, 42 ff., 52 ff.).
[2] Mahavagga, I, 11 (XIII, 113 f.).
[3] Dhammapada, 7 f., 37, 274, 350 (X (1) 5, 12, 67, 83).
[4] Dhammapada, 46 (X (1) 17).
[5] Mahavagga, I, 11, 2 (XIII, 113 f.).
[6] Dhamma-kakka-ppavattana-Sutta, 25, 27 (XI, 153, 154).
[7] Dhammapada, 174 (X (1) 47); it need hardly be said that a different view is found in the more sectarian writing, the Saddharma-Pundarika.
[8] Akankheyya Sutta, 17 (XI, 216).
[9] Mahavagga, VI, 28, 4 f. (XVII, 100); Dhammapada, 126, 306 ff. (X (1) 35, 74 f.).

ligion so bent upon escaping pain even to worms and plants, it is strange that it could entertain its own imaginings of the tortures of the human evil-doer: such a man has food that is like a red-hot ball of iron; his bed is of embers and a blazing pyre; his tongue is seized with hooks; he is hammered and boiled; he rots; he is eaten by vultures and jackals.[1] These torments shall not be escaped until he attain the truth.[2]

And in a like temper there is a happy future for well-doers:[3] the righteous go to heaven; those who are free from all worldly desires attain Nirvana.[4] Heaven has its rejoicing, its song and music and dancing.[5] There is a great assembly of the spirit world,—angel hosts, guardian angels, the Great Thirty-Three, Mara, and Brahma.[6] But the delights of heaven are not to be confused with the ways of true holiness: the rewards of the first step in holiness are greater than going to heaven; he who attains the true knowledge, and the freedom which it gives, him the gods themselves may well envy.[7] The bliss of the righteous seems in no wise the efflux of divine approval, good-will, or love. It is rather the natural outcome of a long self-discipline, of conquering the desire for life,[8] of becoming "well-tamed."[9] As to the actual quality of its blessedness, there seems to be some want of full agreement: it is described as though it were a blissful reality, a positive happiness, a highest happiness in which, free from desire, one is still conscious of happiness all around;[10]

---

[1] Mahavagga, 531, 664 ff. (X (2) 91, 122).
[2] Kullavagga, 230 (X (2) 38).
[3] Mahavagga, VI, 28, 4 f. (XVII, 100).
[4] Dhammapada, 126 (X (1) 35).
[5] Sutta-Nipata, 679 (X (2) 125).
[6] Maha-parinibbana-Sutta, III, 21 (XI, 48), cf. Tevigga Sutta, 46 (XI, 187).
[7] Dhammapada, 94, 178 (X (1) 28, 48).
[8] Maha-parinibbana-Sutta, I, 11; II, 9 (XI, 10, 27).
[9] Dhammapada, 323 (X (1) 77).
[10] Dhammapada, 23, 203 f., 368 (X (1) 9, 54 f., 86); Sutta-Nipata, 227, 953 (X (2) 38, 180).

while again its bliss consists wholly in escape, in utter negation, in the loss of all reality: those who attain Nirvana are "completely extinguished," they disappear, they cease to exist, they go out like a lamp,[1] they pass away "in that utter passing away which leaves nothing whatever to remain."[2]

Buddhism, then, represents an extreme and marvellous attitude toward emotions. Far back, as we approach the early expression of this faith, we find that its goal and the way to this goal have no secure place for any of them, save that of quiet revulsion from them and all other activities of personal life. It is of divided mind regarding joy and love or good-will, while in deepest principle it is opposed even to their presence. But it has no indecision with regard to anger and all the qualities that partake of anger. Of these it is unhesitant in its rejection.

IV

As our final example of faiths that are unangry, the religion of the Jains, so close in many ways to Buddhism, is most importantly at one with it in its attitude toward the emotions with which we are here concerned: it is a religion of patience; there is no acceptable place whatever for anger and its kin.

Jainism is wholly unaggressive, studious of the negative virtues,—detachment, calm, indifference.[3] It aims not at the aggressive conquest of evil, but at a passive conquest, by avoiding all the causes of pain. All beings, even the gods, are subject to pain; and not a minor part, but the very quintessence, of wisdom is to kill nothing.[4]

[1] Sutta-Nipata, 234, 765, 1073 f. (X (2) 39, 145, 198 f.).
[2] Maha-parinibbanna-Sutta, IV, 50; V, 21 (XI, 81, 91).
[3] Sutrakritanga, I, 8, 18 (XLV, 299 f.).
[4] Sutrakritanga, I, 1, 4; I, 2, 1 and 9 ff. (XLV, 247, 250, 311).

114 ANGER: ITS RELIGIOUS AND MORAL SIGNIFICANCE

The escape from Karman is by avoiding cruelty: not only should no "breathing, existing, living, sentient" creature be slain, but it should not be treated with violence, nor abused, nor tormented, nor driven away.[1] "Tolerate living beings, do not kill them, though they eat your flesh and blood." [2] Not only do plants experience pleasure and pain, so that it is a sin to injure them; [3] but even earth, water, fire, and wind desire happiness; and by injuring them, men harm their own souls, and will not escape from life.[4]

But the escape from life is not alone by bringing no pain even to the lowliest beings; one must, in one's self, escape from the sources of pain, which comes of passion and desire. Self-mastery is of more value than any outward charity: "Though a man should give, every month, thousands and thousands of cows, better will he be who controls himself, though he give no alms." [5] One must patiently bear what befalls him, without giving way to passion; it is idle to blame others; the sage will conquer his own passions, and will practice indifference.[6] The righteous man is free from all desire; for him friends and enemies are alike; he is without interest in this world or the next.[7]

We are not left doubtful as to the application of this general truth to the particulars of anger. Among the fifteen good qualities, for the most part negative virtues, of a learned monk—to be humble, steady, free from deceit and curiosity; to abuse no one; not to persevere in wrath; to heed friendly advice; to be not proud of one's learning; to find no fault with others; not to be angry with

[1] Akaranga, I, 4 (XXII, 36 ff.).
[2] Uttaradhyayana, II, 5 (XLV, 11).
[3] Akaranga, I, 1, 5 (XXII, 9 f.).
[4] Sutrakritanga, I, 7 (XLV, 292).
[5] Uttaradhyayana, IX, 40 (XLV, 39).
[6] Sutrakritanga, I, 2, 1 and 2 (XLV, 251, 253).
[7] Uttaradhyayana, XIX, 25, 44, 92 (XLV, 91, 93, 99).

friends; to speak well even of a bad friend behind his back; to abstain from quarrels and rows; to be enlightened, polite, decent, and quiet [1]—avoidance of the various forms of anger and irritation holds a large place. And elsewhere anger or wrath is named among the cardinal evils that are to be conquered in oneself—along with pride, deceit, greed, and "the five senses." [2]

Yet it is possible that at times self-culture is seen to be not by mere passivity, but by an inner struggle resembling warfare. When urged to be a true warrior, the reply of King Nami, now enlightened, is that inner victory is far greater than that of warriors, is greater than a victory over thousands and thousands of valiant foes without; "fight with oneself; why fight with external foes?" [3] And the inner state thus reached is described in terms, not of mere negation, but of possession and strength; the true monk is as unmatched in might as is an irresistible elephant, a bullock, a lion; as a monarch with armies; as Vasudeva, the god who fights with irresistible strength; as Sakra, the king of the gods, the wielder of the thunderbolt, the fortress-destroyer.[4] Yet this is the exceptional note; more central is the thought, not of aggression, but of retreat, of escape as in those animals whose only response to danger is by an utter passivity as of death. And in this, hatred is not of opposite worth from love,—love to be sought, hatred to be avoided;—love and hate are equally to be shunned: the enlightened one reaches perfection by cutting off both love and hatred.[5] Karman arises from the passions in sinners subject to love and hate; [6] love and hatred are connected

[1] Uttaradhyayana, XI, 10-13 (XLV, 47).
[2] Uttaradhyayana, IX, 36 (XLV, 38 f.), and cf. Sutrakritanga, I, 6, 26; I, 14, 7 ff.; II, 2, 16 and 44 ff. (XLV, 291, 235, 361, 369), where various special displays of anger are denounced.
[3] Uttaradhyayana, IX, 34 f. (XLV, 38).
[4] Uttaradhyayana, XI, 18-23 (XLV, 48).
[5] Uttaradhyayana, X, 37 (XLV, 45 f.).
[6] Sutrakritanga, I, 8, 8 (XLV, 298).

with rebirth; the righteous man will be free from hostility, indifferent both to pleasure and to pain.[1] "Quitting your former connections place your affection on nothing; a monk who loves not even those who love him, will be freed from sin and hatred."[2] "Every attachment is but a cause of sin."[3]

Yet while the good man will be free from anger and love, and will be indifferent; he is not required to be indifferent to truth: he will delight in the truth.[4] There is, moreover, explicit truth for him to delight in, a truth that is partial, taking sides; in this respect there appears the very opposite of that transcendent mysticism, perfect in India, which affirms whatever it denies, and denies whatever it affirms. For in Jainism, of a long series of contradictions, one is true and its opposite is false: it is true, and only true, that the world exists; that virtue and vice exist; that there exist pride and anger, deceit and greed, love and hate, gods and goddesses, perfection and imperfection, good and evil.[5] When one is questioned by another, one is free to expound the truth.[6] But the quietness, the unaggression, the un-Pauline spirit of Jainism is manifest in that the well-instructed man will not go about volunteering assertions on these and other matters; he will avoid professing his individual persuasion.[7] There are heretical doctrines; but the good man, while not uttering them himself, will not even ridicule them in others.[8]

This religion, as we have seen, holds that the enlightened man will be without interest in this world and the

[1] Akaranga, I, 3, 1 (XXII, 28).
[2] Uttaradhyayana, VIII, 2 (XLV, 32).
[3] Sutrakritanga, I, 3, 2, 6 (XLV, 264).
[4] Sutrakritanga, I, 10, 12 (XLV, 308).
[5] Sutrakritanga, II, 5, 12 ff. (XLV, 407 f.).
[6] Sutrakritanga, I, 10, 16 (XLV, 308).
[7] Akaranga, I, 7, 1 (XXII, 62 f.).
[8] Sutrakritanga, I, 14, 20 f. (XLV, 327).

next. Yet it is itself not without such interest. It invites men to its own faith and discipline by depicting the future life of the soul. Men who sin go to hell; the righteous go to heaven.[1] But heaven is one's place only for a while;[2] the perfect, the pure soul, is at last set free, and attains final beatitude, attains Nirvana, and for him all misery is at an end.[3] In the effort to escape life and attain Nirvana, suicide itself is permitted or even prescribed.[4]

The evil-doer wanders from womb to womb, from birth to birth, from death to death, from hell to hell, from pain to pain.[5] The hells, fifteen in number, are described with a savage cruelty strange in a faith that so shrinks from pain even in vermin, plants, and in life still below these. Hell is of an infinitely intenser cold, an infinitely intenser heat than is to be found here on earth. And there one is not only roasted; he is crushed, his flesh is torn by dogs, by devilish vultures; one is hacked to pieces, consumed with thirst and made to drink burning fat and blood. Horrid and exquisite and enduring are hell's pains.[6] Yet it must not be thought that this is an angry punishment imposed by an offended god. It is the outcome of one's own acts, the sad necessity wrought by desire and passion which have not been renounced.

Jainism is thus at heart a study of renunciation, of escape from life which is essentially evil. Like Buddhism, of which it is own brother if not the child, its way is the way of retirement instead of advance and attack. But more singly and constantly than in Buddhism even, there is in it no eternal place for love; much less is there an

[1] Uttaradhyayana, XVIII, 25 (XLV, 83).
[2] Sutrakritanga, I, 8, 12 (XLV, 299).
[3] Sutrakritanga, I, 6, 24; II, 2: Uttaradhyayana, XXIX, 73 (XLV, 173, 291, 372, 380).
[4] Akaranga, I, 7, 4 and 8 (XXII, 68, 74).
[5] Sutrakritanga, II, 2 (XLV, 376 f.).
[6] Uttaradhyayana, XIX, 47 ff.; XXXI, 12; Sutrakritanga, I, 5; II, 2 (XLV, 93 ff., 182, 279 ff., 376).

eternal place for anger and hatred. Even in this world these are not possible instruments of righteousness. The good man is called upon to rid himself wholly of them with all other passions; they are all fetters of the soul.

In contrast to the angry faiths, this present group of religions are without self-assertion; so deep a calm settles upon the spirit that it ceases to prefer, much less to struggle or to be angry; it is blest in the loss of all desire, all purpose.

The second answer of religion to the question, What shall we do with anger? then is, Do nothing with it, except destroy it; it is wholly an enemy; it cannot be reconciled with devotion to the Best.

CHAPTER VII

THE RELIGIONS OF ANGER-SUPPORTED LOVE

Confucianism, Christianity

We have thus seen the two opposite ways of regarding anger,—the one, all cordial, viewing this passion as the spirit's proper minister; the other, giving no sign of recognition, cold, turning its back upon the unbidden guest. And are these all that religion holds in store; are the full possibilities now spread before us?

There is yet a third course, of moderation, neither rejecting the pugnacious impulse nor yet receiving it to be the ruler of the house. And this course is followed by two, and by only two, great faiths, that have prevailed upon opposite sides of the world and are in many other ways a full world-diameter apart. Yet each makes love supreme and does not thereby exclude hatred, but admits it to the service of good-will. We shall at once see how unlike they are to Islam and all similar faiths; and how unlike to Buddhism with all its kind.

I

In the great religion connected with Confucius' name,—a religion and not, as is sometimes said, a mere system of ethics—there is deep in the universe no such moral conflict as is found in the religions less far to the East. The spiritual foundations of the world are not threatened by evil at war with the good; there is no great leader of Wrong. There is, above man's own misconduct, hardly more than a mild opposition of nature's forces, an ebb and flow with the seasons, in which men may help: at midsummer the forces of darkness and decay quietly meet those of brightness and growth, and at that time superior men will remain quiet, to assist the readjustment; while in midwinter when the balance is again critical, superior men will fast and wait and wish all affairs to be quiet.[1] This passive furtherance of a cosmic readjustment—how different its tenor from the terrible and age-long spiritual warfare to which Zarathustrism and Christianity called their followers!

Yet the divine power—now called God, and now Heaven—is far from being indifferent to the conduct of men. Heaven's attitude is shown in its action only, for it says nothing.[2] Heaven, that may be called our own parent,[3] bestows its favor, its bright favor, on the virtuous,[4] on those who revere the prescribed path;[5] its affection is to the reverent;[6] on the righteous it bestows length of years.[7] Heaven thus in its affection is not partial[8] nor is its favor easy to hold.[9] Its love, however, is particularly toward the people, and the sovereign should heed this divine inclination: "Heaven sees as my people see," says the Great Declaration; "Heaven hears as my people hear." [10]

While God blesses the doer of good, God also sends misery upon the evil-doer.[11] Heaven is capable of anger, indeed now shows its anger.[12] Compassionate Heaven sends angry terrors,[13] sends down calamities on him who

[1] Li Ki, IV, 2, 2, 15; IV, 4, 2, 13 (XXVII, 275, 305).
[2] Analects, XVII, 19 (Legge's tr. 326).
[3] Shih King, V, 4 (III, 361).
[4] Shu King, IV, 6, 2; V, 28, 1 (III, 101, 266).
[5] Shu King, IV, 2, 4 (III, 89).
[6] Shu King, IV, 5, 3 (III, 99).
[7] Shu King, IV, 9 (III, 119).
[8] Shu King, V, 27 (III, 212).
[9] Shu King, VI, 16 (III, 206).
[10] Shu King, V, 1, 2 (III, 127 f.).
[11] Shu King, IV, 3, 2; IV, 5, 4 (III, 90, 95).
[12] Shih King, II, 10; III, 3 (III, 409 f., 418).
[13] Shih King, V, 5 (III, 358).

THE RELIGIONS OF ANGER-SUPPORTED LOVE

opposes the right.[1] Those whom Heaven does not approve sink in ruin;[2] famine is sent because of dissoluteness, and in divine anger is the land laid waste;[3] drunkenness is punished by terror and the ruin of states;[4] calamities from Heaven, the curse of Heaven, comes of disregarding certain rules respecting the seasons;[5] the cruelty of men rises to God as a rank odor;[6] Heaven punishes the taker of bribes.[7]

Nor is the condemnation of God vaguely directed only to *classes* of persons and acts, without farther point and focus; it falls upon individuals, even upon royal individuals; King Hsia is under God's disfavor; Heaven requires that he shall be destroyed for his many crimes; God punishes the wicked King Shau, cursing and ruining him;[8] God's anger is aroused against Khwan because he disturbed the five elements.[9]

Heaven, God, thus is stirred both to affection and to anger; but there is not so hot and fateful a divine passion that it pursues man into the life beyond death. Its expression is chiefly, if not only, in the present life; there is no clear picture of reward and punishment in a Heaven, a Hell. The dead are said to be in a ghostly state [10] and are to be treated as though they were neither wholly dead nor yet entirely alive;[11] at one moment they are said to go to the dark regions of the north; at another, to rest in the ancestral shrine or temple.[12] Yet kings after death,

[1] Shu King, II, 2, 3 (III, 51 f.).
[2] Shih King, III, 2 (III, 414).
[3] Shu King, IV, 10 f. (III, 120 ff.).
[4] Shu King, V, 10 (III, 174).
[5] Li Ki, IV, 1, 1, 22; IV, 2, 3, 11 (XXVII, 256, 279).
[6] Shu King, V, 27 (III, 256).
[7] Shu King, V, 27, 6 (III, 264).
[8] Shu King, IV, 1, 1; IV, 2, 2; V, 1, 3; V, 19, 3 (III, 85, 87, 130, 222).
[9] Shu King, V, 4, 1 (III, 139).
[10] Li Ki, XX, 4 (XXVIII, 203).
[11] Li Ki, II, 1, 3, 3 (XXVII, 148).
[12] Li Ki, II, 1, 22 and 34 and 40; IX, 1, 16 (XXVII, 167, 170, 171 f., 423).

are said to "ascend," to be "on high," to be "in heaven," to "ascend and descend on the left and the right of God." [1] Besides such spirits of the dead, there are vague references to demons and the regions which they inhabit.[2]

Toward the world of spirits men will show respect without familiarity.[3] Toward Heaven, the source of all things, men will feel gratitude and will render thanks, even as they are grateful to their ancestors, the source of their own life.[4] Villagers are described as actively driving away pestilential influences—evil spirits, it would seem,—but without hint that this is conduct suited to "superior men"; Confucius himself on such occasion merely stood at the top of his eastern steps, dressed in court robes, to keep undisturbed in their shrines the spirits of his departed.[5]

Confucianism is therefore not unappreciative of due feeling toward an invisible world. But is it not, like some of the far-Eastern faiths, negligent, at times contemptuous, of the feelings of men toward men? Quite the contrary, these feelings are as a field to be cultivated; [6] indeed, one's feelings are a guide to those of others, and so to conduct: "What you do not like when done to yourself, do not do to others." [7] And as for the particular feelings that are to be cultivated, benevolence is the very substance of man, and finds its greatest exercise in the love of relatives,[8] and exists where superiors and inferiors love one another.[9] In cultivating the feelings of men to

[1] Shu King, V, 23; I, 1 and 9 (III, 244, 378 f., 393).
[2] Shih King, 1 and 4 (III, 412, 420).
[3] Analects VI, 20 (Legge, 191. For this particular interpretation cf. Jennings' tr. 1895, p. 83n, and that of Ku Hung-Ming, 1898, p. 44).
[4] Li Ki, IX, 2 and 6 ff. (XXVII, 427, 429 f.).
[5] Li Ki, IX, 1, 16 (XXVII, 423).
[6] Li Ki, VII, 3, 8 (XXVII, 383).
[7] Li Ki, XXVIII, 1, 32 (XXVIII, 305).
[8] Li Ki, XXVIII, 2 (XXVIII, 312).
[9] Li Ki, XXIII, 4 (XXVIII, 257).

THE RELIGIONS OF ANGER-SUPPORTED LOVE 123

bring them to righteousness, love is the fundamental subject;[1] in government the whole purpose of ceremonial is to give a proper direction to the love of men, underneath which is reverence and affection; "love and respect lie at the foundation of government"; a ruler of men fails if he cannot love his people.[2] Love, widespread far beyond the family, prevailed in the ancient days;[3] and a love of all is still demanded of youth.[4] Particularly is compassion to be shown to orphans and widows, and special consideration to the aged, the ill, the bereaved, and the lame.[5]

The "superior man," while ready to incur the hatred of his associates, desires their sympathy and support.[6] Filial piety is the root of all virtue, the stem of all moral teaching: one's love of his parents will cause him to avoid the hatred of men; although a son must remonstrate with an unrighteous father, he will revere his father, he will love his mother; the father, in the son's reverent awe, will be connected with Heaven; reverence, pleasure, anxiety, grief, and solemnity, are feelings that have their right place in the family life; from these spring the social virtues. "Perfect filial piety and fraternal duty reach to and move the spiritual intelligences, and diffuse their light on all within the four seas:—they penetrate everywhere."[7] But again, filial affection itself is felt to be due to something still deeper, the affection between husband and wife is the spring of that between father and son, and of righteousness and universal repose.[8]

But the acceptance and appreciation of feeling or of

[1] Li Ki, VII, 4, 8 (XXVII, 389).
[2] Li Ki, XXIV, 9 and 14 (XXVIII, 264, 268) and cf. Analects, I, 5 (Legge, 140).
[3] Li Ki, VII, 1, 2 (XXVII, 364 f.).
[4] Analects, I, 6 (Legge, 140).
[5] Li Ki, III, 5, 12 f.; IV, 4, 1, 10 (XXVII, 243 f., 298).
[6] Yi King, II, 43, 3 (XVI, 152, and cf. 249).
[7] Hsaio King, I, XVIII (III, 465-488); cf. Li Ki, XXI, 2, 12 (XXVIII, 227).
[8] Li Ki, IX, 3, 9 (XXVII, 440).

124 ANGER: ITS RELIGIOUS AND MORAL SIGNIFICANCE

sentiment goes still farther: mere knowledge is not enough; there must be the driving force of affection and high pleasure behind the knowledge of duty, behind the moral sense which has been granted by the great God even to inferior people;[1] for Confucius said, "They who know the truth are not equal to those who love it, and they who love it are not equal to those who delight in it."[2]

Yet there is no demand that only love and kindness and delight be shown; the virtuous man will both love *and hate;* he will hate those who slander, those who have mere bravery without propriety, those who are self-confident, insistent and of narrow understanding.[3] But the upright man will guard against quarrelsomeness, especially when he is in full strength; even as in his youth he will guard against lust, and in old age against covetousness.[4] The love commended does not rush on to universal forgiveness; there are wrongs that call for vengeance: the death of a father or mother must be avenged and without delay. And there will be retaliation likewise for a brother's death, or a cousin's, or an intimate friend's.[5] Ruler and household shall turn in vengeance on the parricide; and when a man kills his ruler, all who hold office with him shall kill the murderer without mercy.[6]

Nor has warfare an abhorrent place in this religion of a people so long regarded as utter pacifists. In the ruler, martial qualities are praised and his resources for war. He may well have gifts both of peace and of war; one who is to be a pattern of the people will have his war-gear ready.[7]

Indeed a military general may be the appointed of

[1] Shu King, IV, 3 (III, 90).
[2] Analects, VI, 18 (Legge, 191).
[3] Analects, IV, 3; XVII, 24 (Legge, 166, 330).
[4] Analects, XVI, 7 (Legge, 312 f.).
[5] Li Ki, I, 1, 5, 2; II, 1, 2, 24 (XXVII, 92, 140).
[6] Li Ki, II, 2, 3, 18 (XXVII, 195).
[7] Shih King, II, 7; III, 2, 3, and 9; IV, 4 (III, 325, 335, 339, 414).

THE RELIGIONS OF ANGER-SUPPORTED LOVE 125

Heaven to execute its judgment.[1] God commands the king to prepare for war against his foes; [2] the ruler, the Son of Heaven, goes forth to punish his enemies, with due rites to God, to Earth, to his father, and to "the Father of War."[3] The canonical Book of Ceremonial has, moreover, prescription for the seasons of campaign, for weapons, for banners and war-horses, for drill and instruction, for appointment, and—as though written for old Prussia—for the *bearing* of officers: "When wearing his coat of mail and helmet, one's countenance should say, 'Who dares meddle with me?'" Other rules that deal with military topics of a strangely modern flavor touch upon the unauthorized sale of army-property, upon selling to the army such goods as are not in accord with specifications; touch upon cowardice, and excuse from military service.[4]

Less modern, the tablets representing the spirits of ancestors were provided in the army with a special guard.[5] And there are rules for divining whether a given circumstance requires war, and what would be its outcome.[6] Victory may appropriately be celebrated with religious rites.[7] But the moderation of the ideal here recorded is shown in Confucius' contempt of mere bravery, bravery that lacks wisdom; he did not want, he said, the help of anyone who would unarmed attack a tiger.[8]

It is clear, therefore, that Confucius was not the dull formalist of western tradition. He was not a sage bereft

[1] Shu King, III, 4; V, 1, (III, 81 ff., 124 ff.).
[2] Shih King, I, 7 (III, 392).
[3] Li Ki, III, 2, 21 (XXVII, 220).
[4] Li Ki, I, 1, 5; I, 4, 2 and 9; II, 1, 1, 13; II, 2, 2, 22; III, 2, 21; III, 4, 6 ff. and 17; IV, 1, 1, 22; IV, 2, 1 and 3; IV, 3, 3 and 9; IV, 4, 2, 20; V, 2, 27; XVII, 3, 15 (XXVII, 84, 89 f., 91 f., 125, 185, 220, 234 f., 238, 256, 270, 279, 284, 294, 300, 341; XXVIII, 120).
[5] Li Ki, VI, 2, 13 (XXVII, 358).
[6] Yi King, I, 15, 5; I, 7; II, 43 (XVI, 90, 71 f., 152).
[7] Shu King, V, 3 (III, 133 ff.).
[8] Analects, VII, 10 (Legge, 198).

of sensibility; his religion recommends no mere rites, no fulfillment of purely external obligations; the grief, the reverence to be expressed by the ceremonial is of more worth than the outward show; Confucius himself is described as weeping bitterly at the death of one with whom he once had merely lodged.[1] Music, in particular, is said to have had the power deeply to affect him: on one occasion he was so pleased with what he heard that for three months he did not know the taste of flesh; "I did not think," he said, "that music could have been made so excellent as this." [2] And while it was not his custom to talk of spiritual beings, yet he commended one who displayed the utmost filial piety toward spirits. Nor did he hold himself from prayer: when he was sick and some one asked leave to pray for him, he replied, "My praying has been for a long time." [3] I have found no mention of anger in him, or of any action approaching the pugnacious; although, as we have seen, the religion bearing his name requires anger and hate, yet in all ways subordinated to a wide good-will.

The spirit of the religion, therefore, is kindly rather than passionate; its anger is well-disciplined, uncontentious; it is no seeker of heretics, nor is it aflame to subdue the world; it is no threatener of eternal wrath and punishment. Far from mystic indifference to good and evil, its approval and condemnation are clear as noonday. It commends, to be felt toward all men, the family affections; and toward Heaven, reverence and thanksgiving. Its temper befits a people whose high and unaggressive civilization has persisted, essentially unshaken, for thousands of years.

[1] Li Ki, II, 1, 2, 16 and 27 (XXVII, 137, 141).
[2] Analects, VII, 14 (Legge, 199).
[3] Analects, VII, 20 and 34; VIII, 21 (Legge, 201, 206, 215).

II

Moving now westward, we shall at once see in a different world a religion that, with all its contrasts to Confucianism, agrees with it in accepting and fostering both anger and love. The eminence of love in Christianity is so familiar—with its numberless teachings of scripture that God is love, and that men are to love him and one another—that this present account will not be misunderstood if it leave this aspect unreported, but dwell rather on the anger of Christianity, which is often quite lost to view.

In the precepts of Jesus are the words "Judge not, and ye shall not be judged; condemn not, and ye shall not be condemned." [1] Yet against this is his biting judgment of Scribes and Pharisees: "hypocrites," "blind guides," he calls them, "fools," "whited sepulchres"; each of them is a "son of hell"; "ye serpents, ye generation of vipers, how can ye escape the damnation of hell?" [2] "Put up thy sword," he says to Peter who would defend him, "they that take the sword shall perish with the sword." [3] Yet he also says, "He that hath no sword, let him sell his garment, and buy one." [4] At one time, he says, "Peace I leave with you"; [5] at another, "Think not that I came to send peace on the earth: I came not to send peace, but a sword." [6] "Resist not evil," [7] is his precept, yet he himself overturns the tables of the tradesmen in the temple, and drives them forth with denunciation and blows. This man who commanded that the gift should

[1] Luke VI, 37.
[2] Matt. III, 7; XXIII, 13 ff.
[3] Matt. XXVII, 52.
[4] Luke XXII, 36.
[5] John XIV, 27.
[6] Matt. X, 34.
[7] Matt. V, 39. This side of Christianity, taken by Tolstoy as though no other side were there, is not given its due correction even by so discriminating an interpreter as W. E. Hocking. See his *Human Nature and its Remaking*, 1918, pp. 348 ff.

be left unoffered at the altar until there was reconciliation with one's brother;[1] and who could say, "Whosoever shall smite thee on thy right cheek, turn to him the other also,"[2] "Love your enemies, bless them that curse you,"[3] who will make no defense before his Roman judge; who prays, "Father, forgive them, for they know not what they do," is himself angry with those who oppose his healing on the Sabbath.[4] And he freely suggests that wrath is found on high: "There shall be . . . wrath upon this people."[5] And in the parable of the debtors, when the master was wroth with the merciless servant and delivered him to the tormentors till he had paid all, there are these ominous words: "So likewise shall my heavenly Father do also unto you, if ye from your hearts forgive not every one his brother their trespasses."[6]

Taking the varied elements of this conception in the Gospels we see in outline the portrait of a man affectionate, without resentment, and yet upon occasion hot in his resentment. God was for him a friend, a loving father, yearning for the absent son's return,—and yet hardened to flint against those who are unmerciful. Many would say that the parts of the picture are irreconcilable. I do not myself find them so. Love is supreme, but there is in it no softness, no relenting toward its enemies: there is here "the love of love, the hate of hate." So strong are its opposing elements that one can easily mistake its character. So passionate is its anger that some can see it hardly different from Islam, that other child of Judaism. So strong is its love that others can see it only as at the opposite pole from Islam, contrasted with it as the feminine is opposed to what is masculine, its love so strong that it seems a brother to Buddhism. In truth it is with

[1] Matt. V, 24.
[2] Matt. V. 39.
[3] Matt. V, 44.
[4] Mark III, 5.
[5] Luke XXI, 23.
[6] Matt. XVIII, 34 f.

neither of these extremes; it is opposed to each; yet not so violently as these are to each other.

For Jesus is not the fanatic warrior Mohammed; nor is he the Buddha, seated under the Bodhi tree, studying how he may lose the last trace of passion. Jesus was not an emotionalist, but he showed emotion; he loved, he wept, he lost heart, he grew angry, he attacked. But his anger was never aroused, to our knowledge, by some affront to his person, some threat to his life or his dignity. He never contends for property or for convenience. His anger is detached from all selfish interest; he is enraged against those who have had opportunity and yet remain opponents of the truth and of mercy. He sees his own doctrine to be at once a source of peace and of conflict. Perhaps he had in mind only an inner peace, an inner conflict; perhaps he saw his work leading straight to contention between men, to wars between nations. The expression of his doctrine may have changed with the years or with the needs of those to whom he spoke, his eye resting now upon the eternal Goal there in the untroubled distance, and again his eye looking to the Way, the laborious and cruel way by which the eternal peace is won. Those who are competent must restore the living figure from the fragments. But to my own mind Jesus represents a tempered faith, where love neither excludes anger nor is ruled by anger. Love uses anger as a servant to fight the enemies of love. Jesus is aware of the danger in this heady passion, how it becomes impatient of service and would be master. But he does not for that reason cast it utterly away.

And this in the Gospels is also the temper of the *Acts* and, in general, of the *Epistles,* coming to a perilous intensity of wrath in the great drama of *The Revelation.* The immediate followers of Christ impress one with their natural and manly emotions. There is little of that indifference to success and failure, that sad resignation, which has at times been counted the true state of Christians. They are glad: they rejoice even to be counted worthy to suffer shame. They are *bold* as they face Jews, Greeks or Romans. Peter and John are bold; Paul and Barnabas are bold; Stephen speaks out boldly before his stoning.

Nor is anger lacking, especially in St. Paul. As Jesus had shown intense anger, so the one who had power beyond all others to spread the Gospel in the ancient world was a man of wrath. When Bar-Jesus, the Jew of Paphos, opposed him, Paul replied in words that are only a little less violent than those used by Christ against the Pharisees: "O, full of all guile and all villainy, thou son of the devil, thou enemy of all righteousness, wilt thou not cease to pervert the right ways of the Lord?"[1] And, again, at Antioch Paul had what is described as "no small dissension and disputation"[2] with certain Jewish Christians who insisted that no one could be saved unless he were circumcised. Paul had a sharp conflict with Barnabas over the selection of a companion upon their journey; and each thereafter goes his separate way. Where others merely speak their cause boldly, Paul is contentious. At Corinth he becomes openly angry with the Jews who opposed his teaching: he shook his raiment, saying, "Your blood be upon your own heads; I am clean." He was ready to cease preaching to the Jews: "from henceforth I will go unto the Gentiles."[3]

He was perhaps not proud of these tempests of his humor; I cannot find that he commends them to others as a pattern. If, as Emerson says, we praise what we ourselves lack, we can understand Paul's earnestness in advising the Colossians[4] to put away wrath and anger. He fears that when he returns to Corinth (so he writes the

[1] Acts XIII, 10.
[2] Acts XV, 2.
[3] Acts XVIII, 6.
[4] III, 8.

brethren of that city),—he fears that he will find in them and they in him perhaps wrath and strife.[1] He tells the Galatians [2] that hatred and wrath are among the works of the flesh: whereas among the fruits of the spirit are peace, long-suffering, kindness, meekness. He here draws no line between righteous and unrighteous anger, recommending to them the righteous; anger is condemned without distinction. Yet to the Romans he is less sweeping: "If it is possible," he writes, "as much as lieth in you, live peaceably with all men." [3] He thus sees some limit to the power to live at peace with others—a moderation which appears also in a letter which may not be Paul's, where a wise use rather than a total abstinence of anger is commended: "Be ye angry, and sin not: let not the sun go down upon your wrath." [4]

If in now turning from Paul's temperament and advice to others we recall his picture of the divine character, we find that he conceives God not as one whose tenderness is unmixed. Earthly rulers are his ministers, executing his vengeance on evildoers; [5] yet God is rich in mercy, and through Jesus we are delivered from this wrath; [6] while upon the Jews who reject Jesus, God's anger is come to the uttermost.[7] Paul even entertains the thought that some men are formed by the Divine Potter into vessels upon which he may show his power and wrath.[8]

With this contentious strain not only in his thought of God but in himself, it need not surprise us that Paul should view his life as in effect a fighter's life. He likes to describe his method and career as that of a warrior, a boxer, a gladiator. "I box," he tells the Christians of

[1] II Corinth. XII, 20.
[2] V, 19 ff.
[3] Romans XII, 18.
[4] Ephes. IV, 26.
[5] Rom. XIII, 5.
[6] I Thessal. I, 10.
[7] I Thessal. II, 16.
[8] Rom. IX, 21 f.

Corinth, who would appreciate the simile, "I box, not as one that beateth the air";[1] his heavy fist found his opponent, landing where the blow would count. His strenuous days at Ephesus[2] seemed to him as though he had fought with animals; as though he had been in the arena contending with hungry beasts.

This variable attitude toward anger, now wholly condemning it in men, now condemning it with a proviso, but often displaying it in act and always maintaining it in God, finds an echo beyond the writings of St. Paul. In the *Epistle of James*[3] the peaceful side is clearer; men are exhorted to be slow to wrath, for man's wrath does not work the righteousness of God. Strife even in the heart should prevent one from glorying; for envying and strife lead to confusion and every evil work. In contrast with earthly wisdom, the wisdom that is from above is pure and peaceable and gentle. "The fruit of righteousness is sown in peace to them that make peace."[4]

But in the book of *The Revelation* a more trumpet-like note is sounded: hate and wrath and battle are brought to an epic vigor and proportion. The Nicolaitans are not merely condemned; the Spirit declares that it *hates* their doctrine.[5] In heaven Michael and his angels fight and prevail against the dragon.[6] And in God himself there reappears that wrath in which St. Paul believed, but now represented with a terrible splendor of imagination. The four and twenty elders thank God Almighty that his wrath is come, and the time when he shall destroy those who corrupt the earth.[7] The kings of the earth implore the rocks and mountains to fall on them and hide them

---

[1] I Corinth. IX, 26.
[2] I Corinth. XV, 32.
[3] I, 19 ff.
[4] III, 14 ff.
[5] II, 6, 15.
[6] XII, 7.
[7] XI, 16 ff.

THE RELIGIONS OF ANGER-SUPPORTED LOVE 133

from the wrath of the Lamb.[1] There are the seven golden vials full of the wrath of God.[2] The men who worship the Beast must drink of the wine of God's wrath, a wine poured out pure into the cup of his indignation.[3] God gave unto Babylon "the cup of the wine of the fierceness of his wrath."[4] And out of the mouth of him who sat upon a white horse, whose name is the Word of God, "goeth a sharp sword, that with it he should smite the nations: and he shall rule them with a rod of iron: and he treadeth the winepress of the fierceness and wrath of Almighty God."[5]

The book of *The Revelation* tells of the love and compassion of God but also of his might and his avenging anger. In awful pictures its sentence is illustrated, "As many as I love, I rebuke and chasten." The virtues of the seven churches are recognized; but God has somewhat or a few things or much against them. We behold the multitudes who come up through tribulation; the woe upon woe; the plagues and plagues and yet seven more plagues. We hear the voice that blesses the Bride of Christ, but that also judges the Woman arrayed in scarlet and purple until the smoke of her burning arises forever and ever. A new heaven and a new earth is foreseen, without death or sorrow or crying or pain; the first heaven and earth have passed away. And yet, mysterious and hidden somewhere without, there remains for the abominable and all liars the lake burning with fire and brimstone, which is the second death.

The little book which the angel compelled John himself to swallow, in the mouth sweet as honey but bitter in the belly, gives the contrasts which appear throughout the religion set forth in the New Testament. It does not try to divorce love from hate; the two live together as though

[1] VI, 16.
[2] XV, 7, and cf. XVI, 1.
[3] XIV, 10.
[4] XVI, 19.
[5] XIX, 11 ff.

joined of God; yet love is the motive feeling, is the ruling passion throughout the whole. Anger and hatred spring up in support of good-will to men, and not as a diabolic hate which turns to destroy good-will and to strengthen the tools and ministers of hate. The Gospel proclaims a love that is substantial, that casts a shadow. God is love, but he is also of portentous wrath against the destroyers of love. His wrath is moved and guided by his love of men, and not by an original hate of them. Love then is lord, and God can rightly be named by this his ruling passion.

Some have regarded this early Christianity as the religion of slaves; but if its followers were enslaved in body they were not bondsmen in spirit. There is neither fawning nor despair. They hold their heads erect, in their eye is love and indignation: theirs is the tradition of that early Christian, John the Baptist, who acknowledged with reverence a carpenter as one greater than himself, and yet denounced a king for his sins and would lose his life rather than abate his condemnation. Men with such fierce love of righteousness are not the servile creatures of modern satire; they are of the company of heroes.

To the question, What should be religion's attitude toward anger? our third answer, clearest to us in Christianity, is in substance this: anger is of itself neither bad nor good; its value depends upon its use. *Employ anger freely if the including, the ruling, impulsion is good-will. But it must never itself be the ruling passion.*

With this there are before us the different answers given by the great religions. The Jew, the Arab, the Persian saw a God whose heart is for contention, driving his true subjects to wrath and fierce strife. In the group of faiths farther to the East—Taoism, Vishnuism, Jainism, Buddhism—such a thought is far away: instead of **anger and** conflict, they study tranquility undisturbed by hatred or by love. Finally, in a strange meeting of extremes, the great religions that have prevailed in China and in Europe together with America, agree against both these attitudes; they favor both anger and good-will, the one as servant, the other as the master-passion directed to all men and flowing eternally to and from God.

PART III
ANGER IN RELIGION'S GROWTH

CHAPTER VIII

MAN'S ANGER TOWARD THE SUPERNATURAL

Anger we have seen busied shaping morals. We have seen it also in its varying place in the great religions. These great faiths may now be connected with those not great, to observe how religion in root as well as branch holds itself with respect to the hostile passions. And to notice well the facts without a tourist's haste, the several passionate relations should be traversed, one by one,— the feeling of men toward spiritual beings; of these toward one another and toward men; and finally, under religion's prompting, the emotions which men feel toward their fellow men.

I

Viewing then first the feeling of men toward the powerful beings not living men, but to whom in some way living men are bound, there is upon certain lower levels of religion a place for anger directed at the spirit or divinity. Anger so directed not only occurs, but is accepted without shame. A few instances will make this clear.

It is of course easy to understand that when sickness or other misfortune was thought by a people to have been sent upon them by the gods of their enemies, enmity should be felt toward these gods, and a desire to have vengeance upon them.[1] But the anger might not always be directed thus toward the gods of the foe; it was felt toward one's own divinity. Ellis found in Polynesia that when peace

[1] See, e.g., de Rochefort: *History of the Caribby-Islands*, tr. Davies, 1666, 280.

was desired, gifts were taken to the temple and the god was besought to cause the war to cease; but behind the prayer was a threat: "If you do not attend we will not worship you. . . . If you do not deliver us, you are an evil-working god."[1] And in Tahiti in particular, after vain efforts had been made to appease the god, when a chief who was sick did not recover, "with singular promptitude . . . they executed the idol, and banished him from the temple, choosing in his place some other deity that they hoped would be favorable."[2]

A certain Caribbean, working on Sunday, (we have it on the authority of Monsieur de Montel) was told that he who made heaven and earth would be angry with him for working on that day. "And I," replied the savage bluntly, "am already very angry with him; for thou sayest he is the Master of the world and of the seasons: he it is therefore who hath forborne to send rain in due time, and by reason of the great drought hath caused my *Manioc* and my *Potatoes* to rot in the ground: since he hath treated me so ill, I will work on every Sunday, though 'twere purposely to vex him."[3]

Truculence may pass even to active aggression, with flogging and armed attack upon the offending ones. Thus among the Eskimo of Hudson Bay, the guardian spirit which attends each person often has a material form, that of a doll; and if the spirit is stubborn, this image is stripped and chastised or given to some one without the spirit's knowledge.[4] And the Arabs, before the coming of Islam, dealt in like manner with an offending god; if, after vow or offering, the suppliant's hopes were disap-

[1] Ellis: *Polynesian Researches*, 1831, I, 317.
[2] Ellis: *Polynesian Researches*, 1831, III, 47.
[3] de Rochefort: *History of the Caribby-Islands*, tr. Davies, 1666, 277.
[4] Turner: "Ethnography of the Ungava District," *Eleventh Ann. Rep. Bureau of Ethnol.*, 1894, 193 f. For the beating of fetich see Schultze: *Fetichism*, tr. Fitzgerald, no date, pp. 27, 44; Knox: *Historical Relation of Ceylon*, 1681, p. 83; Waitz: *Anthropologie*, II, 185.

pointed, "the deity was assailed with childish abuse"; while if the request was obtained, the promise was evaded by substituting some sacrifice less costly.[1]

Less individual, more united, anger and attack upon offensive spirits may occur. The Caunians, so Herodotus relates, on one occasion "determined that they would no longer make use of the foreign temples which had been long established among them, but would worship their own old ancestral gods alone. Then their whole youth took arms, and striking the air with their spears, marched to the Calyndic frontier, declaring that they were driving out the foreign gods."[2] And close to this is the general expulsion of evil, at certain seasons, with excitement and outcry if not with actual weapons. "On the Gold Coast" writes a witness, "there are stated occasions when the people turn out *en masse* (generally at night) with clubs and torches, to drive out evil spirits from their towns. At a given signal, the whole community start up, commence a most hideous howling, beat about in every nook and corner of their dwellings, then rush into the streets, with their torches and clubs, like so many frantic maniacs, beat the air and scream at the top of their voices, until some one announces the departure of the spirits through some gate of the town, when they are pursued several miles into the woods, and warned not to come back."[3] Similar doings have been observed among peoples far distant from these.[4]

Doubtless upon occasion such acts might be perfunctory or dramatic, without actual wrath. But even then they

[1] Introduction to Palmer's tr. of the Koran, p. xv. Cf. Tiele: *Elements of the Science of Religion*, 1896, I, 71.
[2] Book I, Ch. 172 (Rawlinson's tr.).
[3] J. L. Wilson: *Western Africa*, 1856, 217.
[4] For occurrences among the American Indians, see *Jesuit Relations*, ed. Thwaites, XLII, 155 ff.; Timothy Dwight: *Travels in New England and New York*, 1821-1822, IV, 213 f.; E. A. Smith in *Second Ann. Rep. Bur. Ethnol.*, 1883, 112 ff. The Sulka, among the Melanesians, drive away the souls of the dead; Parkinson: *Dreissig Jahre in der Südsee*, 1907, 185. It also occurs that the god of rain is driven by stones, from his spring or pool; Frazer: *Golden Bough*, 1900, I, 81 ff.

would point back to a time of excited onslaught, with the full anger stirred by an enemy present in the flesh. Such a loss of the original emotion is probable also in the scourging of an individual to expel an evil spirit from him—done at first by others, but finally by himself. The Indians of New Granada kept in close confinement for years those children who were to be their rulers or commanders and "their keepers at certain Times went into the Retreat, or Prison, and scourg'd them severely." [1] And among the Banmanas of Senegambia little children beat each other to keep off the spirit of one who had died,[2] —a practice which elsewhere was not confined to children, and might recur at the anniversary of the death of a chief or other man of note.[3] Self-scourging as a means of penance is doubtless a variant or vestige of this ancient method of dealing with hostile spirits, whose earlier meaning is still seen when a priest or sorcerer in Guiana prepares for his office by fasting and flagellation.[4] And if spiritual evil can thus be forced to leave, it is but a short mental step thence to the conviction that spiritual good can in the same way be compelled to enter; when certain white visitors were entertained by the "Roucouyennes du Sud" in French Guiana, one of their number besought the visitors to honor him by beating him with rods, and when this was done he expressed unbounded pleasure believing that physical and moral virtue had entered into him.[5]

[1] Herrera: *History of the Vast Continent and Islands of America*, etc., tr. Stevens, 1726, V, 88.
[2] Frazer: *Golden Bough*, 1900, III, 130 f.
[3] See, e.g., J. Crevaux: *Voyages dans l'Amérique du Sud*, 1883, 548; and Bernau: *Missionary Labours in British Guiana*, 1847, 52. Some of this flogging in connection with a chief's death may originally have been a softened substitute for the sacrifice of human life. Such an origin, however, would not exclude a change of meaning, whereby the ceremony came to be an attack upon the ghost or spirit which might "possess" a living person.
[4] Tylor: *Primitive Culture*, 1903, II, 419.
[5] Coudreau: *Chez nos Indiens: quatre années dans la Guyane Française*, 1895, 543 f.

It is not at all strange that there should be felt toward a spirit the fury which would be aroused by an attack by man or beast, when one remembers some of the evil that a malevolent spirit can do. For to the primitive mind such beings can cause all manner of untoward happenings without: they may destroy property, cause accident to limb and life, they may eat the bodies of the dead, take captive their souls; they may "possess" a living man or steal away his soul. The Dyaks of Borneo, for example, "believe that every individual has seven souls, and that when a person is sick, one or more of these are in captivity, and must be reclaimed to effect a cure." [1] And in the belief of certain Melanesians, if the place haunted by a ghost be encroached upon by a man, the ghost punishes him by taking away and impounding his soul and thus bringing upon him sickness.[2]

Now in some cases, as with these very Melanesians, the evil is met by obtaining the service of a "dreamer," through whom the captive soul is released by asking pardon of the ghost on behalf of the sick man, who then is restored to health. Or incantations may be used against demons, ghouls, and vampires.[3] With some peoples, however, the spiritual attack was to be met in wrath and repelled *vi et armis*.

II

But there comes a time when anger or contempt of man toward spirit, and especially anger toward a god, either does not occur, or, when occurring, is felt to be a transgression, even a blasphemy, which others cannot behold without fear and abhorrence. The son of the Israelitish

[1] H. Ling Roth: "Natives of Borneo," *Jour. Anthropol. Inst.*, XXI, (1892), 117.
[2] R. H. Codrington: *Melanesians*, 1891, 208.
[3] See, e.g., R. Campbell Thompson: *The Devils and Evil Spirits of Babylonia*, 1903-4; for other references showing the use of protective magic, see pp. 161 ff.

woman is stoned to death for cursing and blaspheming the name of the Lord.[1] A charge of cursing or blasphemy is trumped up by Jezebel as a sure means of bringing death to Naboth.[2] Job in his prosperity offers sacrifice lest his sons may have cursed or renounced God in their secret hearts. And when his own misfortune overwhelms him, his wife in urging him to hurl back his indignation at the Lord, feels that such an act is a last and unpardonable affront to Jehovah, for which Job's own life must be paid. "Curse God" is her word to him, "and die."[3] Wherever in communities of advanced religion it still is found, it is of rare and usually of private occurrence.[4]

Even from the beginning there seems to have been an exceptional attitude toward anger. Other emotions toward God,—love, for example, and awe, and humility—are, at one or another time, singled out for overt culture. Religious frenzy is intentionally brought on by dance and fast and drug-intoxication and sexual orgy. The emotions so incited are felt to bring illumination, to bring a sense of union, of divine "possession"; by their means the long and narrow way from man to God is opened.[5] But artificial means are never used to heighten anger toward a god, unless it be perhaps of one's enemies.

Such means to anger are quite within men's reach: there are anger-producing devices which he readily employs, even with all religion's approval, to stimulate rage

[1] Leviticus, XXIV, 11 ff.
[2] I Kings, XXI, 10 ff.
[3] Job, I, 5; II, 9. For further light upon the Hebrew attitude toward blasphemy, which of course need not always be the expression of anger or hatred, see II Kings, XIX, 6, 22; Isaiah VIII, 21; XXXVII, 6, 23; LII, 5; LXV, 7; Ezekiel, XX, 27.
[4] One who knew Mark Twain, told me of witnessing in him, at his home, a passionate outburst, with defiant gestures of anger against God, because of so much poverty and suffering among men.
[5] An account of some of the practices toward this end will be found in Tylor: *Primitive Culture*, 1903, II, 416; Frazer: *Golden Bough*, 1900, II, 366; de la Saussaye: *Manual*, 153 ff.; as well as in the present writer's *Psychology of the Religious Life*, 1911, 109 ff.

toward his fellow men.[1] Moreover there are drinks which until quite recently have not been counted of disadvantage in war and which would assist toward religious anger if anger were methodically sought in religion. The intoxication that *unites* was wanted, and not the intoxication that withdraws and severs. Thus the Zend-Avesta, although showing an eager combativeness toward evil, praises the sacred drink Haoma because it alone breeds no hate; "Homage unto Haoma, because all other drinks are attended with Aeshma, the fiend of the wounding spear: but the drinking of Haoma is attended with Asha and with Ashi Vanguhi herself."[2] The tobacco used for religious intoxication by American Indians would also rightly be classed among the unangry drugs.

Wine as used in the worship of Dionysos must often have brought—as in alcoholic intoxication to-day—a phase of quarrelsomeness; but the religious effect prized was assuredly not this anger. If anger toward the gods was ever artificially stimulated, such rites have disappeared leaving no trace. In contrast with the early means to separate oneself from an unwelcome spirit or god—including the use of emetic, flagellation, uproar, and armed attack,—there is soon a dominant desire to become one with the god, to commune with him, to partake of him; an end toward which the worshipper is brought nearer by eating, music, vigil, fasting, exhausting dances, sex-orgy, drugs, and dreams. These brought the feeling that the god had come nigh, and in very touch and thought and emotion had revealed his presence to his votary.

We should hardly take this as of course, knowing that (as we shall soon see) intense enmity between spirits and of them toward men seems more frequently and vividly conceived in very early religion than is intense affection. Yet the passion of hostility, apparently dominant in early

[1] See pp. 165, 168.
[2] Ashi Yast, II, 5 (XXIII, 271). Ashi Vanguhi is a goddess of fortune and wealth (XXIII, 270).

man, evidently meets the opposition of less stormy but more powerful passions. Practical considerations may hinder a riddance of hate and anger toward his fellow men; but in his emotions toward the gods he escapes the choking hold of these emotions.

Of the course of the developing mind it may accordingly be said in brief, that *the anger of men toward supernatural powers, which in many backward religions is accepted as right and proper, in due time finds no religious place; it has come to be viewed as impious. And from the very beginning it appears never to have received that intended and artificial stimulation which other emotions in religion have received.* Anger is not a revelatory emotion, it is only fortifying; it establishes no permanently satisfying relations. Therefore in the approach to God it is not cultivated, it falls into disuse if not condemnation, not only by the quietists and mystics, but even by those who most of all prize purpose, effort, and action.

CHAPTER IX

THE ANGER OF THE GODS

With this glimpse of the course run by man's anger toward spirits and gods, let us turn to the relation of these beings to one another and to men. Here too we shall find important contrasts between the lower and the higher levels of faith. As we look to these different heights, it will be of interest to see the emergence and the slow fading of the divine wrath.

I

At the lower levels, there may be no clear attitude of spirit powers toward one another. Their interrelation seems to have escaped creative interest. It is as though their beholders had been preoccupied with individuals or at most with the posture and look of these toward men, and there had been no imaginative power remaining to advance the sketch into a group-composition where the separate figures look with friendly or inimical eye to one another. They are given no common life, with purposes that mutually agree or clash.

Especially does the idea that supernatural power is impersonal or is of ill-defined connection with persons— an idea expressed in such terms as *mana, oudah, wakanda* or *wakonda*,[1] reveal a want of keen interest in the definite-

[1] Codrington: *The Melanesians*, 1891, 118 ff., 191, 307 f.; Marett: *The Threshold of Religion*, 1914, 99-121; Durkheim: *Les formes élémentaires de la vie religieuse*, 1912, 273 ff.; W. J. McGee: "The Siouan Indians," *Fifteenth Ann. Rep. Bur. Ethnol.*, 1897, 182 f.; Fletcher and La Flesche: "The Omaha Tribe," *Twenty-seventh Ann. Rep. Bur. Amer. Ethnol.*, 1911, 597 ff.; Riggs and Dorsay: "Dakota-

ness and interrelation of these powers. In so far as they are not clearly thought to be personal, they of course have no emotional bearing toward one another.

But even where the supernatural world is of personal beings, there is often a great number of spirits that stand in no clear psychic relation to one another. Or if they are related to one another, they are not to men. In Borneo, for example, although there is a god above the innumerable spirits who, for the natives of the Valley of Barito, fill the air, yet these spirits seem to be neither hostile nor friendly among themselves; but each object has its particular spirit which watches over it and defends it.[1] In Korea, likewise, the spirits who are said to number "thousands of billions" seem to have no definite mutual attitude.[2] And the Arabian jinn are without stated relations with men; they live in desert places, and are outside the pale of human society, although they have kinship among themselves.[3]

In all these the absence of definite attitude toward one another or toward men seems to indicate mere failure to enlarge the sketch.

II

But elsewhere the disconnection is not from lack of men's interest in completing the picture. It springs rather from a positive desire to have the disconnection. The English Dictionary," *Contrib. N. A. Ethnol.*, VII (1890), 507 ff. There is no sufficient evidence in the facts so far reported, to prove or even to make it highly probable that very primitive man recognizes "a kind of ague power diffused through things" *before* he recognizes definite and personal beings of powerful action, or that, as Durkheim holds, he may first recognize the divine in this impersonal form. It seems hardly likely that the recognition of impersonal power antedates the recognition of power as an expression or efflux of personal beings, whether in secular or in religious thought.

[1] Frazer: *Golden Bough*, 1900, III, 47 f.
[2] Bishop: *Korea and her Neighbors*, 1898, II, 227 f.
[3] Smith: *Religion of the Semites*, 1901, 119 ff., 127.

sketch itself indicates that the separation, complete or nearly complete, is by intention.

Often a great divinity is declared to dwell afar off, of unknown character or known to be indifferent to mankind. Such a belief is far-extended in West Africa: Nyong-mo, Heaven, the Eldest, the Supreme Deity of the Gold Coast negroes, sits at rest, like a Grand Monarch while his children serve him and act in his stead on earth; even as with the Guinea negroes, the Highest Deity has abandoned the control of the world to lesser spirits;[1] and particularly of Northern Guinea it is said that "the prevailing notion seems to be that God, after having made the world and filled it with inhabitants, retired to some remote corner of the universe and has allowed the affairs of the world to come under the control of evil spirits." [2] In the belief of the Kuribunda race of the Congo, Suku-Vahange, the Highest Being, takes little interest in mankind, leaving the real government of the world to the good and evil *kilulu,* or spirits, into whose ranks the souls of men pass at death.[3] And among the entire Tschwi and Bantu races of West Africa, the god of the firmament is possessed of great power but he does not care to exert it, being without interest in human matters.[4] Such a belief would seem to extend to the East Coast, where the Amazulu hold that the King of Heaven is so far removed from men that they know nothing of his mode of life nor of the principles of his government, nor do they ever pray to him;[5] such a being can hardly be concerned with men. Perhaps it is found also among those Dyaks of Borneo who, questioned by Rajah Brooke, spoke of Tupa, but knew nothing of him nor did they sacrifice or pray to him: "they bestowed on him no attributes of power or greatness, of mercy or wrath; they seek not to deprecate his anger, or gain his

[1] Tylor: *Primitive Culture,* 1903, II, 348.
[2] J. L. Wilson: *Western Africa,* 1856, 209.
[3] Tylor: *Primitive Culture,* 1903, II, 348.
[4] Mary H. Kingsley: *Travels in West Africa,* 1897, 508.
[5] Calloway: *Religious System of the Amazulu,* 1870, 1 ff.

approval."[1] And among the natives of the Philippines the greatest gods seem to be regarded as exceedingly remote from men, both in space and time, and to lack interest in human affairs.[2]

It is a slight tempering of this thought when we find that the god is not so remote, so indifferent, or so unknown, but that—although in the main he is inert and ineffectual—men are aware of some benevolence, some goodness in him; his sluggish inclination is toward good-will rather than toward malice. Among the Ashantee, God, the Creator, knowing all, is the giver of good, but he lets the world go its way. Below him are spirits good and evil, the evil spirits having one who is their ruler, the Enemy of men, who too is far away from the world, dwelling in the Beyond.[3] And the Great Spirit, with many of the American Indians, is described as passive but good, letting the lesser spirits govern the moral destinies of men.[4] The Caribs said of the power dwelling in the heavens, that it is "content quietly to enjoy the delights of its own felicity," and "is endued with so great goodness, that it does not take any revenge even of its enemies."[5] The Great Spirit of the Tuelches of Patagonia is likewise described as "careless of mankind," yet also "good";[6] even as Boa, the Heaven-god of the Tunguz, is felt to be at once "kindly but indifferent."[7]

III

Yet with due time or temperament or circumstance, all is not left so remote or so colorlessly well-disposed. The spirit-powers now have clear passions, largely of hostility.

[1] *Borneo and Celebes;* from the *Journals of Rajah Brooke,* 1848, 197-204.
[2] Kroeber: *People of the Philippines,* 1919, 178.
[3] Waitz: *Anthropologie,* II, 171.
[4] Schoolcraft: *Archives of Aboriginal Knowledge,* 1860, I, 37.
[5] de Rochefort: *History of the Caribby-Islands,* tr. Davies, 1666, 278.
[6] Musters: *At Home with the Patagonians,* 1871, 179 f.
[7] Tylor: *Primitive Culture,* 1903, II, 351.

THE ANGER OF THE GODS 151

In some cases we must regard this as a clear advance of the religious imagination, the beginnings of a deeper or more intimate recognition of one another or of men, and prophetic of organization and ultimate harmony in the invisible world. But apart from this, we can at once see that the conscious antagonism appears in various forms, with differing breadth and depth.

There may be an obscure change and opposition within the divine character itself, as where the Tagomaling, a divinity of the Bagobo in the Philippines, is in turn a god and fiend in alternate months [1]—suggested perhaps by some great traditional case of hysterical dissociation or of cyclic insanity.

Or there may be, rather, mere petulance, irritability, ill-will, easily aroused, and by charm or gift or supplication mollified. Such a trait is in the spirits that "guard" many a common object and place, and that must be propitiated as one passes by; they wish their seat to be unmolested, and if they are left alone, they bring no harm. They seem not wholly unlike pugnacious animals that resent intrusion into their lair.[2] Capricious ill-will is often shown by souls of the dead, who can easily be aroused to anger and who are greatly feared.[3] In Korea even those spirits whose nature in part is kindly are easily offended and act with extreme caprice.[4] Of a like character are all those gods who, often without constant interest in men, become angry when a temple or offering of theirs is violated, or some rite suffers neglect.[5] Polynesians expected their god Oro to avenge by death an insult unwittingly offered by a party of strangers who landed on

---

[1] Kroeber: *People of the Philippines*, 1919, 179.
[2] Cf. the account of the *hantoes*, believed in by some of the natives of Borneo (Frazer: *Golden Bough*, 1900, III, 47 f.). Cf. also the particular experience recounted by Bock: *Head-Hunters of Borneo*, 1882, 80.
[3] See, e.g., Waitz: *Anthropologie*, VI, 277, 308; Jastrow: *Aspects of Religious Belief in Babylonia and Assyria*, 1911, 362.
[4] Bishop: *Korea and Her Neighbors*, 1898, II, 229.
[5] Waitz: *Anthropologie*, VI, 302.

a spot sacred to Oro, and ate there with their women! Sickness and death come as punishment from the gods, because of neglect or violation of taboo. One of the leaders, Pomare, although influenced by the missionaries, is constantly apprehensive of the anger of his own god; and when Pomare is suddenly taken ill and dies, this is believed to be due to the anger of the god Oro. When the Europeans brought new diseases to Tahiti, these were thought to be sent by the god of the missionaries because the natives would not reject their own god Oro. The anger of their own gods, who sent sickness, might be due not only to some offense of the Tahitians themselves, but to the influence of some enemy.[1] Among the Baining of the Melanesians, the Sun summoned all beings to an assembly; men alone disobeyed and were punished by being made subject to death; on the island of Uneri it is believed that certain spirits in snakes punish men for violation of totem-usages.[2]

Different from these spirits which are changeable or petulant or require some special provocation of their anger or ill-will, there are spirits almost or quite steadily malicious. Thus we find that although among some of the Melanesians the spirits of the dead are not feared, yet with more they are believed to do much mischief: they bring sickness and death, they eat men, they are vengeful. Kot, a being higher than these, a being eternal and unchanging, is hostile to men. And on the island of Uneri, it is believed that a spirit Laulaubin, who dwells in hollow trees, loves to pursue little children and kill them. Other forest spirits that dwell in trees enter into men's bellies and feed on their intestines; still other nature-spirits in great numbers inhabit the coral reefs, the sea, air, trees, and rocks, and do injury to men.[3] In

[1] Ellis: *Polynesian Researches*, 1831-42, II, 66 ff., 76; III, 46 f., 397.
[2] Parkinson: *Dreissig Jahre in der Südsee*, 1907, 158.
[3] Parkinson: *Dreissig Jahre in der Südsee*, 1907, 159, 187, 308 f., 386 ff., 441 f., 528.

THE ANGER OF THE GODS 153

Samoa, the spirits of the unburied dead, and in New Zealand the spirits of children or from abortions, or from certain bodily discharges,—these are especially given to evil-doing, apparently without special provocation.[1] And in Korea there are great numbers of malignant spirits, both self-existent and coming from the dead who died in poverty and distress. Of the legions of spirits there, fully four-fifths are said to be thus ill-disposed.[2] In the belief of the Eskimo of Hudson Bay, the guardian spirits of sea, land, sky, winds, of every cave and rocky point, are all malignant and are under a malignant god, Tung-ak.[3] The Dacotas said that their deity was *always* offended with them; heavy storms especially were the expression of divine anger.[4] Other examples of malevolent spirits or gods might be given: that great being, ill disposed, the wife or mother of Torngarsuk of the Greenlanders;[5] Maboya of the Caribs;[6] Locozy of the Youmans;[7] Ataentsic, the moon, the wicked spirit of the Hurons, who makes man die;[8] and Huythaca, the moon, of the New Granadans, who brings all manner of trouble upon men.[9]

IV

Thus far we have seen indifference or weather-vane anger or steady malignity toward men. We may next see strong passion defining the attitude of gods and spirits toward one another. The spirit-world itself is

[1] Waitz: *Anthropologie*, VI, 304, 306.
[2] Bishop: *Korea and Her Neighbors*, 1898, II, 228.
[3] Turner: "Ethnography of the Ungava District," *Eleventh Ann. Rep. Bur. Ethnol.*, 1894, 193 f.
[4] Schoolcraft: *Archives of Aboriginal Knowledge*, 1860, II, 196 f.
[5] Cranz: *Historie von Grönland*, 1765, 263 ff.
[6] de Rochefort: *History of the Caribby-Islands*, tr. Davies, 1666, 278-290.
[7] Tylor: *Primitive Culture*, 1903, II, 325.
[8] *Jesuit Relations*, ed. Thwaites, VIII, 117 ff.; X, 132 ff.
[9] Piedrahita: *Historia General*, etc., I, Ch. III.

riven, power set against power, in persistent individual hostility or open war.

The animosity may be of that character seen in clans which fight to dominate or to prevent domination. There is mere assertiveness, mere love of battle and conquest because of strength and the love of power. Such would seen to have been the conflict of the sons of Kronos with the Titans as told by Hesiod.[1]

Or the opposition may have at its foundation a widely different principle, the one power being creative, the other destructive. Thus in parts of Africa, a supreme god, Zambi, the maker of all, is opposed by Zambi-a-n'bi, the destroyer.[2] And for the Khonds of India, Boora Pennu, the creator, is opposed by his wife Tari Pennu, who brings death and discord into Boora's work.[3] Or if not directly and explicitly a struggle between upbuilding and destruction, it is close to this, perhaps expressing it in symbol: as when in Egypt there is the great struggle between day and night, and the sun-god, Ra, must daily fight with a gigantic serpent, Apopi, representing the darkness; and in time of eclipse, Ra seems for the while to be defeated.[4]

Or again, the hostile powers may not differ as creative and destructive: each may create, but create very differently, creating well and ill. Among the Iroquois it is believed that the Great Spirit created man and all useful animals and plants, while the Evil Spirit created all monsters, poisonous reptiles, and noxious plants.[5] And similarly, as we have seen, both Ahura Mazda and Angra Mainyu create, in the religion of the Zend-Avesta.[6]

[1] *Theogony*, 618 ff.
[2] Abbé Proyart: "History of Loango, Kakongo and other Kingdoms in Africa" (1776), in Pinkerton's *Voyages*, 1814, XVI, p. 594.
[3] Macpherson: *Memorials of Service in India*, 1865, pp. 85 ff.
[4] Book of the Dead, XXXIX, and elsewhere; Maspero: *Dawn of Civilization*, tr. McClure, 1894, pp. 90 f.
[5] Morgan: *League of the Iroquois*, 1851, 156 ff.
[6] Vendidad, I (IV, 4-10).

With still others in the spiritual world the clash and
enmity begins to have explicit reference to human beings,
but as yet to human beings in general, and without distinction among them by blood or government or character.
The Binbinga of Australia believe in two spirits of the
sky, their bodies covered with white down and with
knives in the place of arms. These two spirits are ill-
disposed toward men, but their designs are prevented by
a friendly spirit who lives in the woods and is on constant watch and stops them. And a like belief is held by
the Mara of Australia.[1]

Farther on, and as an expression of a growing sense
of kin or government, the clash is based on discrimination
between different kinds of men, the differences now political or racial simply, and not as yet primarily moral. So
Athena is opposed to Poseidon, Hera to Aphrodite, because of their different attachments, as between Greek
and Trojan. Likewise Jehovah is early conceived as a
partisan of the Jew, and opposed to other peoples and
their gods. Wherever there is strong tribal, or even national conflict, the motive is there to awaken the belief
in such partisanship on high.

Finally the opposition or enmity among supernatural
beings is based neither on an undiscriminating attachment to all men, nor on an attachment to a particular
tribe or nation; it is based on *moral* distinctions, either
clear or confused. The spirits or gods are themselves
of good or evil character, and must have a different relation to men according as these are good or evil. Thus
among certain of the Melanesians there is, when a man
is sick, a conflict between good and evil spirits; and whoever at death comes among the good spirits is in no danger
of annihilation; but if these delay to come for him, evil

[1] Spencer and Gillen: *Northern Tribes of Central Australia*, 1904,
501 f.

spirits may come and devour his soul.[1] Among certain natives of West Africa, there are two great spirits or classes of spirits, the one benevolent, the other resentful; and with the one or the other of these, according as they have been virtuous or wicked in this world, the spirits of the dead must take their place.[2] A like distinction was felt by American Indians: Enigorio, the Good Mind, is opposed to his twin brother, the Bad Mind;[3] Hä-wen-ne'-yu, the ruling spirit, delighting in virtue and in the happiness of his creatures, is set over against Hä-ne-go-ate'-geh, the evil-minded, versed in deeds of evil;[4] Kitchemonedo, the Great Spirit, is good and beneficent, while Matchemonedo, the Evil Spirit, seeks to overturn all good measures, and two classes of beings—the one, benign, the other, malignant—are in perpetual antagonism to each other,[5] the great lord, Glooskap is good, while Malsumsies, or Wolf the Younger, is bad and killed his mother at his birth.[6] Kechi Niwaskw and Machi Niwaskw are opposed in moral quality.[7] In Mohammedanism the proud Iblis, who would not obey Allah when commanded to bow down and worship Adam, is the leader of a host of rebellious spirits. But in the religion of Zoroaster, to a degree reached by no other, is there fierce and continued and universal conflict between Ahura Mazda, the God of Righteousness, and Angra Mainyu, the Spirit of Evil.

[1] Parkinson: *Dreissig Jahre in der Südsee*, 1907, 387. For a somewhat similar battle for the soul, in Zulu belief, see Tylor: *Primitive Culture*, 1903, II, 318.
[2] J. L. Wilson: *Western Africa*, 1856, 217.
[3] Leland: *Algonquin Legends*, 1885, 24.
[4] Morgan: *League of the Iroquois*, 1851, 156 ff.
[5] Schoolcraft: *Archives of Aboriginal Knowledge*, 1860, I, 40, 320, 413.
[6] Leland: *Algonquin Legends*, 1885, 15; cf. Schoolcraft: *Myth of Hiawatha*, 1856, 254 f., where the "Master of Life" is opposed by a wicked spirit who induces men to evil.
[7] *Bull. 30, Bur. Amer. Ethnol.*, 1907, 4. For the belief in a good and evil principle, and of reward and punishment after death, found in the Oregon region, though the belief may be colored from outside, see Waitz: *Anthropologie*, III, 345.

From the very beginning was the separation: each chose in opposition to the other, and between them is terrible war. Nor does this warfare, as we read of it in the sacred accounts, appear to be but image and metaphor: it is an actual struggle of angry hosts who battle daily, especially when the darkness comes.
In these great religions and in Christianity, there is good-will toward men, but its expression alters with men's conduct, and may show itself in wrath as well as in affection. Jehovah chastises for their sins the very people of whom he is the patron and support; and the God of Christianity, holding to a wide plan of help to men, punishes the disobedient. At times the anger is toward individuals, they singly are responsible, in hell each is rewarded for his iniquities, and by flood there is wide punishment.

Thus we have seen many gradations: from indifference, through a growing interest in one another or in men, until there is perpetual and studied conflict, bursting finally into that contest between moral good and evil that shakes the universe to its depths.

V

Next let us see this enmity, now reached its climax, grow less and less momentous. For while there is a progress *into* conflict, there is also a progress out of it. Let us observe this until we see it end in peace.
Even in very backward peoples, as we have noticed,[1] one of the gods has been elevated, and mutual hostility finds expression only in the spiritual ranks below him. He himself appears free from these jealousies and enmities.
But in peoples far advanced, the spiritual struggle may for the time involve even the Supreme God; yet it is only for the time, and the future victory of the Highest

[1] See pp. 149 f.

is assured. With the Greek the struggle in the spirit realm never was profound or enduring: it never was of those dimensions which Persia illustrated both in religion and in politics, where countless numbers swept down upon their foes; in the Greek religion, although the gods still might bicker among themselves and be of divided sympathy with mortals, yet the great conflict of the Olympians with their enemies long had ended. With the Persians, there was a present fierce contention, yet with certainty that the forces of evil could not hold out forever. So, too, in the Christian scripture Satan is—not yet, but at some distant time—to be utterly subdued.

Or, with the ancient Chinese, the struggle has already ceased to be a conscious antagonism; it has lost its angry look, and has become a mere difference in the direction of change: the Confucian religion sets in opposition the powers of growth and the powers of decay, without however representing them as enemies one of the other.[1]

Finally, and bringing to naught the possibility of real warfare, the Supreme God includes and is All; and since there is naught beside him, no spirit can be at enmity with him, nor can any power move counter to his will. Such an idea is already half-risen wherever the enemy of God is conceived as his creature whom God could easily defeat. Allah *permits* Iblis, permits Harut and Marut, to oppose him;[2] God *permits* Satan to be unbound,[3] even as Jehovah declares that there is none but himself, and he creates evil.[4]

Yet the idea of the all-including God is not clearly risen until he is conceived—not as the creator of free persons, free even to oppose his will—but as the one of whom all particular persons are but the unreal appearance. The battle in which Krishna speaks to Arjuna, a

[1] Cf., e.g., Li Ki, IV, 2, 2, 15; IV, 4, 2, 15; IX, 1, 4 (XXVII, 275, 305, 418).
[2] Koran, Chs. II, VII, and XV (VI, 14, 138 f., 246).
[3] Revelation, XX, 7 ff.
[4] Isaiah, XLV, 5 ff.

leader of one of the opposing sides, is not a real battle: "Whom I have killed do you kill." [1] Reality and illusion [2] are but aspects of Divinity; God is what is, and what is not.[3] In such a creed there may be utter indifference of the divine to the human and mundane; but now an indifference, not of the divinity remote, but of the divinity near and all-pervading, so catholic that all things are alike and no deeds or persons are either precious or abhorred.

Such a view is approached or attained particularly in some of the great religions of the farther Orient; in that of the Jains and of the Buddhists, in the Vishnuism of the *Bhagavadgita,* and in the Taoism of the *Tao teh King.* Conflict has now come to its end, and an utter peace, could we escape our blindness, would be seen to pervade the world.

VI

In summary, then, the opposition and anger in the spirit world may in certain undeveloped religions not be felt at all; and when felt may appear as a private and passing irritation; or there may be a steadier clash, having differing depths and motives, ranging from mere assertiveness, mere love of domination, through tribal and racial partisanship and the opposition of creative to destructive power, into a clear moral cross-purpose; and out beyond this, a spirit world of angerless calm. Enmity is thus amply present in the supernatural, but not equally in religion's full course: for it is less prevailing in rudimentary religion, and again in religion highly developed; it has its chief seat in a zone between. As we pass from lower to higher levels, we consequently find *at first between spirit beings a want of those relations that breed hatred;* then

---

[1] Bhagavadgita, XI (VIII, 96).
[2] Maitrayana Upanishad, VII, 11, 8 (Deussen: *Sechsig Upan.*, 1897, 370).
[3] Bhagavadgita, IX (VIII, 84).

there is seen intense and settled enmity, wherein men and morals come to hold the very center; and finally in the upmost levels the conflict is felt to be not eternal or is felt not to exist at all.

In this then is a suggestion that with respect to anger the development of religion as a whole, but not of each religion, is cyclic: the later stretches resemble the earlier, in that within the divine regions the hostility becomes quieted. Yet clearly these later stages, with all their resemblance, are leagues from the earlier, since a peace by power and permeation can hardly be confused with a peace whose elements are so at variance that they find no common ground for quarreling.

The great god in many a lowly religion is indifferent—indifferent toward men, and careless of the spirit world itself. The social bond is thus without deep sanction; and after it obtains it, may lose it. A survey of religion this reveals the birth and growth and death of a spiritual society and government—of spirits and gods only, or of these and men. Students of human institutions may here find reflected, mirage-like in the heavens, an unwitting expression of the indifference or cherishing or contempt which men themselves feel for social and political union.

CHAPTER X

CURSE, PERSECUTION, AND WAR, IN RELIGION

We have seen the rise and decline of anger in men towards the gods, and of the gods toward one another and toward men.

I

Considering now the feeling of men toward their fellows, we find at low levels of religion that anger, even deadly hostility, is untouched: it is neither approved nor disapproved, but accepted as of course, like breathing and the milky way.

That religion has some of its roots deep in ill-will between men, is shown in magic, whether we regard this as an early form of religion or—preferably, I believe—as religion's precursor and accompaniment, early adopted into religion itself.[1] For in any event the substance of religion is colored and shaped by attempts, not only to help one's own and one's tribal interest by magic, but—by secret name or song or phrase, or by the manipulation of wax, twig, spittle, hair, nail-paring, or a thousand other things,—to injure someone, bringing upon him property-loss or sickness and death. I shall not try even to name the direct goods that magic can bring, including, as they would, many varieties of success—success in hunting, agriculture, mining, trade, gambling, war, debate, and love;[2] but looking at once to the magic of ill-will, we shall

[1] Illustration of this may be found, for example, in the *Zend-Avesta*, in the *Kalevala*, and in the *Rig-Veda*.
[2] For examples, see Skeat: *Malay Magic*, 1900; and the *Atharva-Veda* (XLII).

see its many forms. Nor, in this, need we carefully separate cursing and hostile will-power and magic, since the borders of these are not important for us here. India is rich in these pearls of imprecation, religiously treasured. "May this slay my enemies," we find in the sacred canon, "those whom I hate and those who hate me!" "Bind in the toils of death that cannot be loosened those enemies of mine whom I hate and who hate me." "Of the enemy who bewitches with his eye we hew off the ribs." "He that shall curse us when we do not curse, and he that shall curse us when we do curse, him do I hurl to death as a bone to a dog upon the ground." [1] There are incantations to be used by a woman to keep her rival forever unmarried; to injure as well as help a man in his love; charms to defend one from another's wrath: "As the bowstring from the bow, thus do I take off thy anger from thy heart. . . . I step upon thy anger with my heel and my fore-foot." [2] And within the canon of Zarathustrism are clear signs of a tolerance of magic rites to be used not alone against spiritual enemies, the demons, but against men.[3] To these, if one wished, could be added examples that would circle the globe. The Hidatsa Indians "think that a sorcerer may injure any person, no matter how far distant, by acts upon an effigy or upon a lock of the victim's hair." [4] The Omahas believe that disease and death may be invoked on an offender "by turning on him the consequences of his own actions," somewhat as one can send help to another in the distance, by willing it.[5] In Tahiti, as in Hawaii, death may come from the incantations of a priest.[6] In parts of Melanesia sneezing means that some

[1] *Atharva-Veda*, II, 7; III, 6; VI, 37 (XLII, 91 ff.).
[2] *Atharva-Veda*, I, 14; IV, 5; VI, 138; VI, 42 (XLII, 107, 105 f., 108, 136); and cf. III, 30; VI, 43, 64, 73, 74; VII, 52 (XLII, 134 ff.).
[3] Bahram Yast, XIV, 34 f. and 44 (XXIII, 240 ff.).
[4] W. Mathews: *Ethnography and Philology of the Hidatsa Indians*, 1877, 50.
[5] Fletcher and La Flesche: "The Omaha Tribe," *Twenty-seventh Ann. Rep. Bur. Amer. Ethnol.*, 1911, 583 f.
[6] Ellis: *Polynesian Researches*, 1831, II, 64 f.

one is angry with the sneezer, is "perhaps cursing him by calling on his *tindalo* to eat him; the man who sneezes calls upon his *tindalo* to damage the man who is cursing him." Or with a bamboo magically loaded—among other ammunition, with a dead man's bone, and with proper *mana* song—the thumb held over the end of the bamboo until one's enemy is within range, this deadly spiritual charge is fired at him;[1] even as in Australia one's enemy may be killed by cursing him while secretly pointing at him a magic stick.[2] And many of the magic practices of the Malays are framed to be the weapons of ill-will or to be armor against ill-will in others.[3] Man's fear and hate of man is thus embodied in practices that merge into religious rites.

And man carries over into the next life his animosity toward his fellows; this is one of the reasons for the fear of the dead;[4] they may not forget their earthly grudge, or lose their evil character, but have new powers to give it vent upon the living or their fellow-dead. A Dyak who has been murdered goes to his own place, where he does nothing but fight and murder.[5] Those who live evil lives quarrel and are malignant in the life after death, and return to harm the living, out of spite, eating men's souls; and a woman, dying in childbed, returns from the land of spirits, seeking her child everywhere, in grief and rage; such a ghost is particularly to be dreaded. Other ghosts returning to earth may be kindly; but if earthly friend or property be injured, they are excited to anger and revenge.[6]

Magic as a system passes no judgment on hate; it merely

[1] R. H. Codrington: *Melanesians*, 1891, 216 f., 226, 205. For details of Melanesian hostile magic, see also Parkinson: *Dreissig Jahre in der Südsee*, 1907, 194, 120 ff.
[2] Spencer and Gillen: *Northern Tribes of Central Australia*, 1904, 455 ff.
[3] Skeat: *Malay Magic*, 1900.
[4] See pp. 151 ff.
[5] Bock: *Head-Hunters of Borneo*, 1882, 229 f.
[6] Codrington: *Melanesians*, 1891, 274 ff.

furnishes it weapons and defense. It is not concerned, as is full-flowering religion often, with making men to be friends or enemies of one another. If a man love or hate, magic merely opens a way. It depicts and assists, without guiding, the unschooled passions.

But clear religion also may be at this level: the gods may have no interest in men's attitude toward one another. There are, to have before us but a single instance, certain Australian tribes with no idea of a Supreme Being that cares for the moral conduct of men; all approval and condemnation comes, not from the unseen world, but from the older men.[1] This need not mean, however, that the spirit-world is indifferent to human beings and human actions; spirits and gods may be alert to injure or help men, but there is no interest in men's feeling or conduct toward their fellow men.

II

But religion that is advanced cannot escape judging and attempting to reshape this human bond, and especially does it feel the impulse to rule men's mutual anger. And in such regulation all magic, sorcery, witchcraft, especially as instruments of hate, are condemned [2] or silently fall into disuse. And quite beyond these, the ravages of unlimited vengeance are eyed with suspicion. Places of refuge are established and sanctioned, where the pursued is at last safe from the avenger. And outside such precincts the revenge must not in its severity go beyond the original injury; if one kill another's son, that other may not return and kill all four sons of the slayer: only an eye for an eye, a tooth for a tooth, and there the feud must stop.

But that the death of a man should be avenged by his

[1] Spencer and Gillen: *Northern Tribes of Central Australia*, 1904, 491.

[2] See, e.g., Exodus, XXII, 18; Leviticus, XX, 6; Deuteronomy, XVIII, 10 ff.

CURSE, PERSECUTION, AND WAR, IN RELIGION 165

next of kin is not only tolerated; it may be required by religion itself; there is a demand of such action, lest the family tie be of no effect. Confucianism, strong in its support of family obligation, clearly and positively summons to avenge with death the murder of those near of kin.[1] The family bond is here given a peculiar religious support, quite as is the political bond the world over, where religion urges men to kill the state's enemy, even though, as in America, there be no visible union of church and state. In time, however, religion comes to oppose all revenge that comes of family feud.

Other killing by the individual, outside of family feud and unauthorized by court or government, has also had something like religious approval. Extreme anger, even to the pitch of frenzied murder has been included in the acceptable expression of saturnalian excitement, which early always had some connection with religion. The beginning of the New Year, among the Wasuahili of East Africa, was a time of general license. "Everyone did as he pleased. Old quarrels were settled, men were found dead on the following day, and no enquiry was instituted about the matter."[2] In a like manner, in Hawaii at the death of a chieftain, there was a time of riotous "mourning," a time of license which included not only the gratification of lust, but arson, plunder, and sometimes even murder;[3] even as in the carnival at the death of the king, in certain parts of Africa, the brothers, sons, and nephews of the king were permitted to rush forth and kill indiscriminately and unpunished.[4] Religion here winks at or approves killing by the individual. But in nearly all

[1] Li Ki, I, i, v, 2; II, i, ii, 24; II, ii, iii, 18 (XXVII, 92, 140, 195). For many other instances of a sacred obligation to avenge with death, see Westermarck: *Moral Ideas*, 1912, I, 176 f., 479 f.
[2] New: *Life, Wanderings, and Labours in Eastern Africa*, 1874, 65.
[3] W. Ellis: *Narrative of a Tour Through Hawaii or Owhyhee*, 1826, 148.
[4] Bowditch: *Mission from Cape Coast Castle to Ashantee*, 1819, 288.

religion that is far advanced, bounds are set not only to killing but to far milder expressions of anger.[1]

III

But in the religious acceptance and encouragement of war, we find an intense and persisting approval of pugnacity to the death. In this a notable effect of political institutions upon religious judgment and emotion is to be seen, since the prestige of the State here colors all attempts at impartial praise and blame. Long after religion may, as it believes, have condemned enmity, it may silently except war. War does not until late appear a violation of the divine will, so important does it seem to preserve the political order, and to protect or extend the rich accumulations of culture which foreign peoples always are, or must seem to be, menacing.

This infusion of religion into war appears in varied ways, and first in the purpose and preparation with which wars are undertaken. Wars to convert the enemy to the faith are not confined to Mohammedan and Christian: the Aztecs are said to have had this among their motives, —this and the desire to get captives for religious sacrifice.[2] With the Marquesans, war was waged chiefly to obtain prisoners for sacrifice.[3] In the South Seas also some disrespect shown to gods or king or chief has been an occasion of hostility.[4]

But human sacrifice may be not only among the purposes of war, it may be also in its immediate preparation.

---

[1] In an old Assyrian fragment, copied from a still older text, we find this wisdom in regard to anger: "When thou art angry do not speak at once. If thou speakest in anger, thou wilt repent afterwards, and in silence sadden thy mind." See Jastrow: *Aspects of Religious Belief in Babylonia and Assyria*, 1911, 389.
[2] Waitz: *Anthropologie*, IV, 117.
[3] Waitz: *Anthropologie*, VI, 153.
[4] Ellis: *Polynesian Researches*, 1831, I, 294.

CURSE, PERSECUTION, AND WAR, IN RELIGION 167

In the Pacific, along with other sacrifices,[1] this is true;[2] there the weapons might be made ready by human sacrifice.[3] Indeed there and elsewhere the potency of war weapons, even when poisoned, might be regarded as due to supernatural influence.[4] The Zuñis, when they fought the Spanish, blew shells filled with "medicine" at the enemy and repulsed him.[5] In all this, religion shades into magic as a preparation for war, and magic into a faith in magnificent boasts to terrify the foe and to encourage oneself.[6] Besides armament, the religious preparation might include means to discover the will of the gods.[7] The leader is careful to be thought to act under divine guidance;[8] omens must be observed, divinations resorted to,[9] the heavens watched, the sacrifices scrutinized.[10] As farther preparation interfused with religion, there might be war-dances, days spent in sweat houses, acts of special self-denial,[11] building or restoration of temples of the

[1] Ellis: *Polynesian Researches*, 1831, I, 205.
[2] Waitz: *Anthropologie*, VI, 147; Ellis: *Polynesian Researches*, 1831, I, 276, 281.
[3] Ellis: *Polynesian Researches*, 1831, I, 277.
[4] Ellis: *Polynesian Researches*, 1831, I, 395 f.; Fletcher, in *Bull. 30, Bur. Amer. Ethnol.*, 1910, 914 f.
[5] *U. S. Bur. Amer. Ethnol.* Twenty-third Ann. Rep., 1901-2, 228.
[6] For accounts of magic war-songs among the Pima Indians, and of recitals to gain supernatural power, see Russell, "The Pima Indians," *U. S. Bur. Amer. Ethnol.* Twenty-sixth Ann. Rep., 201. For magic among the African negroes to assure victory and to blind the foe, see Waitz: *Anthropologie*, II, 163 f. For battle-charms, and hymns to the battle-drum in ancient India, see the Atharva-Veda, I, 19; III, 1 and 2; V, 20 and 21; VI, 97 and 99; VIII, 8 (XLII, 117, 120 ff., 130 f.). For weapon-charms and war-charms of the Malays, see Skeat: *Malay Magic*, 1900, 522 ff. In one of these is the swelling prayer that the warrior who utters it may be "Fenced with hell-fire up to the eyes." In another charm the warrior, lighting his speech with imagination, boasts, "Of Iron am I, and of Copper is my frame, and my name is 'Tiger of God.'"
[7] Waitz: *Anthropologie*, VI, 146.
[8] Schoolcraft: *Archives of Aboriginal Knowledge*, 1860, II, 59.
[9] Ellis: *Polynesian Researches*, 1831, I, 303.
[10] Waitz: *Anthropologie*, VI, 147.
[11] Waitz: *Anthropologie*, III, 152.

gods.¹ The war, the war-camp, the warrior himself, might, as with the ancient Jew, be spoken of as consecrated.² And during the war the warrior was taboo.³

But religion did not limit its war-activity to these; it was carried directly into the fight. In certain islands of the Pacific, battle was entered with song to the God of War;⁴ orators of battle animated the braves by recounting to them the martial prowess of their favoring gods;⁵ the first of the enemy to be overcome in battle might be sacrificed on the spot.⁶ In New Zealand, after despoiling one's opponent, he was dedicated to the gods and was taken to the temple and, if still alive, was killed at the altar. Or here and in Hawaii a lock of the hair of the fallen or captured enemy was sacrificed to the god of war.⁷ In Samoa priests hurled maledictions at the enemy,⁸ and images of the gods went with the warriors on their campaign.⁹ In Hawaii priests ran to and fro through the ranks, inspiring their own men with courage, and their enemies with fear; each chieftain had his own war-god with him in battle, terrible to behold.¹⁰

And among some of the natives of the Pacific when peace was wanted, gifts were taken to the temple, and the god was besought to cause the war to end.¹¹ Human sacrifice was offered with the prayer that the god of war return to the world of night, and that there return to men Roo, the god of peace.¹² The conquered, it was thought, had

¹ Waitz: *Anthropologie*, VI, 644; Ellis: *Polynesian Researches*, 1831, I, 280.
² Robertson Smith: *Religion of the Semites*, 1901, 455.
³ Waitz: *Anthropologie*, VI, 147.
⁴ Ellis: *Polynesian Researches*, 1831, I, 285.
⁵ Ellis: *Polynesian Researches*, 1831, I, 287.
⁶ Waitz: *Anthropologie*, VI, 149; Ellis: *Polynesian Researches*, 1831, I, 289.
⁷ Waitz: *Anthropologie*, VI, 149.
⁸ Waitz: *Anthropologie*, VI, 153 f.
⁹ Waitz: *Anthropologie*, VI, 146.
¹⁰ Waitz: *Anthropologie*, VI, 147.
¹¹ Ellis: *Polynesian Researches*, 1831, I, 317.
¹² Ellis: *Polynesian Researches*, 1831, I, 311.

CURSE, PERSECUTION, AND WAR, IN RELIGION 169

been punished by the gods for some impiety; the victors were the instruments of the divine wrath.[1] Among the negroes of Africa occasionally there were religious ceremonies of peace.[2] The victorious warriors of the Jews offered sacrifices;[3] and even as in war-time in the South Seas the requirements of religion were heeded with double care,[4] so also in Mexico when the war was over, a special temple was built to the war-god, bearing the name of the newly conquered region and tended by its natives,—a temple so constructed with militarist foresight that, in a pinch, it could serve also as a fortress,[5]—a suggestion which ought to be considered by our own zealots of "preparedness."

As in Greece and Rome, so there were in many other places special gods of war, some of which have already appeared before us, war-gods in Hawaii, Samoa, Mexico and elsewhere.[6] Men fought in the belief that the conflict between the gods of the warring peoples was as great as that between the peoples themselves.[7] Or if there was no special war-god, war was an important interest of the Supreme God,—of Jehovah of the Jews, and of Allah of the Mohammedans, who drives men into battle by command, promise, and threat.

But with difference of time or temperament, a change occurs in the divine interest in war. In the religions less intensely national and political, the supreme God, while still not opposed to war, is less concerned with it. The

[1] Waitz: *Anthropologie*, VI, 147.
[2] Waitz: *Anthropologie*, II, 164.
[3] Robertson Smith: *Religion of the Semites*, 1901, 491.
[4] Waitz: *Anthropologie*, VI, 147.
[5] Waitz: *Anthropologie*, IV, 117.
[6] Among the Sea Dyaks of Borneo, Singalang Burong, the ruler of the spirit world, is the god of war; he delights in fighting, and head-hunting is his glory; Gomes: *Seventeen Years Among the Sea Dyaks of Borneo*, 1911, 196. The Zuñi Indians had more than one god of war; *U. S. Bur. Amer. Ethnol.*, Twenty-third Ann. Rep., 1901-2, 34, 116.
[7] Ellis: *Polynesian Researches*, 1831, I, 276, 278, 285, 311.

war-god becomes a subordinate divinity, and the ruling god inclines to aloofness or neutrality, as with Zeus in the great struggle between Greek and Trojan; or with Ukko who, in the *Kalevala,* is God both of the Finns and Lapps. It is important that Ares is depicted in Homer as a war-god hateful to the Greeks, while Athena, a warrior also, is beloved as the patron of wisdom and the arts. Krishna, too, as we have seen, loves the warrior Arjuna, but Krishna himself is on both sides of the conflict in which Arjuna is a partisan. And even with the warlike Persians, Ahura Mazda although intent upon the daily struggle with evil, so that he battles prodigiously for the good, yet is far less interested in actual wars between states or peoples than is Allah or Jehovah. In this respect early Christianity is closer to Zarathustrism and to the religion of ancient Egypt than to its immediate blood-kindred, the monotheism of the Jew and of the Arab. Nor does the divine spirit of Heaven in the Confucian religion,—even though it passes no condemnation on all wars of state but lends a mild favor to those that defeat wickedness—enter with might and will to bring victory to the favored side.

This lessened position of the war-god and of the war-interest felt by the Supreme God, we must believe reflects some of the cooling ardor for war and for the social and political rivalries expressed in war; these come to be less confused with the greatest moral and religious aims. Yet the organized killing of the foreigner for purposes of state, continues to receive religious approval long after the human killing in the interest of the individual or of the family or of church or of trade union is generally condemned. Yet we can hardly wonder that religion, like morality in general to this day, finds itself of two minds, finds itself using two standards of judgment in regard to anger and slaughter, according to the width of the conflict, whether it be of individuals and of lesser groups or between states. In the one case animosity helps to bring anarchy in; in the other, it is in support of an institution pledged to keep anarchy out. The glamour, indeed the moral splendor, of the communal life is reflected even upon its conflicts, however partial and selfish these may be. For in war, even when moved by communal greed, the individual shows a phase of virtue; namely, self-sacrifice for a good or an evil which runs far beyond himself. And the moral satisfaction which thence arises, when linked with the adventure and the satisfaction of unrestraint from morals (since the soldier can now, with home-praise ringing in his ears, do savage killing from which in peace he is sternly held back)—this constitutes a psychic alliance which is hard to defeat. What wonder that there is a double standard; and that long after private hate is approved only by exception, religion only by exception condemns at the time the war-hatred felt by one's own tribe or nation.

Reviewing, however, the main course of religion's attitude toward war, a trend is clear. Fighting and religion are linked together from earliest times. Far down, there are many spirits which are without special interest in war; they are the guardian or animating spirits of places and animals and things, interested in the maintenance of their own free life; they take revenge upon individuals who disregard or molest them. Whether these spirits interested in no clan or tribe commonly precede or accompany the spirits which have a social interest is not clear. But it is clear that the war-use of supernatural means reaches far back into rudimentary religion. Then come eminent war-gods as signs of an important corporate life, where warfare has come into honor. Later comes a lessened religious approval of war, a lessened divine interest in the success of arms.

There is a movement here which is quite different from a cycle; while yet it is not in a straight line. There is from the beginning a bond between religion and all im-

172 ANGER: ITS RELIGIOUS AND MORAL SIGNIFICANCE

portant human purposes, of fighting no less than of love and hunting and agriculture. But with the concentration of the fighting-interest into a great tradition, supported by wide tribal or national feeling, then war-religion comes to its crest, and from there declines as religion becomes less confused with some particular government. In few world-religions is the God first of all a God of War.

IV

The rivalry not only of governments but of faiths has linked religion with the anger of men toward men. Intolerance that persecutes has rarely been purely religious, wholly without mixture of other antipathies, political or racial; mingling, these have heated one another. The wars of savage tribes are not wholly religious; and yet at times, as we have seen, the gods of the opposing sides were as much in conflict as were the men. Lowly as well as high pantheons, however, are at times accommodating and admit new or once-excluded members. In Peru, in Egypt, in ancient Rome, the divine society was enlarged by the gods of other peoples. The Kaabah at Mecca before the coming of Islam was filled with deities of many tribes.[1]

Not until we reach the religions with a single great and jealous God is there a flaming intolerance, where the political motive in time becomes subordinate to the religious. The Jew, early lax in his exclusive loyalty to Jehovah, was disciplined into intolerance of Baal, Astarte, and other gods of neighbors; until he was finally disciplined into the thought that Jehovah was not the God of the Jew only, but of the gentiles, of all the world. When the later Jew persecuted, therefore, he did not attack only those of another race: he put to death those of his own blood who seemed to him to have abandoned Moses and

[1] Introduction to Palmer's tr. of the Koran (VI, pp. xii f., xvii).

the Law. The Arabian tribes, led by Mohammed, changed their easy toleration and became haters of other religions, destroyers of men who would not bow to Allah. The Christian, less at the beginning than later when he held political power, has been a persecutor of Jew, of Mohammedan, of Christian who stood for some unaccepted view of Christianity. The propagation of the faith by persecution is thus a wide-spread though not a universal method.

But as though feeling some breath of air from another level, the great intolerant faiths soften their intolerance either into an opportunism by which they postpone their persecution to a more convenient season, or upon principle they turn from all persecution, attempting both to keep pure the faith and to extend it only by persuasion and prestige. Destroy your rival religion, is their thought, not by sword and rack and prison, but by showing a more acceptable way. This intolerance, unwilling that others have less than the best, differs vitally from that intolerance which compels conformity by violence, as well as from that easy indifference which is sure that any one thing is as good as any other.

It is clear, then, that antipathy between religions, or between votaries because of religion, has appeared of different force and under different restraint in different religions, and often it has led to persecution. But over wide regions it has been tempered with a zeal to be rid of rivals by no other active means than preaching and good works.

V

But in the advanced religions, we find those for whom all hesitation, all compromise, in regard to anger between men has ended: all wrath, whether private or public, is condemned. The more mystic faiths readily come to this. Early Buddhism faces straight against private quarreling, against war, against religious persecution. Yet it does not easily live true to such a conviction: along with that notable edict of toleration issued by the Emperor Osaka in the third century B. C., we have later Buddhists persecuting for religion's sake others of their faith.[1] The Quakers in Christianity, the Taoists who have been called the Quakers of the East, set themselves against war. The more mystic faiths come less dubiously to this conviction because with them the relations of men to men are less central to their creed: at the center, rather, is the relation of the individual to God. Taoism, Buddhism, Jainism, Vishnuism, as we have seen,[2] find the social bond to be only passing or illusory; reality is not social, it is essentially without all individual distinctions. Christianity, the religion of the Parsee, Hebraism, Islam, and Confucianism are committed to the upholding of social life, as of value both here and hereafter. The remark of Tagore, that Oriental poetry is as though written in the forest, while the Occidental is as though written in the town, points to this deep difference between West and parts, at least, of the Farthest East. Every religion pledged to perfecting human society is inevitably more embarrassed in its attitude toward all aggression, all conflict: a perfected society is free from strife, and yet strife for the institutions of law and order and personal discipline seems the only way to a perfected society. Every religion nobly unsocial sees the One as alone eternal and real; distinctions of rite, of creed, of government, of morals, belong mainly if not entire to a realm of illusion, and are to be viewed with no such concern as that which the Real evokes.

There is a striking contrast, then, between advanced and retarded religion in their attitude toward the anger of men. *Near the beginning the supernatural becomes*

[1] See, e.g., Forbes: *Eleven Years in Ceylon*, 1841; and Anesaki: *Nichiren, the Buddhist Prophet*, 1916.
[2] Pp. 96 ff.

interested in human relations, aiding the angry man in his purpose, defending him against his fellow's indignation. But the anger itself is not yet approved or condemned. Later this passion itself comes to religious judgment or control: it is aroused, then quieted. Finally there may even be indifference to all relations, including the anger-feeling, of men. But short of such indifference, pure and universal love or love reinforced with anger may be commanded, but never a pure and universal wrath.

CHAPTER XI

THE WORSHIP OF MALIGN SPIRITS

In comparing lower with higher levels of religion, there has been seen a clear difference in the place held by anger and its kin. Even at low levels the open anger of men toward eminent spirits and gods soon ceases to be acceptable. The hostility of spirits and gods toward one another, so widespread in backward religion, becomes in the advanced more measured, more subject to moral control; or it wholly disappears. And upon the upper levels a bound is set to anger between men: deadly hostility, early accepted, falls under suspicion, and is justified only by the vital interests of family or civil government or of religion itself; neither private advantages nor the minor advantages of the community bring it praise.

Thus religion's prohibition of anger comes to out-voice its consent. Its consent is a half-hearted, distressed consent; until, in several of the advanced religions, all permission to have anger, whether in gods or men, is withheld and there is only a sweeping and flinty "no." *In spite of some appearance as of a cyclic movement in regard to anger*—religion seeming to regain late a very position early held—*this movement is rather in a single general direction, away from the acceptance and admiration of anger, toward its control and even toward its utter prohibition.*

The order in which these changes come is of interest. In general, the first to disappear is the anger of men toward their gods. Next is excluded the anger of gods toward other gods. Later is lost the persistent anger of gods toward men. Last to go is the religious sanction of men's wrath toward men. The early disapproval of human anger toward the gods, while there is still an acceptable anger of gods toward one another and toward men, is like the disparity in purely human emotions that are approved. Ruler and subject, for example, are not granted equal freedom for their emotions: a king may feel and express anger toward a citizen, when the public sense of propriety would be outraged were this man to express a like anger toward his prince. And while this inequality may upon occasion disappear in politics, it is firmly maintained in several great religions. There is felt to be no right of rebellion, no right to remain part of the religious community and yet be angrily defiant of the Lord of that community. The fact that anger between large groups of men is the last to be condemned is due, as we have seen, to the conflicts and necessities of government, with which the fortunes of religion and of religious men are closely bound.

With this, let us pass to our proper topic of the moment,—malign spiritual powers, their rank, and the worth and worship which they have from men.

I

It would gratify our love of order if we might find that, among least cultured peoples, malevolent powers were always of higher rank than the spirits of good-will. Often there is indeed a subordination of good to evil, but not invariably. The rank of benign beings is inconstant even when we make due allowance for differences which lie merely in the symbols and not in the meaning of the symbols. For we should expect that the higher place and dignity of malice would be expressed, not merely by its power to thwart and overcome all kindly powers, but by greater age or receiving higher honors.

Thus the Mandans of aboriginal America held that the Evil Spirit existed long before the Good Spirit; while both the Mandans and the Abnaki believed that the Evil Spirit was far superior in power.[1] Eataentsic, the Moon, who elsewhere was said to be the creator of the world and of men, makes men die and is thought to be wicked; while her child, Iouskeha, the Sun, has care of the living and is counted good.[2] And in the American North-west is a thought, not wholly unlike this, that, upon high, anger was early mingled with good-will, and that a son of this Great Power it was who did only good.[3] Likewise certain Indians of Brazil believe that the Evil Being is more powerful than the Good, at least with regard to the fate of men.[4]

But among the Pottawatomies there was difference of opinion as to which of these beings was more powerful.[5] Some American Indians, like some in India itself, held the two powers to be coeval.[6] And among the Iroquois the good and evil spirits were twins and had equal part in the creation of the world, yet the Good Spirit alone is Lord of Life, and the Evil Spirit is of less power than he,[7]— even as among the Tandjoeng Dyaks the Supreme Being is the source of all good and of good alone,[8] while, as we

[1] Catlin: *North American Indians*, 1842, I, 156; *Bulletin No. 30, Bureau of Amer. Ethnol.*, 1907, 4.
[2] *Jesuit Relations*, ed. Thwaites, 1897, VIII, 117 f.; X, 132 ff. And cf. Waitz: *Anthropologie*, III, 183.
[3] Waitz: *Anthropologie*, III, 330; and cf. the culture heroes and culture gods in many lands—Quetzalcoatl, Prometheus, Athena, Nebo, Agni,—beneficent spirits, who are made subordinate to gods of less clear good-will to men.
[4] Tylor: *Primitive Culture*, 1903, II, 325.
[5] Schoolcraft: *Archives of Aboriginal Knowledge*, 1860, I, 320.
[6] Leland: *Algonquin Legends*, 1885, 15 and 24; Morgan: *League of the Iroquois*, 1851, 156 ff.; Macpherson: *Memorials of Service in India*, 1865, 85 ff.
[7] Waitz: *Anthropologie*, III, 183; Morgan: *League of the Iroquois*, 1904, 147 f.
[8] Bock: *Head-Hunters of Borneo*, 1882, 232; cf. Gomes: *Seventeen Years Among the Sea Dyaks of Borneo*, 1911, 198, where it is said that of the gods no evil is predicated—though by our standards

have seen among the native Australians, spirits well-disposed toward men are ever able to defeat the spirits of ill-will.[1]

Among still other peoples who are clearly to be counted among the backward, the ancient and highest place is held by a spirit-power of unknown character; or, if known, is felt to be "good" and yet without interest in men or in this world's distinctions of right and wrong.[2]

But the high significance of malevolent powers in backward religion is shown perhaps most clearly in those many instances where worship is only of the evil spirits or gods, while to the good or the indifferent are paid no honors. Thus the Oraons of Bengal neglect Dharmesh, the Supreme Being who preserves men by his goodness and mercy, and they propitiate the malignant spirits who thwart Dharmesh's benevolent designs. The natives of the Barito Valley in Borneo pay ritual heed only to powers hostile to men, although in their myth and creed these are not supreme.[3] And in Dutch Guiana the supreme and good Deity is entirely neglected, while supplication is made to Yowahoos, devils whose delight is in doing harm.[4] Such custom is also found wide-spread in Africa: the Bantu and Tschwi neglect, in their prayers, the great and indifferent god of the firmament; the Amazulu pray neither to the supreme and unknown God of the heavens, nor to the "old, old one," the Creator of all things, but only to "men who have died."[5] And even where honors are paid to spirits and gods well-disposed, it is to spirits ill-disposed that the

something is wanting in Singalong Burong, the god of war, who glories in his power as a head-hunter.
[1] See p. 155.
[2] See p. 150.
[3] Frazer: *Golden Bough*, 1900, III, 52.
[4] *Natural History of Guiana*, by a "Gentleman of the Medical Faculty," 1769, 308 ff.
[5] M. H. Kingsley: *Travels in West Africa*, 1897, 508; Calloway: *Religious System of the Amazulu*, 1870, 1 ff. Cf. also J. L. Wilson: *Western Africa*, 1856, 209; and Waitz: *Anthropologie*, II, 171, 419.

more frequent sacrifices are offered.[1] Yet even with lowly peoples there may be no formal honor whatever to evil powers: prayer is made only to those gods and spirits who are believed to be good; upon their help alone may men count for protection against evil.[2]

There is, then, diversity on the lower levels; preëminence is granted now to ill-will, now to good, and now to powers indifferent to good and ill. But, more important, such divergences are seen only on the lower levels. No religion so far advanced as to have an important scripture and to have a wide company of adherents ever grants the chief place to fixed malignancy. The spirit of ill-will disappears or is made subordinate to a Power either indifferent or of clear good-will to men. Nowhere does high religion approve rites of honor or propitiation directed to an Evil Power.[3]

Yet in high religion the subordination of evil to the good is not always of like degree. In ancient Persia the Spirit of Hate, Angra Mainyu, is strong and eminent enough to test to the utmost the power of the Good Mind, Ahura Mazda. The Evil Power is not a creature of the Good: both powers exist from the beginning. The conflict between them does not appear to be permitted by Ahura Mazda; the rather it seems forced upon him, a present and terrible conflict, almost uncertain in its outcome. Yet the outcome is not truly doubtful: dim in the future is seen by faith the coming of a Beneficent One, the Sao-

[1] Gomes: *Seventeen Years Among the Sea Dyaks of Borneo*, 1911, 201. In regard to the negroes of the Gold Coast, see Tylor: *Primitive Culture*, 1903, II, 348.

[2] See, e.g., de Rochefort: *History of the Caribby-Islands*, tr. Davies, 1666, 278 f.

[3] This, of course, does not preclude the appearance of such rites in degraded forms of high religion. In the Lama Buddhist Temple at Peking, the writer observed prominent images that seem to represent with extraordinary vividness powers of evil. It may well be that in this impure form of Buddhism there is retained or restored what is proper only to a lower stage.

shyant, who shall bring peace and victory and a purification from all sin.¹

Different from this, the Iblis of Mohammedanism and the Satan of Christianity, while powerful, are spirits of clearly subordinate power: each for the time is permitted his evil freedom; but when God wills, their hostile sway must end. In Buddhism the Tempter Mara is far below whatever is supreme. In Brahmanism and in Vishnuism evil is still farther depressed: it appears only as an illusory manifestation of the One. In Confucianism and Taoism there is on high no active and personal spirit of ill-will.

Thus as we pass from low to high forms of faith, there is a clear direction of change. *In backward religion spirits of ill-will are often at the very center of creed and worship. But in all great religion the highest place is denied to a spirit that is malign, and all worship of such a being becomes abhorrent.*

II

May we now enquire why there is ever an exclusive worship of malign powers? Where good-will and ill-will are believed in, why do some peoples give all their active heed to beings of ill-will?

The reason often given, that kindly spirits, the good god, can without prayer or offering be relied upon to be well-disposed, while the hateful powers must be placated, —this quiets one's curiosity only to arouse it. For at once we would know why the good powers are thought to be so constant, while the evil powers are not.

Among the causes of this strange turn of judgment is the quality of external nature or perhaps rather the wide adaptation between man and nature. For he finds so many of the goods of life—his health and strength of body,

¹ See p. 81.

the satisfaction from family and companions and the sun's warmth, the rewards of hunting and fishing, of the trees, the soil, and rain—he finds these many goods coming with fair if never perfect constancy and to be expected even if there is neglect of special appeal to a great spirit power. To the plain man, unlike the wan poet, lover, or philosopher, the blessings of life come not by exception but by rule. Not so the dreaded things of nature—tornado, flood, famine, the attack of beasts, earthquake and pestilence. These are irruptions into the normal; something uncommon must cause them, something wayward and changeable. There is in them a suggested need of appeal to the powers that do such harm to men. So the passions that answer to misfortune may have quite solitary effect, and lead to a neglect of all but evil powers.

The exclusive worship of malignant powers is supported further by the excessive interest which anger always excites, especially when directed toward oneself. If even a king could hardly give individual attention to a flatterer, hard by whom were a minion fuming against the royal person, of how much more compelling interest to one of us would be the anger that came not from some underling but from a being above kings in rank and power! Since the violent and exceptional events of nature seem the utterance of divine wrath, these dire misfortunes tend to inhibit interest in all but their direct and personal source. The fascination of the enemy must therefore join in causing the exclusive worship of hostile powers. A worship that includes friendly spirits with the unfriendly indicates a wider span of the emotions, and marks a more flexible and promising order of mind.

Moreover there is occasionally to be found in the very conception of goodness a motive for rites to the evil and for neglect of the good. For in early thought the idea of goodness is often negative, pointing mainly to an absence of evil. Evil is here the positive notion, involving overt and hurtful action; while to be good requires only to refrain from doing harm. Early morals are mainly prohibitive, seen in the "Thou shalt not" of Sinai and of children's discipline, save in Eskimo-land and the United States. Gods who are remote and negligent of men are therefore too often "good" by that very fact, while the Evil Power cannot be evil unless he acts. This power then is practically important and calls for rites to avert his anger or recklessness.

But deep among the reasons for conceiving good-will to be steady even where ill-will is not, is that it is closer to the common experience of men themselves. Intimate and early influences suggest it. In childhood are the family affections that, for all their surface-gustiness, have undercurrents strong and constant. Then and later are found companionships; and, added to love, there are the unfailing bonds of the tribe. These stand up larger in the normal environment, run closer to the natural course, are nearer to the springs of daily behavior than is hatred. Enmities are experienced, but enmities that usually end in truce, end by compounding for the injury inflicted, end by favor or by the pressing needs of some common enterprise. For all its stout wrappings, hostility is more frail than the favoring sentiments, than those unpassionate recognitions which we call good-will, and by which the family, the village, the tribe, is founded and sustained through generations. This then fortifies all the other motives whereby the savage, assured that the friendly power will continue friendly without special plea, is also assured that the anger of evil powers is inconstant and can be turned by suitable appeal.

III

But with religions not on the lowest level, there disappears not alone the exclusive worship of malignant powers but any worship of them open and approved. Only by stealth do men now appeal to spirits and gods of fixed ill-will.

184 ANGER: ITS RELIGIOUS AND MORAL SIGNIFICANCE

The decline of devil-worship is part of the broad movement whereby anger generally finds less honor in religion. The worshipper, as we have seen, no longer openly upbraids and chastises the divinity that brings no gain; the rancor of supernatural powers toward one another is softened; the gods are less cruel toward men; the anger of men with men finds less general favor in heaven or on earth. As man himself becomes less wanton and vengeful, so must those become who can rule his spirit. His personal and public life gradually turns from rapine and killing and toward the strengthening of law. Important as are one's enemies, yet kith and kin and friends are more important and the great company of all those who without friendliness of feeling are ready to be co-workers. Thus malice becomes less the very breath in one's nostrils. Men come to expect from their fellows, not only of the family but far beyond its borders, less of violence and more of a common interest in suppressing violence. The magistrate, the chief, the civil ruler becomes a more imposing and honored figure than the bravo or surly outlaw. Man has now come to look to powers that by habit intend to help rather than to destroy him. The loyal tribesman feels the need of supporting his chieftain who favors him and all his kin, rather than of placating some dangerous neighbor-chief. His lord rather than himself will consider his enemies.

This secular experience, this schooling in communal feeling, inevitably colors his outlook into the spirit-world. Religion now comes to direct an undivided loyalty toward men's spiritual protector, toward the foe of their foes, requiring men to trust in him alone for their defense. With the powers of evil direct, there can be no approved communication, to them can be paid no ceremonial heed. It would be as traitorous as private overture to the enemy in war-time.

One can hardly without surprise observe this change. It means that we can overstate the stability of the religious emotions. For it is well recognized that the rites and conceptions of religion alter: the mental picture of divinity suffers change, and the character of divinity, and the impulses which it arouses in the worshipper. But the emotions which suffuse the imagery and the thought and the ceremonial act, though they are steadier, are not fixed. Their seeming fixity is rather from a failure to discern what occurs than from a failure of the occurrence. Could we observe with all precision, we should doubtless notice in these passions the surge and tide as of the sea. Not only because of their intrinsic fluctuation is there an ebb and flow in the emotion within the span of the individual's experience, but within the larger scope of religion's history there is a profound change in the quality of its passion.

For religion is the utterance of man's supreme fear and hate and love; religion cannot change in its lesser aspects without affecting these. The object worshipped, the end striven for, cannot alter without modifying the emotions which these excite; the mind is so organized, so sensitive to its own parts, that deep changes anywhere within must in the end reach every vital function. The change in the creed and in the rite by which the center of regard passes from hostile to friendly powers carries with it a revolution in the passionate life. Whatever be the emotions with which fickle or hostile spirits are worshipped—whether with dread or cringing submission or complaint or open anger—these must yield their dominance to the wholly contrasting feelings awakened by beings who are constant, humane, supporting justice and all right obligation.

The growing confidence that the world at its center is of good-will to men marks a victory within man's own spirit the more amazing when we consider how inbred is animosity, never having been absent, indeed having a large place, in man's animal and human ancestry. When he comes to himself he gains assurance that hate is not the central power in himself or in the world. In creed and rite and feeling he refuses longer to be dominated by a passion of even such driving force, of such biological compulsion. There is in this a promise of the final mastery in him of a power that bears no malice. So that the decline of the worship of hostile powers, like the decline of anger generally in religion, expresses in its peculiar way the force of those motives which give to religion the still-unaccomplished task of making men to have good-will toward one another.

CHAPTER XII

ANGER AND THE ORIGIN OF RELIGION

With the main facts of anger in all the different relations within religion thus before us, let us subject them now to a farther gentle pressure, and see whether some oil of truth, though perhaps unclear, will flow.

And first, does anything come forth as to the origin of religion, in which there is deep and abiding interest? Do we find anger active at the source? Shall we obey or resist that touch of enthusiasm, not unknown in science, which urges an investigator to become a partisan of some single factor, and which here would cause one to discover in anger religion's sole source; even as some have found religion's sole cause in fear;[1] and others in love.[2] These three—love, fear, and anger—are the major emotions; and if we are to search in our emotional life for the springs of religion the psychologist would hardly stop with fear and love, but would press on to enquire concerning anger also.

Yet to learn its source we must know what religion *is*. For according as it appear to have one or another nature, shall we find its head-waters in regions far apart. Nor shall we be persuaded that we can directly examine re-

[1] E.g., Renan: *Histoire du peuple d'Israel*, I, 29. Other references will be found in Leuba: "Fear, Awe and the Sublime in Religion," *Amer. Jour. of Relig. Psychol. and Educ.*, II, 1 ff. The oft-cited passage in Statius (Thebaidos, III, 659 ff.), *Primus in orbe Deos fecit timor*, since it occurs in a dramatic dialogue, need not be taken as the belief of Statius himself nor of any other ancient writer.

[2] E.g., Tiele: *Elements of the Science of Religion*, 1896, II, 135; W. Robertson Smith: *Religion of the Semites*, 1901, 54 f.; Durkheim: *Les formes élémentaires de la vie religieuse*, 1912, 320 f.

ligion at its historic source. Especially is the earliest life of those peoples who have possessed religious genius shrouded in mystery, their religion emerging from an antiquity which palaeontology only begins doubtfully to disclose.[1] Our enquiry will have in it less of guess-work and more of solid evidence if we do not attempt to reach directly the nature and motives of religion back in the most distant past, but let this be inferred, with all possible corrections, from the character of religion in those peoples far developed, as well as in those whose development has been arrested, and of whom we have direct and reliable observation. What is their religion, what sustains it, making it to be not a listless heritage, but inescapable, controlling themselves and their children? For religion has its birth not alone with the first men in whom it welled, but with all who because of a like mind freely repeat those ancient processes. We shall know, too, that the earliest forces need not all be identical with the latest: what introduces me to a stranger and leads me to begin some surface-action with him may not as yet touch the deep springs of my later respect and affection for him and of my readiness to give myself to his large plans.

I

Looking then to the nature of religion, we at once discover in it imagery, beliefs, practices, instinctive facilitations and inhibitions, strong emotion.[2] Nor do we find some one emotion more and more prevailing as we near

[1] See H. F. Osborn: *Men of the Old Stone Age*, 1918, 272, 359, 465, 501.
[2] So acute a writer as Durkheim (*Les formes élémentaires de la vie religieuse*, 1912, 50), recognizes but two kinds of religious phenomena, namely (a) *beliefs* (opinions, representations) and (b) *rites* (determinate modes of action),—distinguished as *thought* and *movement*. This, though of course defensible, greatly cramps the facts. My own reason for dissatisfaction with it will soon appear.

ANGER AND THE ORIGIN OF RELIGION 189

religion's lowest forms; here are friendliness and joy, and there fear and depression, and still elsewhere dislike and anger and contempt. And in the same people and religion not one emotion only need appear, but emotions mingled or in alternation. For even early religion, like late religion normally, is man's full response, both inner and outer, to beings who are not the readily visible [1] and normal members of his community nor of any other human group with which his own is friendly or hostile; and yet it is a response to beings psychically like those who are such readily visible and normal members. The inner and outer behavior to gods and spirits resembles man's inner and outer behavior to other men—to the mischievous and erratic solitary, to the dangerous alien, to the family head or chieftain or despot-conqueror, or to some person of non-ruling but heroic mold.

Now what, we may ask, is awakened in plain men when they feel themselves within the influence of some man of fateful power? No one emotion usually, but several mingled, and these differing in their quality with his known or guessed attitude toward them. The despot well-disposed will arouse in them friendliness answering to his, with elation that such greatness is ready in their behalf; and there will be admiration of his superior power and a sense that he in some measure dominates them inwardly as well as outwardly, that he makes them mentally subject to him, glad to do his will; and to all this there will be added a dash of anxiety lest they give offense or he otherwise be turned from them and they suffer his known and cruel wrath. If he already be indifferent or unfriendly, there will be strong fear; but, even with the fear, attraction will come because of his exalted place and power which are admired and coveted, and there will be a sense of subjection,

[1] Strictly, the religious objects are often "seen" in early society and, less frequently, in late. For this reason one needs some qualifications of the term, such as I have attempted. Nor am I forgetting the exceptional character of at least one line of development in India, where there is no personal object of worship.

of "negative self-feeling," and expressions of humility and of good-will from which a trace of good-will itself need not be wanting since often it unbidden arises as a very means toward the good-will desired in another. Should he be not greatly exalted and yet have shown ill-will and done them injury, our men will respond hardly with fear even thus alloyed, but with hostility, their fear now metamorphosed into resentment, into a defensive anger. For anger the more readily arises where the personal and inimical power is not overwhelming, and where there remains to those threatened the hope of tempering if not averting the disaster that impends.

It would be wrong to regard men's emotional response to the powers of the spirit realm as analogous to their response to the great or exceptional of earth; rather, the responses are identical in outline. And they are in outline the same because the situations are psychically the same; they are in either case occasions of complex social reaction, if it be true (as has just been said) that religion, in all but a single exceptional form, is a response, inner and outer, to those who, while apart in abode or mode of appearance and manifestation, yet share the basic qualities of our nature and toward whom we can therefore feel as toward powerful strangers or foes or friends. And just because these social responses appear to be complex, even where men meet men, so in all likelihood are the emotions when men face spirits and gods.

But the very considerations that persuade us that no one emotion tells the early story of religion, persuade us also that the emotions as a whole cannot tell that story. We must look to them but also to powers beyond them, indeed to all the great activities of the mind. The human and living hero, the mysterious stranger, the father, the chief, the king, does not awaken emotions merely; he arouses anticipations, memories, beliefs; arouses also dim and dumb instincts, flitting impulsions, conflicts of impulse, perhaps steady purpose. There are impulses born of self-interest, impulses born also of interest in others. There is some attempt to complete the sketch of the momentous character, which the known facts always leave incomplete; memory is tricked into saying at least all that it knows; there is some forecast of what may come. And if so much of psychic complexity is disclosed in a relatively simple though important secular relation, we shall expect no less when the relation becomes religious.

Yet we should stray were we to deny all difference between secular and religious psychic action. Early religion differs from the responses of secular prestige, not in the general kind of emotions, impulses, and beliefs called forth, but rather in the quarter from which the stimulus comes and toward which the reaction is directed. And this difference of quarter gradually affects the response, giving a peculiar blend and strength of emotion, a peculiar form to the action and its governing purpose, a peculiar structure to the imagery and judgment, that with time marks them ever deeper as religion's own. The spirits', the gods' mode of action is not precisely the same as that of fateful men; where a man strikes with club or arrow from ground or cliff or tree, the spirit strikes also from spring, lake, cloud or the cloudless air; and instead of gift or threat, brought in person or by simple messenger, there comes from him who is invisible the rain, the ripening fruit, the pestilence, the storm. But even as a man has for a distant king a different psychic response from that which he has for his strong father or his chieftain near at hand, and yet reacts to each and all as to beings of like nature with himself; so it is with the distant human king and with the divinity. What is common to the two kinds of social response exceeds by far what is peculiar to each. The god's aims, motives, passions or indifference are like those of the great of earth; and the lesser spirits, whether they be of human or animal appearance, and live in rock, tree or pool or in the winds,—these lesser spirits are of the pattern of mischievous or sullen or kindly children, women, or men. The responses to them, by the imagination, judgment, emotion, and overt act, may have their own specific marks to distinguish them from the secular, but they are of the type and kind to which secular life is constantly giving birth. Human society and its ways of behavior have but been extended into the invisible realm.

II

With the nature of religion thus seen in outline, we may turn with high hope to see at least some of the particular psychic forces acting to create it. Evidence has already virtually been given not only against those who claim to find religion's origin in fear alone or in love alone, but also against all those who would find that origin in any particular power or process of the mind. For it has been almost a custom among students to declare that some narrow mental power or group of powers brings religion into being,—a special religious faculty, for example, or the activity of dreaming, the interest in causal explanation, the feeling of complete dependence, the sense of conflict, the emotions felt toward ancestors, the fear of ghosts, the awe inspired by the great facts of nature, the fear of great spirits, the awe of them, or the impulse toward the Infinite.

If religion be the extension of society's bounds to include those who are not the readily visible and normal members of a human association, friendly and hostile, and be the continuation and specialized development, toward the beings in this farther realm, of the responses inner and outer which are at home in the visible association of men,—if this be so, as the preceding section has suggested, then we shall be impatient of each of these explanations by a particular psychic process, and of all explanations built on their design. Some will be received without favor for they appear untrue outright; others, because they have but a crumb of truth. Instead our enquiry will be into the creative extension of society and into the extension of social responses to an enlarged fellowship that includes the unseen world. For herein we shall find the origin of religion itself.

Without attempting to array in the order of their origin all the different beings of the religious realm, we may well consider first the acceptance of a continued life of the dead. For it is not hard to understand the main causes of the belief that there exist after death persons who before were well-known—friends, children, parents, greater ancestors, important tribesmen, important enemies. These do not escape from other men's minds and interest as readily as from their own bodies; they continue in memory, in day-dreaming, kept in place by the affections, the fears, the grudges of the living; they reappear at times of emotional crisis, in waking illusion or hallucination; they reappear in dreams. And early man, far less ready than are we with the critical distinction between real and fancied, takes these reappearances to mean that death has not ended the individual life.

But in dreams are met not only men who have died, but beings unknown to common life, beings of strange look and of still stranger power. Marvellous beings appear also to those of disordered mind (who, for early men, have superior mental powers, rather than powers all awreck)—their derangement coming with insanity, loneliness, and fear,[1] with hysteria, starvation and deadly thirst, with intoxicating drinks or drugs or with those hidden poisons which come by utter muscular exhaustion. The wild visions of such persons, joined with the experience of the dreamers and of the fanciful, convince men that person-like beings exist at hand, or in a realm not wholly cut off

---

[1] For a modern instance, see Grenfell: *A Labrador Doctor*, 1919, 328, where we are told of a family that believed they had seen and heard a monstrous creature, like a hairy man, with hoof-like feet and a stride eight feet in length.

from at least the favored, beings not to be seen as common men are seen.

Animals, too, and by another mental course, come to be included within this larger association, since the higher animals in particular have for early men a nature apparently near to the human. They, like men, are cautious and bold, they seek food, seek shelter, grow tired and fall asleep, have mates and young toward which they show attachment and for which they fight; like men they have their own friends and enemies. And man himself feels toward the friendly or domestic animal somewhat as toward a human friend; and toward the dangerous and hostile animal, as toward a human foe. Animals thus in themselves stir men to social reaction, positive and negative, because they are like men; and because of the emotions they directly awaken they are, in imagination, made more like men than they really are: a more human character is ascribed to them, as is always done by children and in animal books for children. And this motive is fortified because so many animals have some powers greater than man possesses—fleetness, greater strength or greater endurance, an acuter sense of smell, an endowment of instincts which within limits leads more precisely than does human experience and deliberation. Because of these, and because their appearance is so extraordinary, and because they inspire in men sympathy and terror and vengeance, do we have ample motives for ascribing to them powers still more beyond man's—greater subtlety and foresight, greater power to befriend and to injure, more of magical power. These awesome creatures thus help to people a manlike yet superhuman and invisible world.

And if we enquire why psychic life is ascribed to sun, moon, and stars; why trees, headlands, rocks, pools, streams winds, and a thousand other inanimate things should seem to have indwelling spirits, this too can be understood. For if a man once come to experience what he holds to be a living spirit he must by a natural mental momentum continue the process beyond this spirit's bare existence; he must give to the spirit a local habitation, if not a name. The spirit is apt to have been,—perhaps it stays,—near the place where the vision came to the man.[1] Or some other association, perhaps purely emotional in tone, may give to the spirit an important object as its body or habitat. Thus D'Estrella, a deaf-mute waif in San Francisco and cut off from current creeds, believed that his mother, whom he had known before she died, was now the moon looking down upon him from the sky.[2] The interest, the fatefulness, the glory, of a natural object or place, especially if some good fortune or some disaster there befell, easily makes it the seat of some known spirit whose character gives forth the appropriate emotional tone. Not many generations need pass, to provide thus an indwelling dæmon for the more prominent objects of nature.

But a more direct personification of the lifeless object seems probable, and not a personification merely to give local completeness to a spirit already known. Sun and moon, volcanoes, fierce storms, and all like things call forth in early men the sense of an indwelling *psyche,* in the very perception of these objects, in the persistent interest, in the emotions they call forth. This is not wholly nor mainly because such a psyche would *causally* explain these objects' actions; not because our intelligence, our curiosity, is best satisfied by endowing these objects with souls; but because the object, so supplemented, better answers to the instinctive action and the emotions which these great natural things excite. For early men, as for late, conscious beings are the most interesting, the most fearsome, the most anger-provoking of all things. Nothing can be fully hateful or admirable or love-awakening that fails of this psychic life. If an inanimate object by ex-

[1] E.g., the place of Jacob's vision was called "the House of God," "Bethel," as a place where the Lord had actually been and still had his abiding-place. (Genesis, XXVIII).
[2] W. James: "Thought before Language: A Deaf-Mute's Recollections," *Philos. Rev.,* I, (1892), 613 ff.

ception stir us deeply, it at once becomes enlarged, completed by the mind into the form of things that from an immemorial past have so stirred us. Purpose, emotion, thought, character, it is felt, must inhere in anything that moves us as persons do. Not by reasoning, but by a more elemental supplementing—as when, in the flower only seen, we already feel at our finger tips the untouched petal, and catch faintly the still unsensed perfume—early men personify whatever deeply stirs feeling and impulse.

The one side of early religion—the activity of mind whereby the world of psychic life is widened to include an invisible realm—thus begins to be intelligible. No one mental process is active to accomplish this result, but many that work together. If it were not for sensory perception,—our power to see animal and tree and storm, the headland, the great heavenly bodies, and to hear and touch some of their manifestations; if it were not for the imagination that gives to these things inner and outer qualities which the senses do not report from them, the imagination creating also new objects in the hallucinations of waking, of sleep, and in manifold forms of intoxication whether by fatigue, or drugs, or disease; if it were not for our power to infer, to organize, to seek to explain what the senses and the imagination offer,—except for all of these the boundaries of society would never be extended to include a vast company of spirits great and small. No one psychic power creates these beings; the whole constitution of the mind is in the work, driving men to represent and to believe in spirit and god.

III

But there would be no full religion did the mental process end with representing, with stoutly accepting into belief these ominous beings. Religion has its origin not merely in the picturing, not in the belief only, but also and in no less degree in the active response to the beings thus recognized as real. And this response must be thought of, not as some merely muscular performance that crystallizes into rite; there is an *inner* response also, mainly but not wholly of the emotions. To explain religion, one must explain this full answer of the person to the strange beings to which his own nature has introduced him. Nor is there first the belief, and thereupon the response; the rather is it true that only in the reaction, inward and outward, does there come effective belief, do the beings become real.

Now in his inner drive toward persons, creating them, discovering them, man inevitably conceives them as endowed with at least the rudiments of a social nature like his own, and thereby the readier to awaken in him social reactions. He responds then to the extra-natural order with such behavior, inner and outer, as men show toward those within their normal society. The veneration of the idealized ancestor is a continuance, perhaps heightened, of the impulses and emotions which children have toward their parents,—impulses and emotions partly instinctive, but modified and strengthened by training in childhood and youth. We could not explain religious behavior were it not for the behavior which men excite in men. If there were no love for the brother, father, friend whom the man had seen, how could he love God whom he had not seen? If man did not fear and hate his brother-man, neither would spirits and gods hate him, and he in turn both fear and hate them.[1] Religion thus has its origin as well as its sustenance in the innate and acquired inner attitude and expressed action of men toward members of their normal society, taken to include friends, strangers, and evident foes. Later these religious responses become specialized, differentiated from those toward the secular

---

[1] For illustration of the influence of a people's enemies in giving to demons their characteristics, see Moncure D. Conway: *Demonology and Devil Lore*, 1879, I, 150 ff.

society. But nearer to the beginning are the unchanged secular impulses and emotions seen to be at the source of religion also.

IV

The evidence thus makes it clear that anger is important, even though not all-important, in the nature and origin of religion. We have seen anger in the attempt to coerce and punish and repel supernatural powers. Men do not always cower before the little-known: they may feel outraged by it, and may revile and flog and drive it off. Furthermore, the gods themselves are plenteous in anger: they show wrath toward one another and toward men. It is usual for men to attribute anger even to the divinity toward whom they themselves may feel no anger. Where fear and never love is the normal religious emotion in men, the god is feared chiefly because he does evil to men *from anger,* from anger perhaps settled into malice, into hate. *The fear-awakening character of the god is thus a product of man's own anger and ill-will projected into the objects of his religion.* Unless anger were in early religion, moving the god or spirit even when not the believer, there would be little or no occasion of fear.

For it is difficult, where not impossible, for simple men to reach forward into our own studied conception that evil may come impersonally; and, where personal, may come without intention, without ill-will. Mr. Roosevelt showed the elemental human temper when he habitually branded any statement that seemed to him false, especially if it were about himself, branded it not as false merely, but as a *deliberate and malicious* falsehood. Anger thus creeps into all passionate and uncritical recognition of evil. Anger is inseparable from early fear; we cannot make the one a *vera causa,* without admitting the other. And the same is true of love; it is early fraught with anxiety lest offenses come; the well-liked god brings good to men, but he usually is exacting, and becomes angry when his exactions are not met.

Anger thus is one of the great emotional constituents as well as sources of religion. Religion, when we look to its emotional springs, does not arise from fear alone nor yet from love alone, although these are active at the very start. Neither does it spring from anger alone, nor from any other one emotion. The emotions interplay; they tend to come in companies and not alone. Love, if we take the term to include all positive desire—the desire linked with an appreciation not only of others but of oneself and of the goods ministering to all of these,—love is the driving force of life, and fear and anger are subordinate and assisting.

CHAPTER XIII

THE GEOGRAPHY OF HATRED

I

Is there anything of interest in the distribution upon the earth's surface, of some of these traits we have been considering?

Taking first the backward religions, America stands opposed to Africa. A persistent hostility and cross-purpose of eminent spirits is not infrequently found in aboriginal America. Such a belief we have seen among the Iroquois, Pottawatomies, Hurons, Mandans, and Wabanaki.[1]

In parts of Africa, on the other hand, the heights of the spirit world are often at peace and rest; and there is unconcern with human affairs: such seems to have been the belief among certain of the Negroes proper, as well as among the Tschwi and Bantus of the West Coast, and also among the Amazulu.[2] Yet this belief in powerful but indifferent gods is not confined to Africa; it is found in Borneo, in the Philippines, and—though not characteristic, since conflict is more frequent—in native America;[3] but of all backward lands Africa seems the especial seat of this belief.

Religions far advanced also reveal an interesting contrast of geography when we compare the great irenic

[1] See p. 156. After listening to the witnesses there cited, one finds it difficult to accept the statement by Schoolcraft, in his *Archives of Aborig. Knowl.*, 1860, I, 37, that the conflict of spirits was wholly between Manitoes below the Great Spirit.
[2] See p. 149.
[3] See pp. 149 f.

THE GEOGRAPHY OF HATRED

faiths with those which give some honored place to anger. Except the remarkable placing of the religions pledged to monotheism, of which something will later be said, the most striking fact of locality is that the great unangry faiths—Buddhism, Jainism, Vishnuism, Taoism,—are gathered in a single quarter, in south-central, south-eastern, and eastern Asia,—in India, Burma, Siam, Thibet, China, and Japan.

Over against these are the seats of the great anger-admitting faiths, in western Asia, Africa, Europe, and the Americas whose culture is from Europe,—the seats of the religion of Zoroaster, of Mohammed, of the Jew, and of the Christian. These, here and there, have entered the territory of the peaceful religions, especially upon its western border, in India. While within its eastern stretches, in China and Japan, is Confucianism which holds fast the human affections, including anger; and in Japan the Buddhism which there is not wholly free from contention shares the ground not only with Confucianism but with Shinto.

II

Wherein does this geographical grouping of religions have its origin? Is it from any difference in the constitution of peoples, some of them being more energetic, perhaps more irascible? And does this difference, if it exist, lie deep in the original substance of men, or is it mainly or in whole a result of training, existing in the culture rather than in the nature of the stocks?

The final answer to these questions must await a wide gathering of facts that no one yet has made; but the deep interest of the enquiry will in time provoke many to make the gathering sure. In the meanwhile it may not be amiss to try one's feet upon confessedly quaking ground. Full discovery by others will hardly be delayed by some adventuring.

As to the difference in the general quality of the religious outlook in native America and in Africa, it is probably an expression of a contrast in psycho-physical "build." Energy, vigorous reserve, lasting resentment, seem to stand forth in the Redskin; and his religion could hardly represent him unless with the thought that conflict, interested partisanship, reached up to the very peaks of life. On the other hand, the African in general,—for there are bold exceptions—has taken his purposes less seriously; although he is capable of being stirred to anger and can wage terrible wars, yet in general he is inclined to seize the moment, to be cheery, to be indolent. The picture of a great Power, indifferent to the world and to mankind, leaving to others the care of planning and control, seems to express something especially deep in the human nature of Africa. And since anger is so often dependent upon energetic desire, and usually arises from a thwarting of purpose, it is apt to be strong in the energetic and purposeful. In the broad difference of the religions of America and Africa, consequently, we may well have a symptom of a deep contrast in the nature of Redskin and Black.

Such a difference in native pugnacity would do no violence to our other knowledge. There are clear contrasts within far narrower limits: the aborigines of America, compared with one another, were not equally aggressive, nor are the natives of Africa. The Polynesians as a whole, although they have waged exterminating wars, have seemed a friendly, sunny race. Ellis, who saw them early and lived with them long, noted their few domestic broils; he estimated that there was not more than one-twentieth the personal friction amongst them that Englishmen would have had. They did not appear to delight in provoking anger in one another, but were more given to mirth and humor.[1] And to the visitor in the Philippines to-day, coming from the West, there appears a mild look and action in the Tagalog that seems to go deeper than

[1] Ellis: *Polynesian Researches*, 1831, I, 96.

mere manner and to separate him from the forceful and self-confident Igorot and from the Moro. In Europe there have been signs of a like distinction. The ancient Greek could fight if need be, but with no stomach for the enterprise; he loved to hear of fighting on the plains of Troy, but his heaven was a place rather of peaceful conversation; he loved Athena and hated Ares. Even the Roman, less averse and with a genius urging him, waged his wars stolidly, with no heroics, as part of the nation's work. But the ancient German loved war itself and became the father of a long line that loved it, his pagan paradise, his Valhalla, being a place of war-heroes uncontented without a daily battle.

If then it is probable that the religious ideals of Redskin and Black African find support in the differing temperaments of these stocks, is there any like cause for that love of calm found in the religions of south-central and south-eastern Asia?

The divine indifference in this part of the East is also, as we have just seen, wide-spread in Africa, and is scattered in Java and the Philippines, and even in aboriginal America. Tangled racial strands, it seems probable, bind all these regions one with another; and physically the connection between India and Africa has been strong in times remote. But into the region of the great peaceable faiths so many currents of blood have flowed—Mongoloid, Negroid, Caucasic, besides or including the obscure Dravidian—that it would be rash to ascribe the religious ideal to the direct hereditary influence of a single strain. With certain strains may have come a temperament whose outlook influenced others by spread of culture rather than by blood itself. In India to-day there are backward folk markedly peaceable in all their ways.[1] Such a people may represent, as a mere fragment and trace, what in remote times was strong in blood or culture.

[1] Rivers: *The Todas*, 1906, 555, 586.

We need not be over-impressed by the temper of the Vedas. They are an ancient but far from primitive expression, connected in some obscure way with the aggressive vigor of the great Persian faith, and represent therefore an intrusive strain of religion from the unpeaceable North. Those who imagine that vigor comes only from Nordic stock here rush their pet doctrine to the front.[1]

But in more ancient times, perhaps long before the coming of this more doughty blood and culture, there may have prevailed in India a people or perhaps many groups of peoples whose larger inclinations by intrinsic temperament were away from war, and who accepted it, when at all, with great reluctance. Their attitude, imitated in time even by those who conquered them, may well have contributed to the pacific strain in so many far-eastern faiths. But that such faiths have not only here had seed and root but have spread mightily would make it probable that no purely local influence, say in India only, was at work, but that widely in all south-central and south-eastern Asia there was a temperament different from that of the invading Aryan, and far more congenial to the spirit of peace. If in the very bodily and psychic blood no greater dislike of strife had been found there than in Persian or Assyrian, in Arab or Teuton, the peaceable faiths would hardly have had their welcome. The religions of Parsee and Mohammedan, if not of Christian, would have run a freer course.

Too great importance, it is clear, may easily be ascribed to an original weakness of pugnacity. Alone it hardly explains all. Along with some lessening of the native pressure of aggression, there must have been both the endowment and the circumstance which made for a commanding religious life. This is possible only with great culture, emerging after ages of struggle with forces opposed to civilization. The arch enemy of civil develop-

[1] Cf. Madison Grant: *The Passing of the Great Race*, 1916, 223 ff., where the Vedas are held to be of Nordic origin.

ment is not unintelligence so much as it is particularism, mad loyalty to the minor group, cherishing its little animosities, keeping alive each old and petty grudge.

Everywhere outside of social chaos we find two opposing efforts in dealing with pugnacity: there has been a spur into the flank of resentment, driving it to headlong feud, to separative fighting that would prevent any large social and political life; and opposed to this there has been a social, a moral, a religious effort toward accommodation, toward coöperation, proclaiming aggression an intolerable wrong. Now in the quarter of Asia which here holds our interest these opposite tempers have been face to face and uncommonly strong. Social stimulation has been at work to cause those outbursts which we see primitively in the studied vengeance of the Malay headhunter, in the fanatic *juramentado,* and in that particularist madness of the one who runs *amuck.* The incessant conflicts of the older India show the difficulties which civilization there had to meet. That the opposing tempers, pacific and contentious, were facing each other in different races—this may well have intensified the expression of each. Also it was here that religion attained an exaggerated social position, as in its Brahmans. When supported by a natural peaceableness in much of the stock itself, the professional sympathy of such a priesthood and caste with calm and concord, may well have brought pacifism to perfect imaginative flowering. The priestly and prophetic desire for peace now came to classic expression in a great religion and in its great scripture. But the expression must of course be understood as a longing rather than as an attainment. Primitive religions, in their divinities, more nicely reflect the actual moral state, while advanced religions utter what is hoped for, revealing the hidden and undefeated strength of great desires.

III

It is worth our farther notice that the region of Asia whose great religions have honored anger least has lain outside the breeding places of world conquest. The armies that subjugated widely, when they did not come from Africa or Europe, came from Asia of the center and north and west and south-west—the Asia of Babylonian, Assyrian, Persian, Mongol, Turk, and Hun. The people of India, Thibet, Burma, Siam, and China have, within all historic time, been less ready to attempt world-wide aggression.

And yet, even the parts of Asia which hold the mild religions have shown anger and pugnacity. India has fought endless wars; her literature celebrates martial heroes. And within the wide region of peaceable aspiration there has been retaliation and all manner of violence and bloodshed. Mainland and islands have been places of vengeance; head-hunting has been a duty; piracy an approved career. We cannot then sharply oppose West and East, as though fierce assertiveness chose the one and avoided the other. It can hardly be said that world-conquest found other breeding grounds because here was no spirit of aggression whatever.

Doubtless the impulsion to war was less powerful here, finding more persons difficult to arouse to zeal, especially for distant subjugation. But it is probable that the great conquering peoples not only had more native readiness to anger, but—more important—had a greater acquired readiness to immense organization. Mankind in general comes into existence as a "moderate" between "left" and "right" of biological endowment. Below man are the extremes: fox and rabbit, tiger and deer, eagle and dove, wolf and sheep—nearly pure ferocity, set over against nearly pure timidity. In man fierce hatred is joined with fierce affection, foretold in the complex structure of ants and bees, that can battle to the death when need be, but that bind this impulse to the service of tireless coöperations, unbreakable attachments. And within men there appear differences not only of aggressiveness in the individual, but of psychic interconnections, alliances, oppositions within him, which give setting and check and furtherance to his pugnacity, and which make possible a large political life.

Now warfare depends not wholly on individual pugnacity; it comes close to politics. Armies are itinerant pugnacious states, or issue from pugnacious states. And those delicate adjustments of psychic impulse in great masses of people which give enduring strength to statecraft are not at their best in the stretches of earth that begin in the Africa far south of the Mediterranean and extend along much of Southern Asia, and across the Pacific into aboriginal America. This is not always from want of intelligence but rather from some failure of organization of emotions and impulses, from lack of that spirit of energy and compromise which supports extensive and persistent undertakings to which men pledge themselves together by thousands and by millions. Successful warfare is one of the measures, then, of the degree to which pugnacity is politically organized in the large. The ancient Jew, for example, had a will to fight; his religion helped to keep smoking hot his hatreds; but he lacked the numbers and the solid coöperative statecraft to forge his anger into victory. Even more passionate than his neighbors, he was ground to political dust by the powerful machinery of Egypt, Assyria, Persia, and Rome. These, spiritually less endowed, had a better adjustment of varied social impulse. That there can also be solid social adjustment without lust of foreign conquest is clear in China and in Japan before her "awakening."

IV

Absence of conflict, spiritual indifference in high places, is thus seen to be scattered not haphazard through religions; even in our present ignorance there is a hint of rhyme and reason. Certain contrasts among advanced religions as well as those among the backward religions become more significant by placing them upon the map and noting their boundaries. Distinctions of religion begin to join hands with differences of psychic constitution, with temperament, doubtless also with blood. *There seem to exist, then, obscure racial and geographic differences in regard to anger and pugnacity. And these have left their deep mark upon religion.* The existence and locality of the angerless faiths now seem not wholly inexplicable. The emotional and impulsive drive behind the pugnacity in these peoples apparently had a lessened original force and faced peculiar problems and peculiar perils; and these have made intense and systematic the longing for an existence free from strife.

Outside these regions of mildness, the religions which hold to some anger have found a welcome especially among peoples of political talent. With them the attitude toward anger has run a middle course, between license and prohibition, anger being neither cherished nor abhorred, there being recognized exceptional moments requiring wrath but only when it serves communal growth and not communal isolation and decay. The West, therefore, aglow for self-assertion, sets its face against the self-assertion of the anarchist as well as of the tribe or petty state. It would be rid of anger and yet would have its service when great interests are at stake. Religions in all lands where political stability is valued feel impelled to such a compromise.

CHAPTER XIV

JEALOUSY AS A SOURCE OF MONOTHEISM

In considering the geographical contrasts in the great religions there is an occurrence so far superior in interest and so intricate that for the time all else must be set aside while we view this alone and unhurried. For Monotheism is territorial, absent—save in an occasional and passing way—from all the important faiths which arose in the Far East and still possess it. Its origin and sway have been in the Near Asia of the Jews, whence it passed into Islam and Christianity. The course of our present study would seem bounteous indeed if it helped us toward an understanding of this strangest of all the differences in the geography of faiths.

But no full understanding is possible until we see in monotheism something more than the work of the explanatory impulse; as though we had, in the faith in the One God, merely a more daring edifice of intellect, and religion were nothing different from science or philosophy. This new conception of God is, rather, an expression of the entire spirit of the worshipper, a spirit not without intelligence, but with its ideas and formulations all shaped and colored by love and hate. We shall lose our way if we do not look to the emotions and their connected impulses, not for the cause entire, but for the major factors in the cause of the belief that there is no other god than God.

For in monotheism the reverence which is felt by all true worshippers is not only spurred and supported by a mastering emotion of loyalty and subjection, but this is met and opposed by another emotion, without which monotheism would never appear, namely by an almost arrogant assurance of the worshipper's own worth. The believers in this daring creed, unlike the Greek, feel that God needs no many-hued divine society, but finds in men and in the spirits not far from men an object sufficient both for communication and for his love and wrath. God finds in the human struggle with wrong, enough to engage his purpose and his heart.

Into the countless forces of feeling and reflection which drive toward monotheism and do not reach it, there to be joined by others that complete the unfinished task,—into these we must not aim to go.[1] But a strong motive, if not the strongest, is within the field of our present interest, and may not be left aside. For without that peculiar *fusion of anger and love which is found in marital jealousy* it is improbable that any or all of the other strivings would have reached their goal. In trying to lay bare the causes of the monotheistic faith, justice has never been done to this intense emotion.

I

Jealousy, then, must be looked to, that we may see its force and the direction of its working. Its energy will not surprise us unless we forget that the love between men and women and the jealousy it engenders are among the powerful human passions.

It would be a mistake to join jealousy only with the love of lovers. For it will be found as an outgrowth and expression of every form of strong attachment or desire. Children are jealous of their place in the affection of their parents; and friends sometimes resent the presence of a

[1] An essay in that direction may be found in the writer's *Psychology of the Religious Life*, 1911, Chs. XIX and XX. In the attempt there made to indicate the influence of the marital motive toward monotheism, too exclusive stress, I now feel, was laid upon monogamy. Polygamy, as will soon appear, acts, though less powerfully, toward the same end.

rival. Almost all governments expect in their subjects an undivided loyalty: in becoming a citizen of America, the foreigner must renounce allegiance to his former land and ruler. A Christian sect will usually not permit its own to be at the same time members of another sect. And some trace of jealousy, it would seem, is in animals even: dogs have been known to show anger, suppressed or open, when a strange dog, or perhaps a strange child, is fondled by those from whom the dog has long received affectionate attention. Our attachment to things, to property, and our wish to exclude others from its use or enjoyment,—an impulse which all communists will long find to be a lion in their path—is hardly to be given this name, although it is tinged with something very like jealousy; we flare at the threatener of our land or dollars, somewhat as we flare at the menacer of our other loves. But jealousy itself is clearly widespread beyond courtship and marriage. If we find in these its most characteristic utterance, this is not because it issues wholly from sex-love, but only because this love is universal and of power, giving the best-known field for jealousy's display. But wherever the religious bond becomes, as it sometimes does, more powerful than sex-affection, then the corresponding jealousy comes forth more scorching and imperious than that of lovers.

Nor must we think that love-jealousy is a late social achievement. We know of its presence in some of the simplest, the least advanced of living tribes, where monogamy is practiced. But love-jealousy is not connected only with monogamy; it is manifest in polygamy both in modern and in ancient times. For in this form of marriage it is usual for the husband to be angrily against any rival and against the wife who favors another man. The husband, himself free for new attachments, is nevertheless a jealous husband, even where the relation of love is, as here, not equal and reciprocal. Furthermore, if we can trust common report, it may be present among the wives of a common husband; here too there may be jealous rivalry for the favorite's place. Marriage in either its monogamous or its polygynous form [1] elevates a single person to the headship, and this is maintained with jealousy. Only the tepid or the degraded lover is without this passionate defense of an exclusive place in the eyes of his beloved.

Jealousy is a peculiarly personal response: personal not only as all psychic reactions are, in that they issue only from a mind, whose form is personal; but still farther, in that a mind alone can serve as its stimulus and object. Other passions can be stirred by what is inanimate—by gems, noisome decay, food, lightning, a boulder bounding down a mountain side. Jealousy reveals its closeness to the love-passion through its intimacy with persons. It is distinctively an inter-personal emotion.

To understand its religious influence, we must also remember that jealousy serves to check certain consequences of love. Love would, in thought at least if not in fact, blur the outline of individuals. Unjealous love obscures the difference between mine and thine, between me and thee; in its outrush of sympathy even the inner life, the pain, the gladness of another is as though it were my own. The ecstasy of love, secular and religious, brings the desire, and in a measure the actual experience, of union, of a complete fusion of separate persons into one. Jealousy reaffirms the distinction between the lover and the beloved, and between them both and the one who would supplant either in the affection of the other. It thus declares for individuality, serving as a foil and foe of that dreamy commingling which love invites. Love, while personal, is ever threatening individuality. Jealousy is a restorative, watchful of self-interest, serving to draw sharp again the distinctions essential to society and even to the fullness, in the end, of love itself.

[1] Whether, and in what degree, jealousy exists among the women in a polyandrous society I am unable to say. That it is at times weak or absent among the husbands of such marriage has been reported. Cf. Westermarck: *History of Human Marriage*, 1891, 516.

II

Having looked upon jealousy by itself, turning it this way and that, let us now see it in action, potent in the religion of the Jew.

It entered Jewish religion because it was present in the Jews' ancient social life. The jealous husband, jealous with good reason or without, was of such frequent and disturbing occurrence as to require attention from the Law. When the spirit of jealousy came upon a man (it was enacted), he should with an offering bring his wife before the priest. And then, placing barley meal in her hand and preparing a drink of holy water mingled with dust from the floor of the tabernacle, the priest declared to her that if she were innocent the drink would do no harm; but if guilty, she was accursed and the drink would cause her belly to swell and her thigh to rot: "this is the law of jealousies, when a wife goeth aside to another instead of her husband, and is defiled." [1] Furthermore we are allowed to see the heat of this secular passion: the husband's jealousy is described as a rage that spares nothing in the day of his vengeance, that cannot be appeased with any gifts;[2] the cruelty of the jealous man is as fiery as his love: "for love is strong as death; jealousy is cruel as the grave," and burns like coals of fire.[3]

Now to the relation between God and his people Israel, all this passionate love-anger is transferred. The ground is prepared by regarding them as lovers, as husband and wife. The marital imagery is full and recurrent. God

---

[1] Numbers, V, 11-31. It is significant of the Jewish acceptance of jealousy as a right and normal passion that there is here no penalty, no rebuke even, of a husband's jealousy toward his innocent wife. Jealousy was evidently to be brought to a crisis, to discover whether it were baseless or sound; but the jealousy itself, even when baseless, seems not to have been viewed as sin.

[2] Proverbs, VI, 34 f.

[3] Song of Solomon. VIII, 6.

has been a husband;[1] but because of her transgressions the wife has been divorced from her Lord.[2] The prophet sees Zion and Jerusalem not as a woman forever forsaken and desolate, but as one that may bear a name of delight, to mark her as a married woman; she is the bride of the Lord, "and as the bridegroom rejoiceth over the bride, so shall thy God rejoice over thee."[3] The woman that had been barren, ashamed, and widowed is to break forth into singing; her dwelling is to be enlarged, her children are more in number than those of the married wife; she is to forget her shame and her widowhood, for her Maker is her husband, the Lord of hosts is his name.[4] God will make a covenant with Israel and Judah: "I will betroth thee unto me forever; yea, I will betroth thee unto me in righteousness, and in judgment, and in loving-kindness, and in mercies";[5] they are to call God no longer "my Lord," but "my Husband."[6] Jerusalem is not merely the beloved, but is the wife, joined in wedlock to the Lord.[7]

Not only is the soil prepared for a divine jealousy because of this love and marriage: the jealousy actually comes forth, and out of it a flame vengeful and consuming. The worship which is given to other gods is viewed as a spiritual desertion and adultery. Israel and Judah, the beloved of the Lord, have looked with favor upon other lovers; the one has decked herself with earrings and jewels, and has burned incense to Baalim; the Lord denounces her as not his wife, but an adulteress, a harlot.[8] The wife has played the harlot, going after Baalim; the

[1] Jeremiah, XXXI, 32.
[2] Isaiah, L, 1.
[3] Isaiah, LXII, 2-5.
[4] Isaiah, LIV, 1-6.
[5] Hosea, II, 18 f.
[6] Hosea, II, 16.
[7] Ezekiel, XVI, 32-38.
[8] Hosea, II, 2, 13; III, 1.

JEALOUSY AS A SOURCE OF MONOTHEISM 215

bride has forgotten her bridal attire and has sought unlawful love;[1] she has played the harlot with many lovers, as has her treacherous sister, Judah. But if Israel will return, her husband's anger will not be kindled forever.[2] Jerusalem, upon whom the Lord has bestowed such loving care, and who has borne sons and daughters to him, has built a brothel house and played the harlot with the Egyptians, the Assyrians, the Chaldeans and the Canaanites. God in the fury of his jealousy will judge her as a woman taken in adultery: she shall be stripped and stoned and run through with a sword, and her houses shall be burned; "so shall I make my fury toward her to rest, and my jealousy shall depart from me, and I will be quiet, and will be no more angry."[3] And again it is said that the religious faithlessness of Samaria and Jerusalem, shown by practices received from Egypt, Assyria, Chaldea and Babylonia, is the faithlessness of a wife of Jehovah, and stirs him to furious jealousy: the woman is polluted by her idolatry and is to be punished as by the raging husband of an adulteress—her children slain, their houses burned, her own face mutilated, her jewels taken, and she to be stoned and stabbed to death.[4] We here see God's anger pictured as a mad jealousy, a jealousy that, in the words of the Canticle, is cruel as the grave.

But Jehovah's jealousy, often rising to this pitch of love-fury, is not of exceptional occurrence, in discord with his true character; it is regarded as part of the proper description of his character,[5] the term reappearing almost like an Homeric epithet: on Sinai the Lord reveals himself to Moses as a jealous God who will not tolerate the

[1] Jeremiah, II, 20, 23-32, 33.
[2] Jeremiah, III, 1, 8, 12, 14.
[3] Ezekiel, XVI. Here and in many of the passages to be cited, it is important to remember that the Hebrew terms for the Divine jealousy are the very same as those used for the jealousy of the human lover in Numbers V, 11-31, and in Proverbs VI, 34, as well as in the Song of Solomon, VIII, 6.
[4] Ezekiel, XXIII.
[5] Nahum, 1, 2.

worship of an image or likeness of anything in heaven or earth or in the waters under the earth.[1] His people when commanded not to worship the gods of the peoples driven out of the land are told that his very name is Jealous.[2] Neither graven images, nor the sun, moon, and stars were to be worshipped, for these belonged no more to the Jews than to all the other nations of the earth: "the Lord thy God is a consuming fire, even a jealous God."[3] His people must have no other gods before him; they must not go after the gods of the people round about them, "for the Lord thy God is a jealous God among you."[4] Israel, by serving the gods of the Egyptians and of the Amorites, had forsaken the Lord, who would not forgive such waywardness: "he is a jealous God. . . . If ye forsake the Lord and serve strange gods, then he will turn and do you hurt, and consume you, after that he hath done you good."[5]

This jealousy of the Lord is especially connected with the worship of the gods of the other nations;[6] such false service arouses an unsparing jealousy that smokes against the offender and brings down curses upon him, and blots out his name;[7] it is a rage that threatens to consume Israel,[8] that will devour the whole land in the day of wrath, against which neither defenses nor wealth can serve as a protection.[9] The terrible punishment of Jerusalem is recognized as due to this passionate resentment of the Lord;[10] only in famine, pestilence, war, and

[1] Exodus, XX, 5; Deuteronomy, V, 8 f.
[2] Exodus, XXXIV, 13-17. And cf. the mysterious "image of jealousy" which Ezekiel saw in his "visions of God." (Ezekiel VIII, 1-14.)
[3] Deuteronomy, IV, 19-24.
[4] Deuteronomy, VI, 14 f.
[5] Joshua, XXIV, 14-20.
[6] I Kings, XIV, 21 ff.; Deuteronomy, XXXII, 6-21; Psalms, LXXVIII, 58.
[7] Deuteronomy, XXIX, 18-20.
[8] Numbers, XXV, 1-11.
[9] Zephaniah, I, 1-18.
[10] Psalms, LXXIX, 1-5.

exile, can the fury of Jehovah be expressed and be appeased.[1]

There can be no shadow of doubt, then, that prominent in the feeling of the, Jew toward his divinity were the ideas and emotions fundamental in marriage,—passionate mutual attachment, the passionate assertion by Jehovah of an exclusive right to the loyalty of that Israel whom he regarded as his wedded wife, the wounded and indignant conviction that by worshipping other gods, Israel had violated her marriage vow, had become spiritually an adulteress, and that the fierce anger of a betrayed husband was God's fitting answer to such disloyalty.

Nor can it be doubted that the love between man and woman, in thus becoming a fiery mold of the Jew's thought of God's relation to Israel, pressed this thought straight toward the form of monotheism. In such love there often comes with joy a sense of the uniqueness of the object, fit exclusively to receive the lover's homage. The upright and devoted woman, especially among the Jews, could have no thought of other than a single husband. In this region of the Semites, throughout which the sex-passion played such a role in religion,[2] and where as

[1] Ezekiel, V, 11 ff. There is another side of the jealousy of the God of the Jews which is important but perhaps not so directly a force helping to create and sustain monotheism. It is the *zeal for Israel's interests*, the angry *defense* of the beloved against her enemies. This is the psychic completion of the lover's attitude, that besides the claim to a sole place in the heart of the beloved, there is the passionate espousal of her cause when she is threatened by another. Thus Jehovah is not simply jealous *against* Israel and the gods who have her faithless love; but when her punishment is complete and she is forgiven, he is jealous *for* her and against those who cause her suffering (cf. Zechariah, I, 14; VIII, 2; II Kings, XIX, 31; Isaiah, IX, 7; XXXVII, 32; Ezekiel, XXXVI, 5 f.; Joel, II, 18. Other passages, less clear, seem to point in the same direction; e.g., Ezekiel, XXXVIII, 19; XXXIX, 25; Zephaniah, III, 8; Isaiah, LXIII, 15).

This kind of jealousy appears also as a zeal of men for the cause of the Lord (cf. I Kings, XIX, 10; Numbers, XXV, 11, 13; Psalms, LXIX, 9; CXIX, 139; II Samuel, XXI, 2).

[2] See, e.g., W. Robertson Smith: *Religion of the Semites*, 1901, pp.

among the Jews it was curbed and disciplined into a fidelity to one person and sanctioned by consuming jealousy, it drove the erring religious mind back from its rovings and fixed it upon the one and sole divinity.

At first it may well have seemed consistent with the thought that other gods are real, are seducing lovers of Israel, rivals of Jehovah. Indeed logically the jealous god cannot be the sole-existent god; his very rage affirms the reality and importance of his rival. Yet the love-passion here drives both with and against the current of logic. For there is also in the worshipper here the emotional exclusion of the rival, that is insidious; the withdrawal of human interest and affection is more deeply annihilating than would be a purely intellectual denial where the object still had its fascination.

To other peoples came a passing vision of the One God, —to the Aztec, the Hindu, the Chinese, the Greek, the Babylonian, the Egyptian,—and both the Babylonian and the Egyptian may well have helped the Jew toward his great achievement. But not until the Jew himself, in a wide portion of the earth where the sex-passion had so important a place in worship, took this passion purified, bringing mutual and enduring obligation to be angrily asserted and defended—not until the Jew took this group of master passions and let them help to mold his reverence, did monotheism become a central and permanent tradition in a great religion, whence it spread to others who were disciples of the Jew.

III

But the jealousy of the lover was not left to act alone: there was added the jealousy of the father and the king.

55 ff. It is surprising that this author, although he refers to the jealousy of the personal god in higher heathenism, and the jealousy of the husband in Judaism (see pp. 162 ff. and 180 of the work just cited) gives no indication that he appreciates the place of marital jealousy in the conception of Jehovah.

JEALOUSY AS A SOURCE OF MONOTHEISM 219

Not until we look to these, comparing their force with that of the marriage passion, shall we see the full effect of jealousy in the Jew's religion. For other relations than those of lovers are single and exclusive, sensitive against all that tends to rivalry, against all that multiplies the objects of obedience and loyal regard.

Jehovah is not merely the husband; he is the one from whose loins the Jews have sprung: Israel is the son,[1] the firstborn of God.[2] God is a father to Israel, and Ephraim is his firstborn, his dear son.[3] The children of Israel, disowned of the Lord, are to be restored to sonship.[4] God is the father of those of whom Abraham is ignorant and whom Israel does not own.[5] God pities those who fear him, even as a father pities his children;[6] he is the father of the fatherless;[7] he has nourished children who have rebelled against him, who have forsaken him and provoked him to anger.[8]

God is also the king, sitting upon a throne, high and lifted up,[9] sitting upon his throne above the firmament,[10] upon his throne with all the host of heaven standing by him on his right hand and on his left.[11] He shall be king over all the earth;[12] he is the governor among the nations;[13] he sitteth upon the circle of the earth, and the inhabitants thereof are as grasshoppers.[14]

[1] Hosea, XI, 1; and cf. Deuteronomy, I, 31; VIII, 5; XIV, 1; XXXII, 6.
[2] Exodus, IV, 22.
[3] Jeremiah, XXXI, 9, 20.
[4] Hosea, I, 9, 10.
[5] Isaiah, LXIII, 16; Malachi, II, 10. Here the idea of fatherhood is extended beyond the mere blood connection, to a universal spiritual community.
[6] Psalms, CIII, 13.
[7] Psalms, LXVIII, 5.
[8] Isaiah, I, 2-4.
[9] Isaiah, VI, 1.
[10] Ezekiel, I, 26.
[11] I Kings, XXII, 19.
[12] Zechariah, XIV, 9.
[13] Psalms, XXII, 28.
[14] Isaiah, XL, 22.

It is evident that the conception of God as a single person clothed with authority and requiring loyalty is formed and fortified by the thought of that single relation in which a man stands to his father and to his king. These aids and motives then unite with the thought of marriage to impress upon the mind allegiance to the One God.

If now we ask which of these currents contributes most to the final stream, the evidence favors the conviction that with the Jew it was that of wedlock. The image of the king whose subjects have rebelled; of the father whose children have disgraced his name,—these had power and suggested their own forms of wakeful jealousy. But in his accounts of the offended God who is king and of the God who is father, the Jew expresses no such intensity of feeling against the unfaithfulness to the One as when there is in his mind the offended lover and husband. Here the Jew feels it fitting that there be a fire of jealousy exceeding anything which outraged royalty or fatherhood suggests to him. In the love, forgetful of all other men, which the husband expected of his wife, he found the excuse for a passion explosive and annihilating. In the scripture the kingship of God is associated more with emotions suggested by his grandeur, by his wide sway; his fatherhood is associated more with his tender pity, his forgiveness. But the recurrent image of the divine husband, while it was also blended with mercy and the return of love, yet was lit more often by an awful fire of vengeance, a vengeance that could burn the offender's house, slaughter her children, tear from her her garments and her jewels, mutilate her face, stone her, stab her naked and broken body with the sword! In imagining what the king or the father might do to the disloyal one, the Jew's thought comes to no such pitch of retribution as this.

To see the significance of the marriage bond it is also well to remember that both this and filial loyalty come closer and earlier to the individual than does his obligation to his king; nor are they displaced by this when it comes. But the motives strengthened in early childhood favor the thought of a world at whose head is, not a man alone, but a man and woman, who are its creative parents and directors,—a thought which appears so often in primitive religion. Such an idea therefore goes no great distance to explain the monotheism of the Jew. Nor, on the other hand, does the monarchal motive, to which, assisted by the paternal motive, Robertson Smith would ascribe the coming of monotheism,[1] explain enough. For it is active in almost every other religion, great or small, and yet without this outcome; nor can it even help to account for certain other traits so significant in the Jewish faith, which the love-motive can explain. For with the love-bond as the guiding image in religion, the human term in the divine-human relation becomes weightier, less unequal than with the citizen-subject in relation to his monarch. For with lovers, even when we allow for the woman's lesser place in the Oriental world, the bond is more nearly between equals, more nearly balanced and mutual, than even that between father and child.

In the marriage relation even as conceived by the ancient Jew, there is for the wife far more of sympathetic understanding, far less of mystery and of arbitrary will, than would be common for the child [2] or the loyal subject. One might well doubt whether that contempt which the great Hebrew preachers poured upon mere legality, upon the scrupulous outward observance of rites, and the demand for right desire, for obedience in the very heart, could have been inspired by the governmental, the monarchal conception rather than by what is central in lovers'

[1] The *Religion of the Semites*, 1901, 40 ff., 55, 73 f.
[2] In the Christian use of sonship, there is an express elevation of this into mutual understanding, by uniting it with friendship,—"Henceforth I call you not servants, . . . but . . . *friends.*" And in the parable of the "prodigal son" we see no longer a mere child but the mature son who can finally enter with sympathy and intelligence into the father's purpose.

affection and wedded loyalty. A king, a governor, a judge, is commonly well-pleased with strict observance of law. He may upon occasion feel concern for a man's knowledge and intention, in order to decide some point of responsibility. But in general the external act itself is of moment, and all else is without his care.

But not so in marriage even when imperfect. More is required than what is outward. There is a craving for an inward faithfulness, for a return of affection, for some approach to oneness of spirit. All this which is in the secret store of love becomes, in the prophets and the sublime devotional poetry of the Jew, essential also to the relation between Jehovah and his people. The fiery exhortation, the unutterable longing, is so often illustrated by love and wedlock that the thought cannot be escaped that religion was here drawing its very life from the life of lovers. The "inwardness" of the Hebrew prophetic religion is thus in deep debt to marital affection.

Husband, father, and king, all point to singleness on high. But with the Jew they do not appear in equal force. The obligation of the wife, and its sanction by a jealousy cruel as the grave, commanded, as in no other people, the Jewish imagination and reverence. And thus the paternal and the kingly suggestion, elsewhere at work, here for the first time come to their fruition. Instead of mere glimpses of monotheism as from a distance, the Hebrew thus went in and possessed the land and made it a heritage for all the world.

IV

Urged by his sense of the exclusive loyalty found in marriage, the way of the Jew was made easier by his intense and narrow love for those of his own faith and blood, by his coldness and hostility toward what was not his own. Thus it was easier for him than for many others to believe that God needed, indeed could brook, no divine associates. The Jewish temper led not only to zeal, but to a zealous hatred and exclusion.

In Mohammed there was found a fiery spirit prepared to receive and transmit what the Jew attained. The founder of Islam, acquainted in some measure with both the Christian and the Hebrew concept of divinity, became a burning partisan of the Hebraic view. He might compromise with the ancient religions of his homeland as to holy places and images and festivals, but never and in no degree as to the solitary and jealous sublimity of God. Allah is One, he proclaims; merciful but avenging, without companions, without children; God has no sons, no daughters, no associates: in hot anger is the Oneness of God hurled back against the Christian and his belief in the Divine Son, the Divine Trinity. The terribleness of the Arab, fanatic in its love and hate, was like the temper of the ancient Jew. And while the Arab was ill-endowed to originate so bold and sublime a conception; yet, once offered it by a great leader, he eagerly accepted and imposed on others the thought of a sole and jealous God.

The Christian West, less passionate, yet amply endowed with anger and self-assertion, could also under the Jew's tutelage believe in a self-assertive, a rival-destroying God. Yet in the West the great discovery became a shade more tolerant, more compromising, a shade nearer to the polytheism hated of the Jew and Arab; since it now changes to the mystical confession that the One God is a God in Three Persons. The Christian might cling to the wrath of the Jews' Jehovah, persisting in God the Father, and to Jehovah's love now made manifest in God the Son; but the ancient jealousy was tempered by acknowledging that the directions of allegiance are not narrowed to a point, that toward the Perfect there may be a certain complexity, indeed rivalry, of fealties. If the Greek, the Roman, had been accustomed by his temperament to focus his hate and love to the same burning point as did the Jew, Christianity would doubtless have preserved as strict a monotheism as did Judaism and Islam, and we should not have had that profound modification, yet without return to polytheism, found in the doctrine of the Trinity. Greece whose intellect ruled Rome, might in her philosophies attain to a strict monotheism; but her own people and the others of the West were of too varied interests, were too temperate and mobile in their affections, ever to feel long that God required an adoration excluding from very existence a divine equality and association.

V

Although Christianity thus tempered the monotheism of the Jew, yet it felt with approval the Jew's jealousy and self-assertion. Had this not been, Christianity might well have gone the way of the Far East, where religions are unjealous and where monotheism finds no certain place. Apart from anger and jealousy, bound up, as these are, with self-valuing and self-assertion, it seems impossible to understand all the religious currents of India and China and the rest of the Oriental life to which they are neighbor.

For the life there moved close to monotheism, indeed passed around it. It is not that the far Eastern mind was incapable of so distant a journey from its early polytheism. The rather it traveled farther than was needed: its course was as though with a conscious repugnance of monotheism, its eye fixed upon something far on the other side.

In India, for example, the hymns of the Rig-Veda express an adoration that magnifies now one and now another god until all others seem but his manifestation. Agni is declared to be all the gods; and, again, all the gods are Rudra. This which Max Müller termed *henotheism* needed but an appreciating and conserving force to fix it into monotheism. But the motives for such fixation were lacking, and the attainment was lost in the very making;

the religious affection was lured on by the vision of a divinity including and accepting all, rejecting and hating nothing, a divinity against which nothing in man himself stood defensive, ready to resist in the name of sheer human worth and responsibility the divine encroachment and absorption.

Pantheism represents no less of sustained and adventurous thought than does monotheism; it represents, rather, an intelligence mastered by a sympathy and longing without restraint, a sympathy that is in fact unprincipled. There is here no protective resentment, no salutary jealousy; the riot of appreciation obliterates first the line between good and evil, and then between mind and mind, and at last the One alone remains, without preference, indifferent to all the polar qualities of affection and will. In the distant East, love has been acclaimed, until the faith there has seemed one with Christianity in all that is essential; but wanting jealousy, partisanship, anger, there resulted a Being without discriminating affection, said to love righteousness but having no hatred of evil, a Being without definite character and conscious intention, the substance of the universe now become impersonal law.

Anger has had no place in the very center and ideal of many of the Far Eastern religions—Taoism, Vishnuism, Jainism, Buddhism. Their gods, where gods remained in the faith, were unangry toward one another. The religious bodies themselves are habitually tolerant of one another. In China to-day the communicants of any one of the great faiths may freely partake of the rites of the others. And in India a god was readier than in the West to accept as though for himself the homage intended for another.

Whether there has been some approach to equal tepidity, to equal generosity, in the secular intercourse of men, so that even human love has been less proprietary, readier to share its object and feel no bitter rivalry, than in the West, it would be interesting to know. But in so far as an accepted picture of the Burma of to-day [1] represents something ancient and extended, we may well believe that widely there the fires of hostile passion, of self-assertion, are less aglow. Because of its relative quiescence, its love less ready to blaze into wrath, the extreme Southeast, with all its subtle speculation and its ever-present patterns of autocracy, never moved securely into monotheism and held it as a final revealing of the foundations of the world.

VI

In sum, monotheism is seen to have a different emotional plan from that of pantheism, from that of polytheism. The varied directions of wonder and fear and affection which many gods offer, in monotheism are limited, and the mind holds inalterably to the One. There is here a new relief and satisfaction, as of a woman who, long listening in eager distress to many suitors, at last makes her choice and drives from her heart all division, all rivalry. But in monotheism, as we have seen, the emotional flood which in pantheism submerges the distinction between worshipper and worshipped is held back: bounds are set between God and men, as there are between man and man. The individual asserts himself with more self-consciousness, with more self-esteem; the devotee will not yield his own private and personal reality; even God must not crowd him out. These emotions that have their center about the self here help to preserve the *personal* along with the *unitary* character of the Ideal.

We need not come forward to the democracy of the modern West for secular manifestations of this same spirit. It is seen in the temper of the ancient world, in the nearer East where the Jew attained his faith. Self-confidence, self-assertion is clear enough in the war-vigor of Persia, Assyria, Babylonia, and Egypt. Ringed with such peo-

[1] H. Fielding Hall: *The Soul of a People*, 1902.

ples, tinged with the blood of some of them, there came as a culmination and spiritual fulfillment of their secular ideals the religion of the Jews. Less skillful to express their longing and their wrath by conquering armies, the Hebrews uttered by their prophets an ennobled indignation, an aggressive anger for the cause of righteousness. Men here spoke as representatives of an unseen king, a judge, an outraged husband, in words compressed with yearning and command and indignation. In no other land had so many sides of impulse spoken for so sublime an enterprise.

This note of passion, jealous and divisive, is clear also in Islam and Christianity. These too are assertive, intolerant, for long ready on the grand scale to persecute one another and all who opposed their course. Judaism, Islam, and Christianity have found in the character of their monotheism something congenial and encouraging to the fierce temper of the peoples to whom they minister. With these three monotheistic faiths and with the peoples who accept them personal passion is not despised and rejected but has its enduring place even in the life of the Perfect.

By the individualizing, self-assertive force of jealousy, then, religion has been enriched and dignified and made alert, not losing its way in a dreamy infinitude of appreciation. The personal God, and not the impersonal Law is here supreme. The impersonal exists, but is an expression of a deeper and conscious spiritual order. *Monotheism, then, came to its full and enduring life where a speculative religion, conscious of logical and political and moral motives which bring the manifoldness of the universe toward unity, yet feels within itself also the master passion of the jealous lover.*

This creative use of the love-motive and its jealousy was worthy of the religious genius of the Jews. They were in this upon common ground with the other Semites, and

yet separated from them as by a great gulf. For with
their blood-kindred the love-motive had remained erotic;
physical sexuality had entered into the temple service,
representing perhaps to the spiritually gifted the union,
so earnestly sought the world over, of god and worshipper.
The Jew, however, could not live at peace with this abomi-
nation. And yet try as he would to escape its fascination,
there was too much in his own warm nature as its ally;
it held him, and he gained peace only by plucking out its
spiritual core, preserving its strength for use, lifting it up
into a place with moral law and moral institutions.

For with him the lovers—God and his chosen bride—
were no longer creatures of mere passion; they gave and
accepted pledges of honor. Their union was felt to be
abominable unless there came with it a sense of mutual and
lasting obligation. After this manner the lust, the physical
gratification, so powerful in other Semitic worship enters
now, purged into man's intercourse with the divine, and
there remains only what accords with the finer loyalties of
the family bond. We now have love that permits no wan-
dering, love that is severe in its angry maintenance of
duty. Affection, generosity, understanding, zeal for the
interests both of the lover and of the beloved—all that is
central in right marriage—has been received to enrich the
relation between Jehovah and his people Israel, until they
look back upon their worship of other gods as wantonness,
as adulterous and abhorrent love.

With love and wrath steadied and made of power by
such a discipline, it was, as we have seen, but a psychic
step to the denial of very existence of all other gods.
And as the final sublimation of their endowment of anger,
where the warlike neighbors of the Jews went forth to
conquest with armies and were in the end held back, this
conquering spirit in the Jew made his God go forth to a
spiritual war which none could withstand. He thus becomes in the ideal of the ancient Jew, the king, not of the
Jews only, but of all the world. "For he put on righteous-

ness as a breastplate, and a helmet of salvation on his head; and he put on the garments of vengeance for clothing, and was clad with zeal as a cloak. According to their deeds, accordingly will he repay, fury to his adversaries, recompense to his enemies. . . . So shall they fear the name of the Lord from the west, and his glory from the rising of the sun." [1]

[1] Isaiah, LIX, 16-19.

PART IV

THE FUTURE OF ANGER IN THE WEST

CHAPTER XV
THE HISTORIC TREND IN THE OCCIDENT

We have seen anger and its kin in a double rôle, puzzling to all who are concerned with human welfare. Anger has been an advocate of the right, helping men to strengthen their moral code and their moral institutions. It has also been a chief offender, a destroyer of friendship and family and state, ready to bring to naught the good-will which is ever in sore need of increase. Anger has thus been as a hand in molding religion and morals, helping to give character to the gods and to their relation with one another and with men, active early in all religion and especially at the source of monotheism. Religion and morals have been as embarrassed by its help as by its opposition.

It is of no wonder, therefore, that the great faiths have stood boldly opposed to one another in their counsel regarding it. A few religions like Mohammedanism have had no qualms in putting anger in the forefront; others, with Buddhism as the prime example, will have no dealing with it; while Christianity at first stood midway, accepting anger, but on condition that it be subject to love.

Our next endeavor then must be to lay a course for this troublesome impulse, seeing as best we can and with some detachment whether science and plain wisdom speak more in the spirit of Mecca, or of Benares, or of Galilee; or whether indeed they assume the tone of none of these. It is a task inviting to the mind.

But first we should observe the change in Christianity, and in the culture whose ideal it has done so much to form.

I

In the Founder of Christianity good-will was joined to violent animosity. He who called the peacemaker blessed, and declared God to be a friend who would come in and sup with one, nevertheless bade his disciples shake off the dust for a testimony against the inhospitable, and himself drove commerce forth with such violence from the sanctuary, that to those who saw him he seemed as one consumed with his jealousy. There is here an ample anger, an ample pugnacity; but above and guiding it is a zeal to erect a spiritual house in which God and men can dwell together.

But soon there appeared divergent trends; the one, in the *Revelation of St. John;* the other, in the *Gospel of St. John* and in the *Epistle of James*. The one would extend anger until the life of the spirit is to be lived almost wholly without love; the other would enlarge love until it leaves hardly a place for wrath. In a relation so complex and so difficult to maintain as that which early Christianity would have between good-will and anger, it is almost inevitable that there should be these two opposing spirits,—the one with all the wrath of Islam; the other, with the kindly quietism of the Buddha. Especially does the angry side of Christianity appear when later it enters politics. The Crusaders, as I imagine them, were as ready to conceive religion to be a visible conquest and submission as were the Muslims. The opposing attitudes, though not in their extremes, confront each other also in those two geniuses of the Reformation-time, Luther and Erasmus,—the one priest, all for battle and defiance; the other, all for peaceful influence. "I think courtesy to opponents is more effective than violence," writes Erasmus to Luther; "Old institutions cannot be rooted up in an instant. Quiet argument may do more than wholesale condemnation. Avoid all appearance of sedition. Keep cool.

Do not get angry. Do not hate anybody. Do not be excited over the noise which you have made." [1]

A little later the Puritans in battle-array under Cromwell represented in somewhat other form than Luther's that same side of Christianity which still later, in Jonathan Edwards, came to a severity almost equal to anything that Mohammed could express, and which is repugnant to those whose dependence is on sweetness and quiet contemplation and an unmixed love. Quakers, Doukhobors, and the followers of Mrs. Eddy, with all their differences, inner and outer, are alike in refusing to take into the Spirit's service this dark and violent impulse. So far as they utterly reject anger they have departed far from the early pattern and precept. But this they do in protest against a worse departure from the early example and advice, against the elevation of anger into a place not dominated by goodwill.

The efflorescence of the peaceable temper in Christianity is seen in St. Francis of Assisi, the gentlest, the most tender of men, and in the honor, renewed from past ages into our own time, still paid his name. With him hatred is soothed into the quietest aversion; he loves as though the whole world had in it only loveliness.

But were we now to look, not at the extremes of Christianity, but at its mean, do we find that the main body would still observe the relation between love and hate recommended when the faith was young? Has the great company of its fellowship, whatever of failure may have come in practice, held steadily to the old ideal?

We must admit a marked change, a marked softening of the stern and inflexible features of Christianity. All have noticed how much milder than of old is the tone in which are mentioned sin and God's way of viewing it. The word "sin," the word "wickedness," has almost disappeared

---

[1] Froude: *Life and Letters of Erasmus*, (1895), p. 234. For this quotation I am indebted to a privately printed essay entitled *Desiderius Erasmus*, by my friend, Warren Olney, Sr.

from the vocabulary of many; the idea of an angry retribution of sin has for many wholly disappeared. Who would now dare think, much less utter, the awful denunciation of the wicked which in amazement we read in the sermon, "Sinners in the Hands of an Angry God?" Church-members, whatever their official expression may be, refuse to believe that infants are damned to eternal hell, indeed that to hell are damned even the worst adults. This is no longer an approved theme of public discourse.

Furthermore the religious toleration now known, but which was a stranger to the world in no far-distant time, points to this same change. The propagation of the faith by torture, conversion by fear, is no longer the acceptable way. The representative of that Islam against whom generations of Christians waged war could in the World War be the ally of most-Christian emperors. And in times of peace there is an era of good-feeling between sects. It is not good form any longer for Protestants publicly to denounce Catholics, or for Protestant sects to show anger one with another. Both in the organization of Christian conduct and in the Christian view of God, anger is no longer in its old place.

It would hardly be accurate were we to see in all this change merely an excision of what cannot be reconciled with the original plan. There is a deep misgiving in regard to anger in any form and for any purpose. Even anger in the service of love suffers mistrust.

II

In secular life also there is a more frequent attempt at gentleness. The severe punishment of sinners after death as well as of heretics before death is hardly more under suspicion than is the severe punishment of offenders against the civil law. Here, too, as in religion, some would not have us speak of punishment; such an expression implies retribution, implies vengeance; and society's interest in the offender, it is held, is solely an interest in reclaiming him. The torture-chamber at Nuremberg is now a place for curious tourists; the old burning at the stake is now approved by no government but only by the mob. We have not cleared the world of these brutalities, but they have not their former honor. Fewer persons are visited with capital punishment for their crimes; and the few persons who are so punished are not drawn and quartered, or impaled, or hung in chains. Debtors are not thrown into prison; the whipping post, the ducking stool, the pillory, the stocks, are no longer found in the machinery of law in civilized lands. In England a husband at one time was within his rights in beating his wife, provided only that he did not maim her. In America even a wife would hardly have this right over her husband. The whipping of children in the schools is in many places prohibited; the whipping of them in the home is in many families quite unknown. Anger and hatred are, with a goodly number, counted a belittling of the soul: their attitude would be well represented by the negro Booker Washington who "learned the lesson," he tells us, "that great men cultivate love, and that only little men cherish a spirit of hatred." "It is now long ago," he continues, "that I learned this lesson from General Armstrong, and resolved that I would permit no man, no matter what his color might be, to narrow and degrade my soul by making me hate him." [1]

And if one were to array the evidence of this growing coolness should not the increased attempt to rid the world of war be named? It is true that in the anarchy of international affairs anger and pugnacity are held in highest honor. It is also true that war's economic waste is so appalling that some hate war for little else than this. And yet as human beings, interested beyond property, interested in the life of body and spirit which alone gives

[1] *Up from Slavery: An Autobiography*, p. 165.

value to material things and makes them saleable, we must see that the opposition to war goes farther than economists can figure in their tables. The affront to the spirit of the community stands out above the economic loss. Many could bring themselves gladly to spend as much were it chiefly for health and juster institutions and learning and good-will. But to spend it merely to keep a part of what one has, to repel an assault, to meet a crisis created by jealousy,—the human soul cannot forever abide this insult to its dignity and honor. The ugliness of the anger of one nation against another begins to shame us as we have long been shamed out of personal broils, until we no longer count greatest the gentleman quick with his rapier or his pistol, the nobleman with his hired bullies and cut-throat bravoes.

All this is not entirely because we are squeamish of pain. It is true that we are increasingly sensitive to suffering in others, even in animals. The use of anæsthetics has sprung from this feeling and has ministered to it. But the more civilized world grows opposed to anger even when this does not pass into bruise and laceration. That the harsh emotion itself is under a ban becomes evident since for many the child is to be trained, not only without whipping, but without anger. And in a current view of legal restraint in crime, touched upon a moment earlier, there must be no thought of social indignation, even of social condemnation; whatever is done is wholly to correct the criminal's disorder and to restore him to the free life of the community. He is not to be visited with anger; he is to be treated as are the ignorant or the sick.

There can hardly be a doubt, then, but that in the ideal of the West *the current of religious approval, as well as of secular, flows away from anger.* The passion is not of as good repute as once it was in Greece and Rome and western Europe or in America, whether before or after they had learned from Galilee.

III

With the fact of a change thus evident, one would like to see as clearly the causes of the change. But it will hardly be possible to attempt more than a hint of the many influences that have conspired to lessen the honor of anger in our part of the world, once an ancestral seat of the pugnacious impulse. The change is doubtless in part due to Christianity, with its teaching that love is the greatest of the soul's possessions. But we should still find unexplained the change within Christianity itself, where anger is of lessening dignity in the ideal, both of the human and of the divine character. The change is in part due also to the wider fact that men are become more civilized; and, trained in democracy, are more sympathetic, less callous and cruel, toward plain men everywhere.

But looking to particular causes, some would point to the influence of philosophy, which has thrown its weight, in the main, against emotion, translating even the Christian love into terms of the intellect. But philosophy touches few, and follows, rather than leads. Religious ideas influence more. And if the idea of a definite and positive personality of God has in some slight measure made compromise with the nebulous conception held by the pantheist, this would assist in the change to be explained. Krishna is described in Oriental scripture as the producer and destroyer of the whole universe, he is the truth and also the delusion which hides the truth from men. "I am death," he says, "who seizes all, and the source of what is to be." "I am immortality and also death; and I, O Arjuna! am that which is and that which is not."[1] For any who would make God even slightly less personal, even a little nearer to the One that includes all and rejects nothing, there is the temptation to regard him

[1] Bhagavadgita, IX (VIII, 74 f., 80 f.).

as less passionate for the good, less passionate against evil, no longer partial, tolerant toward both sides, whatever be the clash and contrast.

Some urging toward this indifference may also have come from natural science. The doctrine of evolution suggests in nature a power more patient, less eager than our fathers thought, less easily conceived according to the pattern of the human mind. The conservation of energy, also,—energy forever changing and yet forever remaining the same,—readily suggests the Oriental view. It will take time to reconcile the spirit of Christianity with these novel intimations of nature, and in the meantime their immediate influence is toward a less distinctly personal, a less definitely moral government of the universe. Until the moment of a completer spiritual recovery of poise, many will hesitate to project into eternity their human habits of praise and blame.

And apart from any particular truth or teaching of natural science, there is an imperceptible influence which science in general exerts upon its disciples. Those who lose themselves in science become attentive to *causes* rather than to *worth;* they would explain, and not be distracted by questions of better and worse. If, then, the universe were to be modelled after the mind of the scientist, causation would be the world's sole concern; there would be nothing to be condemned, nothing which the heart of the universe would either hate or love. The indifference which often the Oriental mind sees as its ideal is thus suggested also to the devotees of natural science.

The religious thought of our time and of the West feels these currents of discovery and speculation. And with them comes another influence, that of woman. Mystery will long conceal the full difference between her mind and man's but it already seems clear that pugnacity is more ready and vigorous in the male. Women are in time of peace not only less fascinated by war than are men, but in civil matters they lean more to the side of mercy. The gentler affections, prepared for the coming of the child, are helping to reshape the world's sense of justice. One can say this without idealizing, without forgetting that the woman to-day, even as in the French Revolution, can be utterly cruel, utterly rapacious. But the obstacles are greater, there is more to resist the flight of pity from her heart. The mother in her must always first be killed. And with her ever-increasing voice in the conduct of our Occidental society and of Christianity, she speaks against established wrath and for a ready forgiveness. She serves to check the male temper, sweetening the acid humors of his blood, calling him to remember that all his wide-flung designs must be tested also by her and by the happiness of individuals, and is not solely for impersonal ends, for science and commerce and distant empire.

We must leave to others nicely to trace the web of explanation here, saying what makes the novel pattern. We see the great loom of history, and in our day a civil life and a Christianity coming from it, less aggressive, less resentful than in the older days. If this softening were merely in religion's practice we might say that it was due to the loss of zeal, after the Good Tidings had grown decades of centuries old. But the change is not in the practice only; it is in the ideal. An ever-larger body of Christians aim to rid themselves and others of indignation, to be equable of temper, tolerant of all difference, sympathetic even with those who are ravaging the world's most precious spiritual possessions.

Now this purpose if fulfilled would carry us along the way which many religions of the Far East have gone: first, upon a way of love so catholic that it would accept and cherish everything; and then, forward to a stage beyond love, where the intent is less to appreciate than to contemplate and to understand. But before the choice is made and sealed, we should reweigh our thought. The alternatives should be recalled,—the Islamic fierceness, set over against the Buddhist release from all desire, and how Christianity in the beginning chose neither of these, but proposed to men a strange union of love and hate.

The path of Islam is hardly open, save in international affairs. The will to take that course in the World War, as always, led to disaster. Others will try and re-try the barbaric course. But in the end Christianity will not go the way of those who would make it chiefly an instrument of nationalism, interpreting the message of Galilee as though it were from Mecca. Anger as the dominant note, even in national life, cannot but make discord with the Christian theme.

But can our moral and religious ideal, in justice to its own intuition and to the plain light of psychology, move along the other course, into accord with the convictions of the Farther East? Was the original choice of both love and anger a mistake? Are we now to correct an ancient error, freeing love from a comrade-passion that prevents its progress, arousing anger in others when love unaccompanied would be met by love? Or if anger is to be retained, what should be its discipline, what its bonds to keep the peace? These questions will be in mind during all that follows.

CHAPTER XVI

WILL AND THE NATIVE IMPULSES

I

To proceed with hope of solid outcome we must catch sight of the will entire and of the place in it held by intelligence and by the multitude of our native desires and emotions. Only then shall we be more just to anger and its kin.

Four things the will needs: strength, constancy, independence, and a right object. The direction in which the will is turned is as much a part of the will's character as are its force, its steadiness, and its self-reliance.

The trend of the day might cause us to regard belief as of little importance in the will. Yet out on a moor in Maryland when typhoid fever was raging I met a man who held that the disease had no connection with what was eaten or drunk; such a man's will would be influenced by his conviction. But belief or intellect of itself, however necessary, never sets the goal. It presents, sharp or dim, various ends, among which there must be choice; and it suggests ways and means when once the choice is made. Love can do nothing without knowledge; nor can hate. Even conscience gropes and stumbles, except as intelligence shows what ways are open, and to what each leads.

Knowledge then joins with attraction or repulsion to make one decide—cognition being infused with mild or violent emotion that plays over the object which thought or imagination holds before our inner eye. Out before me stands the fact reported by intelligence; but here within is the response which the fact awakens, of liking or aversion. And according as these externals—not physical merely, but also spiritual; for they include the whole surrounding company of persons, of minds,—according as these facts call forth their peculiar response in me entire or in the regnant forces called my ideal, do they have value. The scale of one's valuation constantly appears. No one, in this sense, long conceals his affections; each wears his heart upon his sleeve.

But the affections are many and are conflicting, and we must have some principle of handling them all, and not only anger and love. But the time so spent will hardly be grudged, if the effort promise help for resolution, leaving the will less savage, less sentimental, giving it sinews for a high and steady work.

II

In trying to see distinctly the way to pursue with our great native impulses and emotions let us first confront their whole company and know at least the names of some of them. Besides anger, there is fear, sex-love, parent-love, companionableness, the impulse to humble ourselves before others, to lord it over them, to accumulate property, to work, to idle, to play, to construct, to destroy, to understand, and doubtless many more. And having seen their large and motley gathering we may well ask what are the alternative ways of dealing with the troublesome members of this company, the unruly instincts.

We may try to destroy them root and branch. The impulse to gather possessions, the impulse to domineer, the impulse of love between men and women,—these have to many seemed fit only to be cast into the fire and burned. Men have tried to do this, often in the name of religion, feeling a sworn enmity between them and the spirit. Especially has the love of man for woman been condemned of men themselves; they have renounced marriage, they have vowed not to speak to women, not to look upon them;

they have fled to the desert, they have entered monasteries where no woman might ever come. Terrible has been the struggle to master and then to be rid of this native passion. In a like manner though in less anguish men have struggled with their desire for wealth, which too attains an intensity that awakens fear because of its power to enslave, to drive out pity, to rule or exclude all other interests. This, too, men have wrestled with, trying to kill it, vowing poverty, vowing to hold all things in common, giving away all that they had, carrying no money, begging of others at the moment what food or shelter they might need.

But the very opposite principle may find favor. *We may accept and honor the passions, giving them the freedom of the city.* Thus we have had, not simply in secular practice but in the teaching of religion, an unhindered play,—indeed an incitement—of lust and of the desire for wealth. The religion of the Rig-Veda is strong in its approval of material possessions. "Help us," the pious soul prays to his divinity, "help us to good, resplendent, abundant wealth." [1] And again there is a prayer to the god Agni which would not seem out of place at the opening of some conference of profiteers: "Bring this wealth to us, O powerful Agni, to these our men. May he give us dwelling; may he give us prosperity; may he help us in winning booty. And help us to grow strong in fights!" [2] And one will recall that description in Herodotus, of the obscene practices in connection with worship in Babylonia,[3] and which we know to have existed elsewhere. Unbridled passion has been admitted into the very temple, and in orgies like those of the Saturnalia in many lands. And even Christianity has had in its own communion those who felt that all their promptings must be of God and therefore to be freely satisfied.

[1] Vedic Hymns II, 2, 12 (XLVI, 194); cf. II, 33, 1 f. (XXXII, 426 f.).
[2] Vedic Hymns V, 9, 7 (XLVI, 387); cf. V, 54, 13 (XXXII, 326).
[3] Herodotus I, 199.

But to-day it is outside of religion that one finds the chief advocates of indulgence. That all repression of passion brings harm is a creed that now has quite a following. In its milder forms this new persuasion points out the evil of repressing the instinct to work. Others would not repress the instinct to avoid work: the Doukhobors, an odd sect of Russians, felt a religious enthusiasm for the impulse to remain idle, and to observe and admire; and forthwith they refused to labor, believing that in this they were true followers of Christ.[1] In this advocacy of free indulgence, whether in its somewhat absurd or in its tragic forms, we are thus at the opposite pole to the view that men should deny and uproot these native desires which morality has found so hard to govern.

A third way however is open, less extreme, commending itself to men of moderation: that we should neither imprison nor enthrone our passions, but should *discipline them until they can take their sober place and perform their sober work* in the commonwealth of character. They are to be accepted, not for what they have of original value, but for what they can become and can contribute to the spiritual order. The fire of passion must neither be extinguished nor be wildfire; it must be both fanned and controlled until it blesses the hearth and is transmuted into power and light.

With these possibilities now clear to us, I believe that our choice will not prove difficult. For the first two of the three alternatives,—utter repression and utter indulgence—are at once improvident and repulsive. The healthy mind, at least in the West, turns from the picture of the soul without desire to possess, to enjoy, to understand, the things of body and of mind. The complete denial of the natural order—requiring a man to be detached from wife and child and home, from interest in his present and future welfare as an individual, or in the wel-

[1] Maude: *A Peculiar People*, 1905, 225 f.

fare of the community, and to find satisfaction in the borderless, the indefinite—all this is nihilistic and intolerable. It involves such thriftlessness, such waste of the soul's resources.

The opposite course, that of free indulgence, would establish all that the public-minded are striving to cast down, and would destroy all that they now upbuild. It is impossible to adopt it without surrendering all those institutions that stand between us and a condition lower than barbarism,—the institution of the family, of government, of property, of impartial judgment at law. Repression, it is true, may be inconvenient and may bring suffering to the individual (although this has often been exaggerated); but unbridled passion brings still greater pain and confusion both to him and to his fellows. For the task of science in the service of human conduct is to suggest a plan of living, not in some air-castle where my interest alone is given heed, but on our populous earth-surface where men must be neighbor to one another and in the end can do only what others will witness and approve. Society has found no way to exist without repression, nor is there hope of a discovery.

But more is needed than repression. There is need of prodding. Too much of invitation comes with the thought that our native impulses are all headstrong, over-ready to dominate. In truth some are indolent, while others are inconstant, now sluggards, now zealots. Taking the impulse to rule, for illustration; over against the men who, like Napoleon, are unfailingly assertive stand those who are too yielding, and those who are too assertive and too yielding by turn. And so it is with curiosity, with friendliness, with property-acquiring, down the long list of native urgings; instead of being always too strong, sometimes they are not strong enough. And what appears over-strength may be but lack of opposition, sluggishness in the impulses that should balance and correct them. One would be wrong then in seeing the instinctive forces as initially like raging beasts. They are more like animals caged, where some may unceasingly pace to and fro, while others spend their days sleeping in a distant corner.

But men have as yet mastered the art neither of repression nor of stimulation. Society has blundered in over-doing and under-doing. In the effort to make men's love for women something endurable and beneficent, mankind has done endless wrong to women. In the attempt to bring the wealth-lust within bounds, it has hung men and beheaded them or has left them living to rot in prison for their avarice; while, too-lenient, it has permitted, indeed incited, the avarice of others to maintain serfdom and slavery and "sweating" and the stunting of children in factories. The blunders and the outrage are clear as noonday; these we must correct; but we cannot refuse to maintain the road from which these are blind and willful wanderings. Man must accept whatever repression of his desires is needed for the great Society which alone makes possible the larger satisfaction of his desire. Like those Persians whom Herodotus describes, he is permitted to implore the gods for no blessings upon himself direct, but only upon his entire people, receiving for himself only as he shares with them.

The provident attitude toward the native passions is to view them as energies, as powers of the mind, challenging us to find a use for them, to find some channel for their right discharge. To put no restraint upon them, or to put nothing but restraint is to confess want of wit—as though one were to let some great mountain stream of California flow untouched to the sea, or else were to restrain all its waters stagnant in some vast reservoir; instead of guiding it, here to enrich orchard and farm and field, and there to spin some turbine for car and factory and electric light in distant cities.

Or we may see the alternatives under another guise. We can fence off, chop down, uproot some troublesome or unpromising kind of tree; or can let it grow weedy and wild with bitter fruit; or we can select its better specimen, and transplant, plow, graft, prune, train it, until it yields an abundance of things useful in its wood and leaf and flower and fruit. Such an outcome bespeaks labor and studious imagination. What is bad here may prove good there: the poisonous herb may be medicinal; this gnarled astringent bark will make pliant what is unbending; this pinched bitter fruit becomes in the valley large and sweet. Among the passions, it is to this work that the genius of leaders is now summoned.

III

But lest our minds be left unclear by these considerations, not yet quite convinced that the native impulses need no uprooting, some of the doubtful ones may be examined, after a glance at those which raise no doubt.

For few would question the right of the maternal and filial impulses to remain, with whatever goes into human home-making already prophesied in the action of the many animals that build some form of nest in trees or on the ground, in water or in the earth. Modesty, too, and the impulse to imitate in movement and thought and emotion and purpose, and to play, and to peer at and into things curiously—few persons would raise their voice against any of these.

But the impulse to dominate others, if not to domineer over them and to exult in our power—these do not win so unreserved approval. Nor does an opposite impulse, which is morally perilous, to let others dominate us, to subject ourselves to them and to recognize them as our superiors.

Yet the moral possibility in this latter has been widely recognized—the virtue of humility, little praised to-day in America, and practiced less. Employers would gladly recommend it, not to themselves but to their workmen, yet without hope, as counselling perfection. It is a virtue that does not thrive in the climate of democracy and woman's suffrage and the boycott, being more at home with overlordship and courtly deference. But it lives and must continue to live in the wider relations. There could be no free government, no authority, if there were deep within even us no deference to our fellows and to the authority of their decision. A modern government cannot rest mainly on compulsion,—however much of compulsion may be in reserve for the few obdurate,—but upon consent, upon free obedience to the common will. And when, looking away from government, we consider the heavens, the work of God's fingers, the moon and the stars which he has ordained, the heart cries out as in ancient times, "What is man that thou art mindful of him? and the son of man, that thou visitest him?" End is there none to his universe, whether we look to the inexhaustible variety of life, or to the depths within the organic cell, or to the worlds clustered around the stars, or to the dominion of the mind. What man of right purpose can feel undiminished in such a world,—not from a sense of his ignorance alone, but from a sense of his failure in appreciation and industry, from a lack of moral stature suited to these vast halls!

There is also a place for the impulse of self-valuing, of self-appreciation. It has given rich gifts to human excellence, adding something needed in our sense of personal dignity, of personal honor, and in the right pride of family and of race. This feeling has been a servant of hell, but it has also served another kingdom. The aim to surpass one's fellows, to be their superior, not alone in office and in wealth, but in those solid attainments that rightly draw from others commendation and honor,—this has been a motive whose force has reached to the very heights of character, helping toward those spiritual riches which we owe to men like Milton, Dante, Beethoven, Darwin, and Lincoln. But emulation, ambition, is not to be praised in these great minds only; it cannot be spared in men who never attain to eminence: it helps to make the artist of any rank or craft,—the man of letters known only to the few, the upright magistrate, the skillful artisan, the successful merchant. Even seafarers are not ignorant of its meaning. A friend of mine, a ship's passenger to Alaska some years ago, came to know a petty officer, unschooled, seemingly satisfied with his position; and in conversation touched his latent pride and his ambition, starting him upon a course of self-discipline which made him in time the captain of his ship. There can be no condemnation, nothing but praise, of this impulse when it is duly informed and purified.

Thus as psychologists now see it, the will is not a simple organ of the soul, offering itself for schooling beside other organs. On the contrary, it is the most complex, the most inclusive, of our powers, indeed our all-inclusive power, being the interplay, the organization of all our impulses, all our interests, all our desires, all our intelligence. For this reason there can never be a disciplined will unless all these activities are called to attention, drilled in small and large formation, inspired with a common and sufficing purpose; until like seasoned troops they obey the word of command, lending their force and initiative to an enterprise that before would have found ardor in no one of them alone.

May we not then truthfully say of all the impulsions, emotional and instinctive, that *they are great and useful forces of human nature; and no one of them can be spared*. But they must be disciplined, they must be organized.

CHAPTER XVII

THE RIGHT OFFICES OF ANGER

I

The course we have thus far been following, wherein we find a use for each innate impulse,—can we pursue it also with regard to anger and pugnacity? Does not the recommendation to uproot the poisonous thing seem now less foolish than when we had in mind an impulse like that of good-will? Do we not ourselves feel something of that distrust which runs like an undertone in most of our accepted moral thought and effort, not in the Orient alone, but in our farthest West?—a distrust which stands in strong contrast to the welcome given to native friendliness.

There can be no doubt but that, quite apart from this suspicion, anger and pugnacity occupy a peculiar place with respect to nearly all the native impulses which we have recently been considering. In the sense in which the others are instincts, anger and pugnacity are not instincts at all. For according to the most valued account we yet possess of the native traits which enter into our social life an instinct is stimulated into action by a certain class of objects, and the action which this object calls forth in us is a particular manner of response.[1] In this respect an instinct is somewhat like a reflex action, like the winking of the lids when a mote irritates the eye; a particular stimulus is followed by a particular reaction. But the farther we rise above the simple reflexes and into the more

[1] McDougall, *Social Psychology*, 1914, 29.

complicated forms of innate impulsion, the less does this formula apply. The action is now seen to be aroused by a great variety of objects, and the action itself takes on most varied shapes. The instinct of accumulation may be aroused not only by gold and precious stones but, in the child, by postage stamps, marbles, butterflies, string, trolley transfers, candidates' announcement-cards, beetles, grocers' or druggists' samples, dolls, cigar-bands, and a miscellany of things without end. The things which cause fear are likewise many. And the responses we make to all these things are almost as varied as are the occasions which call them forth. In fear I may stand stock-still and be tongue-tied, or I may scream, I may crouch, I may run away. And yet these are called *specialized* responses to *special* situations; when in sober truth they are highly *un*-specialized responses to highly *general* types of objects or situations. The versatility of the mind is declared even in these its innate emotions and impulsions.

Now if fear and the property-desire and sex-love and domination are unspecialized, still less specialized is anger. In spite of the rich variety of objects and situations which stir some one instinct, its field may lie quite outside that of another instinct: gold, for example, does not arouse mother-love. But nothing that stirs any one of the other instincts is alien to the anger-impulse. The world is its parish. In order to make you angry I do not need to touch you on some particular side, I may touch you on *any* side: I may oppose your interest in your property or your family affections or your desire to domineer or your good-will toward friends or even toward strangers or animals. Ill-treatment not of your horse but of *my* horse may arouse *you,* or ill-treatment of an unknown child; or the stimulus to you may be an insulting word applied to yourself or to one you love, or it may be the sight of someone helping himself unbidden to your choicest flowers, or it may be some wholly reasonable criticism of your political favorite; these and ten thousand others may be the occasion of offense.

Not only are the causes of anger most varied; so, too, are its modes of response. In anger we behave in no single and uniform way. A child enraged may push his enemy away, may grapple him or scratch or bite; or he may do none of these, but may throw himself down and kick against the floor; he may utter no sound, or he may incoherently scream, or may use words that breathe forth threatening and slaughter.

Anger is thus seen to be a highly unspecialized impulsion; it has no immediate interest of its own, but arises to protect and to further any interest that you feel. In so far as you care for possessions, nature has made you ready to be infuriated at anyone who would deprive you of them. In so far as you love your children, are you enraged by one who would do them harm. And so for all your other native impulsions. It is the custom of this passion to be the servant of one's interests and to be indifferent to the character of the interest it serves. It is ready for any work. And although it is used selfishly, it is also used generously: we see it support avarice and lust, but we see it also hewing to right and left in the service of morals.

II

While then we may not for all time slam and bolt the door in the face of anger, yet a passion so powerful and so unprincipled will rightly be admitted with caution. We may not over-value what it promises. For those are clearly wrong who find here a greater power than in good-will. Measuring only by the moment, they are right. Anger may reach a violence which good-will can rarely equal, but good-will more than compensates for its unstorminess by its range and steadiness and its common presence in so many men. If in it we include all the kindly and either quiet or fierce attractions toward men, women, and children, it is the chief motive which creates and upholds society. It joins hands less often with the socially divisive and destructive powers. It even comes to dominate and transform the self-regard of men, so that they reach to no admiration of themselves if they find there no generous interest, no spirit of accommodation, no good-will.

Good-will therefore holds the world's confidence. For it is unlike anger which, as we have seen, is without special interests of its own, without clear and particular persons selected beforehand as its objects; whereas love has the child, the brother, the sister, the parent, chosen for it. Its task is constructive: to bind fore-ordained individual closely to individual, and when this is done, to find others for the union,—playmates and friends and still wider associates. Good-will is thus given its own positive work, which anger is not, a work without which there could be no common life. Family, comradeship, city, and state would without it be undone.

If we had to choose between good-will and ill-will, there could be no moment of hesitation. But we can have both, with good-will in supreme command. Anger and hatred, impossible as masters, make good servants if serving the impulse that is without blame. They are foot-loose, like celibates, ready to be sent where the work calls. And so great is their energy that it would be improvident to refuse them employment, merely because they had been under bad masters in the past.[1]

In imagined circumstances, sound love might be without hate. Were the round world to become a paradise wherein, as a rare family, each had for all others full understanding, full affection, full consideration, there well might be effort without hate. There no persons different and conflicting, unresponsive to affectionate appeal, would be ranged without. But in our actual world,—

[1] For some of these past connections, both good and bad, see pp. 36-72.

rich in good-will but bursting also with antipathies, with well-intentioned foolishness, with ill-intentioned power, with intelligence devoted to some and reckless of others, with stubborn pettiness that would defeat the whole,—in such a welter there will long be excuse for wrath. Where so much is to be done, why spend time idly, trying to destroy a natural power hard if not impossible to destroy, and that can be enlisted powerfully for the right?

The wise course doubtless will be neither to prohibit nor compel the use of anger. It should be permitted, even encouraged; but not required. Let those be calm before evil who can hurl mountains against it and be calm; and let those feel outraged who cannot but feel outraged. Each should be left free to be valiant according to his genius. No one would have St. Francis pushed into wrath. No one would wish Jesus smiling his disapproval of the hypocrite and of him who could see in the ideal only a chance for trade.

If, then, we wish the final increment of vigor in the effort of most men, there must come anger. Wrath, you will recall,[1] is one of the great energizers. I like to remember Thomas Starr King, small of body but one of the spiritual forces in early California: "Although I weigh only one hundred twenty pounds," he once said, "when I am mad I weigh a ton." Wherever the conflict is felt to be mortal, then, this make-weight cannot well be spared. The use of anger in the past—by the animal as well as by man—has been to give a flare to the fire of energy, especially when the obstacle comes from one's fellows. Anger then is for the extraordinary moment, for the emergency, and not—as with those impetuous drivers of the automobile, whose feet are never off the accelerator—for constant use. There is no call upon us to do the day's work with scowl and gnashing teeth. But I see every reason for potential anger that upon occasion becomes kinetic; every reason for steady moral antipathies existing perhaps as

[1] See pp. 8 ff.

banked fires, but ready at the shortest notice to burst into a flame that will set the whole engine awhirl. The multitude of inconvenient subversive antipathies have made us timorous of them all. But let us have little faith in a love of goodness that means no hatred of evil; in an earnest desire for justice to the poor man, that implies no cordial antagonism to the particular instances and representatives of injustice to him.

A recent visitor to America summoned us to feel the insult of much of our city life and government. A more recent writer praises intolerance. With them, I believe, is some weight of wisdom. We find no great difficulty in arousing jealous passion at the least threat from a foreign nation against our government. This limitation of organized anger to the single function of supporting the state, this relative coldness toward the great company of other interests, betokens spiritual poverty and torpor. We need a ready and passionate and united hostility against the threateners of all the other solid moral possessions, against all effort which promises not to build strong and make more spacious, but only to weaken and render less habitable, the social and spiritual structure.

We need more anger of the kind called righteous, but we shall be hindered if we think this the only justified form of anger. Not only is the plain man unready to lay claim to righteousness, but the epithet would reserve our hot opposition for sublime occasions. Indignation should be for lowlier use; for commonplace, although not constant, application. It is needed to offset the advantage which otherwise will accrue to wrong. For the selfish and destructive effort of men is well supported by wrath; they apply with a free hand this bellows to the flame. If men will not forego anger in the service of harm, is there not something like a military necessity to enlist it for decency and good-will? The situation is not wholly unlike that of our governments, which cannot afford to disarm until all disarm. The man of good-will must be prepared to be angry as long as others are prepared. We shall not rightly lay aside this instrument for the communal purpose until it shall cease to be used for partial and ill-considered ends. For the right purposes of life will be still slower to remake the world if they steadfastly refuse to employ that last touch of energy here ready and waiting. The children of this world must not always be wiser than the children of light.

There would seem, then, to be both the possibility and the need of bringing our anger-responses into the service of the interests that deserve to be supreme, and in particular of making pugnacity obedient to good-will.

CHAPTER XVIII

RULES FOR THE FIGHTING MOOD

I

When once we are convinced that in most men anger and pugnacity are needed, and that they may be trained to valiant service, how shall we move to obtain this training?

We may be certain that there will be demanded endless patience and discernment. But it is not all a matter of whip and spur; the reins and a soothing stroke upon the neck are often needed, that there be steadiness before unfamiliar things. We must know that anger, with all its wildness, is really docile. It is an emotion capable of great changes: while it can remain ready to be aroused by some of its old objects, it can also become ready to be aroused by some before which it has been quiet and to remain quiet before some that used to arouse it. It can become fused and tempered with other emotions, and subject to their bidding. The discipline of the boy, the man, the woman, requires, then, not the complete suppression of anger, but the knowledge and habit of *being angry with the right person and at the right time and in due measure.* As to its goal and object, chivalrous anger is the passion at its best. A boy fighting in self-defense draws us to his side; a boy defending another's right—a smaller boy bullied, a lame boy, a girl unprotected, some neighbor's property in danger of pillage—has us eager in admiration and applause. The anger-passion has now become suffused with friendliness, it has become a bondservant of goodwill; while in its crudity it is all joined and mastered by fear and greed and domineering and vainglory. The fighting of the mother-beast for her young reveals within the narrow circle what we should wish to use over wide ranges. The attack of the strong beast upon his wounded comrade shows the opposite quality. We deal then with primitive forces, forces already in the human nerves and blood. We do not have to create outright some impulse, some emotion. The native energies that enter into vice can enter into virtue. But inventiveness must be there.

Let us hate the vague, however. So easy is it to speak in generality, and so useless unless this be brought close to fact, that I am ready to risk offense to some by descending into quite absurd detail, setting forth sententiously a few commonplace rules for animosity. In them I shall not hesitate to sum up things already said and others that lie beyond the point now reached.

1. Use anger with parsimony. It belongs to the reserves, and should be summoned only in emergency. Its use should be an acknowledgment that the occasion is too large for one's ordinary powers.

2. When called in, its strength should just cover the object and no more. A pop-gun is no weapon against the unicorn, nor a thunderbolt to bring down the sparrow-hawk.

3. Jot down soon after the fact and during a stated time—a day, a week, a fortnight, perhaps—a full account of every occasion of your anger or irritation. The humor of many, if not most, of them will then appear,—mere tempests in a teapot. Their absurdity in the review will tend to check the least worthy and to reserve other outbursts for their due occasion.

4. Expect and take precautions against hair-trigger anger in times of fatigue, hunger, oncoming sickness, and old age. In these conditions one's spleen is apt to burst forth in most inappropriate strength and in most inappropriate directions. An uncommonly sharp eye may now be kept upon it.

5. Anger is sometimes unreasonable because there is an underlying and unreasonable anxiety. Misdirected anger can sometimes be scotched if not killed by riddance of this dread.

6. Anger is to be used with the full knowledge that it tends to arouse anger in others. If it is aroused *against* you, it adds to the difficulty of your enterprise. But this is not inevitable: it may well be aroused *with* you, and directed against the same object, now becoming a desired abhorrence of the kind of act you hate.

7. It is not enough that anger be disinterested. It must be right,—right in its outcome as well as in its intent. In driving passionately at an end, harm is often done to other interests; and the act and emotion is to be appraised not only by its motive, but also by the damage and the good done all along the way.

8. Incline to look with favor on anger that is disinterested; still more, on anger whose object is against self-interest, that is generous and to one's own hurt. It may upon occasion be wrong-headed, but its kind needs fostering, being commonly too sluggish and too weak.

9. Even self-interested anger may be amply justified. If I may be angry for another's right, I may be angry also for my own. I count no more than another, but I count.

10. Anger is originally indifferent to justice, and ready to support any interest in power. It is therefore in especial need of light and discipline.

11. Love is consistent with anger. Love can inhibit anger or set it free. These two cannot exist as active emotions at the same instant. But a disposition of love in a particular direction may be the very life of anger toward some other point.

12. The united anger of the community is no less nor more admirable than private and individual anger. It is under the same general rules and is in need of the same discerning discipline. Public opinion needs the support of a public hatred of injustice,—a hatred of the mob's

injustice no less than of the individual's. We need hatred of injustice to other nations.

13. Familiar intercourse, acquaintance, cannot guarantee an absence of anger and pugnacity, whether in individuals or in states. The more we know of some men, the more and the more rightly are we averse from them. Intercourse brings crisis, brings our vague good-will to the test; and unless there be creative foresight, it can bring complete alienation as well as friendship.

14. Delay, opportunity for reflection, weeds out many an occasion of anger, but in itself it will not prevent pugnacity in person or in nation. Some wrongs loom larger the longer they are thought upon. So long as great interests have no adequate support except from the fighting passions, these will stand ready, half-blind and partial, for the conflict.

15. The need of public anger diminishes as there is increase of strength in the civil instruments of protection and of just aggression. The size and frequency of mobs and of armies are a fair index of the defect in institutions to recognize right interests and to adjust their clash.

These minute prescriptions have, then, this in common, that *evil is to be recognized and attended to; against it is to be brought a steady pressure of hate.* Wrong will not disappear by some impersonal mechanics of evolution, in which so many put their trust. It will not disappear by mere inattention, by ignoring it, by declaring it unreal. This is an Orientalism come west, trying to wear a top hat instead of turban, and to seem at home amid cash-registers and dictographs. The old western habit of red shirt and hearty handshake and revolver in hip pocket, is no perfect symbol; but it means good-will with a readiness to face evil angrily, a will to grapple and down it, with fingers fairly twitching for its throat.

I would not deny that evil can be viewed too steadily, until the eye can see naught else. The gaze should rest

by habit upon what is of good report and is lovely rather
than upon what one hates. And there are minor ills, ills
that do not eat into the vitals of the spirit, that we may
best forget; they will be cured by the natural *vis medica-
trix*. But there are other things too menacing, too angry
themselves, for that negative care. As wisely might you,
when in the jungle you saw a tiger crouching for its leap,
trust to closed eyelids and an attempt to think only of
pomegranates and birds of paradise. The mere ignoring
of certain evils will no more cure them than sleep will
cure gangrene. Attentive anger must here come to support a widespread effort.

II

Now in bringing this passion to its place and order
there is work for all who educate,—and not for teachers
only. We may here follow Plato who defined education
as that "which leads you always to hate what you ought
to hate, and to love what you ought to love from the beginning of life to the end." [1] And to this kind of education,
eager for so much more than facts and memory and devices
of livelihood, many are called. It is a task for the family,
the school, the press, the church. Through effort of them
all, the moral impulses must be warmed and directed by
religion. For religion here should guide, its very office
being to put wisdom into the choice of the objects of our
love and hate, and to fan the fires for and against these
things. Religion is a sluggard if not the busy schoolmaster of the affections, giving splendid passion to endeavor and avoidance. It summons us, heart and head, to
the moral conflict, touching with a gleam the colors under
which we fight.

Where and in what ways will religion make anger
serve? Wherever good-will finds the way blocked, finds
patience no longer a virtue, the expense of toleration now

[1] *Laws*, II, 653 (Jowett's tr.).

mounting too high. A man will have need of all his intelligence, of all his wisdom, to make a sound decision, to do more good than harm. But this responsibility comes in the use of any power, of any engine; no steam is raised in a boiler that does not threaten to scald and rend the whole neighborhood. The moment we will do no good if there is in it a chance of harm, we declare for inertia, for paralysis. If religion cannot afford to be adventurous and of fighting temper, what can ? It is committed to the cause of human welfare, not in some other life only, but here; its effort is pledged to the things that serve children and women and men—hired man and millionaire, white man and black. It is pledged to labor for the things that fill men's deepest needs, and against whatever would leave them hungering. We must have good-will and lose patience. Hate as well as friendship cannot be tepid. The mammal, the man, must keep his blood hot or die. Especially does the male feel that he is coming into his own when his blood is up. There is in him the demon that, in the famous story by President Wilson, possessed the American soldier-Indian who complained of camp-life in the army as having in it "too much salute, too little shoot." More work will come from the man if instead of exhorting him not to be angry, he be told what to be angry about. If to the male there be granted the hope of saying in the end, in the spirit of that ancient letter, "I have fought a good fight," there will, instead of desertion of religion, be an embarrassing enlistment.

We need endless suggestion as to where the good fight is to be waged. It is not wholly against oneself; it is also against others. And against them, rather than against oneself, it must be admitted, the native quality of anger finds freest course. The fight is against groups and systems, but also against individuals,—against them as dominated by a certain spirit and will. I cannot as yet agree with those who feel that anger must always be impersonal, directed only against qualities, against abstractions. Love does not work that way, and why should hate? Is one careful to explain to his wife daily that there is nothing personal in his affection for her; that his love is not for her but for certain qualities in her? As love is toward individuals so long as their wills show a particular spirit, so hate is against them only while their powers are bent the one way, are organized against the good. The metaphysician would perhaps say we hate not the substance of the enemy but his form. But his form bulks large; and for the time, if we rightly hate at all, we rightly hate him. We may also turn in anger against collective action, against the habits of the community, the spirit of the time. But even this must in the end come to a fight against a spirit in individuals; for the community is of individuals, and the responsibility cannot be taken from persons and laid upon an impersonal society-in-general, upon a "system."

And if we were to be asked what is the head and front to be attacked in social onslaught, could we not agree that a great menace, perhaps the one great menace, for our place and hour lies in the passion to possess things? This must be thrown and curbed and branded and set to decent work, lest it run wild and wreck all. In our great factory-towns it is imperilling, nay destroying, the lives of workmen and women and children. There are those who dread the uprising of the proletariat and their despotism over all. If this comes, it will be due to the universal failure to tame the economic passion, to make it ruly, to make it know its place. If the possessive impulse be allowed to rule the most intelligent and friendly portion of society, we must not wonder if it rule the ignorant and the base. Making and selling threatens the deepest interests of mankind; its spirit penetrates places of learning; it has long had too great power over the main stream of popular education in America, the newspapers. Here, then, and wherever this menace lifts its head let us strike it.

But perhaps no less, there is need of impatience with

international swagger and self-concern. Among those who proclaim their hatred of anarchy, say in Russia, one finds a strange patience with the existent want of government, which is anarchy, in the intercourse of states. Although war displays great private virtues—endless tenacity, self-oblivion, the mastery of fear and all personal prudence, the discipline, the orderliness by which the will of one becomes the will of every man—although it has in it all this and much else that is heralded when war is upon us, let us see nevertheless its human insult. Its ends must be had by fairer means; we must stop prating of its spiritual blessings, of that love shown by laying down one's life for a friend when, with it, each tries not to die but to make ten foreigners die instead. We need to drive, day and night, against war's causes and for the institutions that will take its place. The last increment of anger is needed to end the chaos between nations, to bring government and organized justice into the life of the world. The barriers will yield the sooner if to our exhortation and education and silent pressure we add upon occasion some outburst of indignation at the intolerable wrong of it all.

The enemy here and elsewhere holds a wide front. There is more that needs opposition than war and wealth-lust. Men must fight steadily, as a soldier fights, against ignorance, stupidity, disease, and vice. Not in a towering rage every waking moment, for so no soldier fights. But if no one, not even behind the lines, feels anger at any time, there will be few soldiers at the front, nor will these few hit hard.

In the schooling of our native passions, in giving them their master and their task, *in making anger a true servant of good-will, religion working through all the institutions of right culture finds a work fit for its great powers.* Unless the highest perceptions of the race be the director of the individual's and the nation's powers, pugnacity will be the more readily governed by love of wealth, by the love of mastery, by sheer gregariousness; swayed by some minor interest, there will be wrath in support of commerce, or of class-interest, or of selfish nationalism.

We need not, then, put our trust wholly in kindliness without sterner adjutants. Good-will is to know itself master. But in our impetuous West at least, we shall long hesitate to dismiss all impatience, indeed all anger, from the service of this good-will.

INDEX

Acquaintance, effect of, on anger, 262.
Acts, The, anger in, 129.
Adrenin, 10.
Adultery, spiritual, in Judaism, 214ff.
Adversity, uses of, 25f.
Affection: in family, 46; in animals, 63; as primary force, 69; condemned, 101; in Vishnuism, 105; escape from, 106; religion as discipline of, 263ff. See Love; Friendliness.
Africans, 41, 149, 150, 154, 156, 165, 167, 169, 179, 200, 202, 203. See Amazulu; Bantu; Tschwi; etc.
Agni, 178.
Ahura Mazda, 77ff., 82, 83, 86, 156f., 170, 180.
Akankheyya-Sutta, 106ff., 111.
Akaranga, 114ff.
Allah, 88, 89, 91, 92, 93, 95, 158, 169, 170, 223.
Alms, 88.
Amazulu, 149, 179, 200.
American Indians, 40f., 42, 145, 150, 153, 154, 156, 162, 167, 169, 178, 179f., 200, 202, 203.
American life, 18, 24.
Analects, 120, 122ff.
Anesaki, 174.
Anger: physiology of, 8ff.; beginnings of, 31ff.; as an achievement, 31, 35; supports family, 43ff.; supports commerce, 47; supports classes, 47f.; supports morals, 48f.; supports religion, 48; as constructive, 49; in conscience, 50ff.; toward oneself, 50ff.; is uncreative, 62ff.; menaces community, 64; supports immorality, 64ff.; and justice, 66ff.; and appreciation, 69; and various passions, 69f.; its motives, 70; distrust of, 71; in Judaism, 75f.; in Parseeism, 77ff.; in Islam, 87ff.; in Taoism, 96ff.; in Vishnuism, 100ff.; in Buddhism, 105ff.; in Jainism, 113ff.; in Confucianism, 119ff.; in Christianity, 127ff.; in religion's growth, 139ff.; toward the supernatural, 139ff.; of the gods, 147ff.; prohibition of, 176; geography of, 201ff.; as a source of religion, 187ff.; future of, in West, 231ff.; growing disapproval of, 233ff.; proper uses of, 252ff.; rules for, 259ff.; communal, 261f.
Angra Mainyu, 77ff., 81, 83, 86, 156f., 180.
Animal impulses in man, 14.
Animals: motives of, 14f.; fighting of, 33, 63; traits of higher, 63f.; in religion, 194.
Appreciation, anger and, 69.
Arabs, 173, 223. See Islam.
Ares, 170.
Arjuna, 100, 105, 158f.
Ashantee, 150.
Assyria, 42, 166, 226f.
Asthenic emotions, 17, 25f.
Atkinson, 44.
Atharva-Veda. See Vedas.
Athena, 170, 178.
Australians, 155, 163.
Autonomic, 9.
Azi Dahaka, 79.
Aztecs, 166.

INDEX

Babylonia, 226f., 245.
Baldwin, 57.
Banmanas, 142.
Bantu, 149, 179, 200.
Barito, 148, 179.
Belief and will, 243.
Beauchamp, Miss, 11, 19.
Bernau, 142.
Bernheim, 10.
Bhagavadgita, 100, 159, 239.
Bishop, 148, 151, 153.
Blasphemy, 143f.
Boasting, 167.
Bock, 151, 163, 178.
Body and Mind, 18f.
Boer War, 13.
Borneo, 143, 148, 149f., 151, 163, 169, 179, 200.
Bowditch, 165.
Brahma, 101, 102, 104, 112.
Brahmanas, 100, 109, 205.
Brahmanism, 181.
Bramwell, 10.
Brooke, Rajah, 149f.
Brown, C. R., vii.
Buddha, 108, 110f.
Buddhism, vii., 105ff., 117, 119, 159, 173f., 180f., 201, 225.
Burns, 60.
Business disappointment, 23.

Calloway, 149, 179.
Cambyses, 86.
Cannon, 8ff.
Canon, sacred: use of, viiif.
Caribs, 140, 150.
Carpenter: the Great, 99f.
Caste, 47.
Catlin, 178.
Caucasians, 41.
Caunians, 141.
Codrington, 143, 146, 163.
Ceylon, 45.
Charcot, 10.
Child, the, in Taoism, 97f.
Chinese, 42, 96. See Confucianism; Taoism.
Christianity, vii., 76, 85, 88, 99, 110, 120, 127ff., 157f., 170, 173f., 181, 201, 221, 223ff., 227, 233ff., 239, 242.

Classes, 47f.
Colohnesi, 46.
Commerce, 47.
Community, spirit of, 37.
Confucius, 99, 122, 124, 125, 126.
Confucianism, vii., 99, 119ff., 126, 158, 165, 170, 174, 181, 201.
Conquering peoples, 206f.
Conscience: origin of, vii.; nature in, 4; anger in, 50ff.; emotions in, 56; its constitution, 58f.; involves dissociation, 60; its imperious tone, 60f.
Contentment, 18.
Conway, 197.
Coudreau, 142.
Cranz, 153.
Creeds, 86f.
Crevaux, 142.
Crime, motives of, 65.
Crowd vs. Community, 37.
Cruelty, 34.
Crusaders, 234.
Culture heroes and gods, 178.
Curiosity in animals, 63.
Curse in religion, 161ff.
Cyrus, 86.

Dante, 37.
Darius, 86.
Darwin, 6ff., 16, 44.
Dead, spirits of the, 121f., 193.
Death, attributed to anger, 152.
Delay, effect of, on anger, 262.
Delusions, origin of, 4f.
Democracy, 24.
Demoniac character, 101.
Demons, 79ff., 84, 87, 102, 110, 122, 143.
Descartes, 32f.
Desire: in Vishnuism, 100f.; in Buddhism, 109; in Jainism, 114.
D'Estrella, 195.
Deussen, 159.
Devil. See Demons; Iblis; Mara; Satan.
Devil-worship, decline of, 183ff.

INDEX

Dhammapada, 106ff.
Dhamma - kakka - ppavattana-Sutta, 111.
Dionysos, 145.
Disciples of Jesus, emotions of, 129f., 134.
Discontent, 18.
Disease and emotion, 17ff.
Dissociation, 19f., 60, 151.
Divine Song, 100.
Divinity School, Yale, vii.
Dogs, 32.
Dorsay, 147f.
Doubt and belief, in Islam, 91.
Doukhobors, 235.
"Drugs," 79. See Demons.
Durkheim, 147f., 187, 188.
Dwight, 141.
Dyaks, 143, 149, 163, 169.

Education of emotion, 21ff.
Edwards, 235f.
Egypt, 42, 154, 170, 172, 226f.
Ellis, 41, 140, 152, 162, 165, 166, 167, 168, 169, 202.
Emerson, 130.
Emotions: significance of, 1ff.; and health, 17ff.; in conscience, 58; in justice, 66ff.; the fundamental, 69f.; in Buddhism, 113; toward God, 144; excitants of, 144ff.; span of, 182; instability of, 184f.; religious and secular, 188ff.; in personification, 195f.; in monotheism, 209ff.; marital, in Judaism, 209ff.; in jealousy, 210ff.; in polytheism, 225; in pantheism, 225f.; discipline of, 244ff.
Energy from emotion, 9f., 19, 26.
England, crime in, 65.
Epistle of James, temper of, 132, 234.
Epistles, The, anger in, 129.
Erasmus, 234f.
Erotic theory of conduct, 15f.
Eskimo, 140, 153.
Evil, 77, 79, 80, 179ff. See Demons.

Family: anger's effect in, 44, 105; in Confucianism, 123.
Far East, temper of, 224, 240f.
Fear: physiology of, 9f.; use of, 46; its relation to other emotions, 69f.; motives of, 70; in religion, 187, 189, 197ff.
Feud, 46, 164f.
Fighting: in animals, 63f.; rules for, 259ff. See Anger; Pugnacity; War.
Fiends. See Demons.
Fletcher, 41, 147, 162, 167.
Forbes, 174.
Forgiveness, 88.
Freud, 11f., 14, 15f.
Friendliness: in war-time, 39; in justice, 66; as originative, 69f.; its relation to other emotions, 69f.; in Vishnuism, 101; in Buddhism, 110.
Francis, St., of Assisi, 235, 256.
Froude, 235.
Frazer, 141, 142, 144, 148, 151, 179.
Functional diseases, 10ff.
Future life: in Taoism, 99; in Vishnuism, 103f.; in Buddhism, 111ff.; in Jainism, 116f.; in Confucianism, 121f. See Heaven; Hell; Punishment.
Future of anger in the West, 231ff.

Gathas, 87.
Geography of hatred, 200ff.
Germans, 39, 203.
Gillen, 155, 163, 164.
God: in Confucianism, 120f.; in Christianity, 128. See Ahura Mazda; B r a h m a; Gods; Heaven; Jehovah; etc.
Gods: in Vishnuism, 102; in Buddhism, 106, 112; in Jainism, 113; anger of the, 147ff.; psychic c h a r a c t e r of, 191f.
Gold Coast, 141.
Gomes, 169, 178, 180.

INDEX

Goodhart, 32.
Good Mind, the, 84.
Good-will: in justice, 67f.; place of, 185f.; value of, 254f. See Affection; Friendliness; Love.
Gospel of St. John, 234.
Gospels, anger in, 128.
Government: and pugnacity, 64f., 166, 170f., 184, 207, 257, 261f.; in Taoism, 98; in Confucianism, 123; and religious differences, 207f.
Grant, 204.
Great Religions: their attitude toward anger, 75ff.
Greece, 154, 155, 158, 169, 170, 203.
Greenlanders, 153.
Grenfell, 193.
Griffiths, 65.
Growth of religion, anger in, 139ff.
Guiana, 142.

Habits of Emotion, 22.
Hall, H. F., 226.
Hanna, Thos., 32.
Haoma, 84, 145.
Happiness and pain, 25f.
Hatred. See Anger: Pugnacity.
Hawaii, 162, 165, 168, 169.
Health, 17ff., 23.
Heaven: in Taoism, 98f.; in Vishnuism, 100; in Buddhism, 112f.; in Jainism, 117; in Confucianism, 120ff., 125. See Future life.
Hell: 79, 80, 82; in Islam, 93; in Vishnuism, 100; in Buddhism, 111f.; in Jainism, 117. See Future life.
Henotheism, 224.
Heretics, 84f. See Tolerance.
Herodotus, 141, 245.
Herrera, 142.
Hesiod, 154.
Hocking, 35, 127.
Hsaio King, 123.
Human sacrifice, 166f.
Hysteria, 10ff., 60, 151.

Iblis, 91f., 93, 156, 181.
Ill-will: its fickleness, 183. See Anger.
Immorality, 19. See Evil; Vice.
Immortality. See Future life.
Impersonal law vs. personal God, 226f.
Impulses, native: in justice, 66f.; their relation to the will, 243ff.; discipline of, 244f.; uses of, 251.
Incapacity, relief by, 12f.
India, 154, 167, 178, 179, 201, 203, 206, 224f.
Indifference: in Taoism, 96; in Vishnuism, 101ff.; in Buddhism, 109; in Jainism, 113f., 116; absent from Confucianism, 120ff.; in gods, 149f., 203, 208.
Indulgence of passion, 245ff.
Infants, behavior of, 32.
Innate powers, 2f.
Insanity, 151, 193.
Instincts: distrust of, 1f.; thwarting of, 65.
Intellect: partisans of, 2f.; in conscience, 58.
Intelligence: tests of, 2; and pugnacity, 63f.; limitations of, 69.
Intolerance. See Tolerance.
Intoxicants, use of, 145.
"Inwardness" of Hebrew prophets, 222.
Islam: vii., 87ff., 110, 119, 156, 158, 170, 173, 174, 181, 201, 223f., 227. See Allah; Iblis; Mohammed; Koran.

Jacob's dream, 195.
Jainism, vii., 113ff., 159, 174, 201, 225.
James, Wm., 7f., 19, 33, 195.
Janet, 11.
Japan, 13.
Jastrow, 151, 166.
Java, 203.
Jealousy: 43, 45f.; national, 65; divine, absent in Vishnuism, 102; as source of monotheism,

INDEX

209ff.; its many causes, 210ff.; its emotional constituents, 210ff.; marital, among Jews, 213f.; of Jehovah, 214ff.; paternal, 219f.; want of, in Far Eastern religions, 225f.
Jehovah, 76f., 155, 157f., 169f., 213ff., 218ff. See Jews; Judaism.
Jennings, 122.
Jesuit Relations, 141, 153, 178.
Jesus: 88, 256; emotions of, 127ff., 234.
Jews, 42, 76f., 85, 88, 207, 209ff., 223ff. See Jehovah; Judaism.
Jezebel, 144.
Job, 25, 144.
Joffre, 20.
John the Baptist, 134.
Judaism, 75f., 144, 168ff., 170, 172, 174, 201, 209ff., 218ff. See Jews; Jehovah.
Jung, 11.
Juramentado, 205.
Justice, 66ff.

Kalevala, 161, 170.
Kant, 62.
Karman, 114, 115.
Khonds, 154.
King, Thomas Starr, 256.
Kingsley, 149, 179.
Kinvat Bridge, 82.
Knox, 140.
Koran, 88ff., 158.
Korea, 148, 153.
Krafft-Ebing, 11.
Krishna, 100ff., 105, 158f., 170, 239. See Vishnu.
Kroeber, 150f.
Ku Hung-Ming, 120.
Kullavagga, 106, 109ff.
Kuribunda, 149.
Kwang-tsze, 99.

La Flesche, 147, 162.
Lama Buddhists, 180.
Lang, 44.
Lange, 7.
Leland, 156, 178.

Leuba, 187.
Li Ki, 120ff., 158, 165.
Love: its early scope, 53; as originative, 69f.; its relation to other emotions, 69f., 261; in Islam, 87ff.; in Buddhism, 109f.; in Jainism, 116ff.; in Confucianism, 120ff.: in Christianity, 127ff., 133f.; as source of religion, 187, 189; in monotheism, 209ff.; in Far Eastern faiths, 225f. See Affection; Friendliness.
Luther, 234f.

Machiavelli, 46.
Macpherson, 154, 178.
Magic, 143, 161ff.
Maha-parinibbana-Sutta, 106ff., 110ff.
Maha-sudassana-Sutta, 106f.
Mahavagga, 107ff.
Maitrayana Upanishad, 159.
Malays, 45, 163, 167, 205.
Malign spirits: 143; worship of, 176ff.
Mana, 147f.
Mani, 85.
Mara, 111, 112, 181.
Marco Polo, 47.
Marett, 147.
Mark Twain, 144.
Marriage: anger in, 44ff.; and monotheism, 209ff.: its effect on Judaism, 209ff.
Maspero, 154.
Mathews, 162.
Mazda. See Ahura Mazda.
McDougall, 33, 41, 44, 252.
McGee, 147.
Melanesians, 143, 152, 155f.
Mexicans, 169.
Mind and body, 18f.
Mithra, 77, 78, 79.
Mob vs. community, 37.
Mohammed, 88, 91, 223.
Mohammedanism. See Islam.
Monarchical motive in monotheism, 219ff.
Monk, virtues of a, 114f.
Montel, de, 140.

Monotheism: origin of, vii.; jealousy as a source of, 209ff.; transitory, 218; tempered, 223f.; rejected in Far East, 224ff.
Morals: origin of, 3f.; Freud and, 16; anger in, 31ff.; 48f., 62ff.; self-review in, 53; in divine anger, 155.
More, Sir Thomas, 25f.
Morgan, 178.
Moses, 88.
Müller, viii., 109, 224.
Multiple personality, 11, 60. See Dissociation.
Musters, 150.
Mysticism, 99, 116.

Nami, King, 115.
Natural objects in religion, 194ff.
Nebo, 178.
Negritos, 45.
Negroes, 149, 200.
Neuroses and sex, 15f.
New, 165.
New Granada, 142.
New Zealand, 153, 168.
Nirvana: in Vishnuism, 104; in Buddhism, 112f.; in Jainism, 117.
Non-resistance in Taoism, 97f.
Nordic stock, 204.

Occident: future of anger in, 231ff.; historic trend in, 233ff.
Offices of anger, 252ff.
Olney, 235.
Oriental mind, 24.
Origin of religion, 187ff.
Orsini, 46.
Osaka, Emperor, 174.
Osborn, 188.
Oudah, 147f.

Pahlavi texts, 77.
Pain: 238, uses of, 25f.; avoidance of, 107f.; in Jainism, 113f.
Palmer, 141.

Pantheism, motives and emotions of, 225f.
Paradise: 82; in Islam, 90, 95.
Paradox: love of, in Taoism, 97.
Parkinson, 141, 152, 156, 163.
Parsee. See Persians; Zarathustrism.
Passion: riddance of, 106ff.; in Jainism, 114.
Passivity in Taoism, 98.
Patimokka, 108.
Paul, St.: on anger, 130f.; emotions of, 131ff.
Peace, military, 85. See War.
Persecution, 161ff., 172f.
Persians, 42, 85, 91, 158, 170, 180f., 226f. See Zarathustrism; Zend-Avesta.
Personal divinity: motives toward, 225f.; vs. impersonal, 239f.
Personification, 195f.
Persons as anger-stimuli, 264f.
Peru, 172.
Philippines, 42, 45, 150, 151, 200, 202f.
Philosophy: influence of, 239.
Piedrahita, 153.
Plato, 263.
Polynesians, 139f., 151f., 162, 167, 168, 169, 202.
Priesthood: influence of, 205.
Prince, Morton, 10, 19.
Prometheus, 178.
Property-passion: struggle with, 245, 248; anger against, 265ff.
Proyart, 154.
Pugnacity: 34, 63; public uses of, 36ff.; is not primarily creative, 68f.; native differences in, 202f. See Anger: Fighting; Ill-will.
Punishment: after death, 81, 82f.; in Islam, 92f.; in Buddhism, 111f.; in Jainism, 117; in Confucianism, 120f.; of spirits, 140ff.; of sinners, 236; secular, 236ff.
Puritans, 235.

INDEX

Quakers: 174, 235; and Taoists, 99.
Quetzalcoatl, 178.
Quietism: Taoist, 96f.; Buddhist, 105f.
Races: strength of, 42f.; differences of pugnacity in, 200ff., 207.
Rage: physiology of, 9f. See Anger.
Rank of malign spirits, 177ff.
Rashnu, 78, 79.
Rebirth: in Vishnuism, 101f., 104; in Buddhism, 111; in Jainism, 115f., 117.
Recreation, 18.
Rée, 58.
Repression of native impulses, 244ff.
Renan, 187.
Religion: origins of, viii, 187ff.; as discipline of emotions, 22; toxic and tonic, 22f.; as corrective of self-importance, 24; angry defense of, 48; anger in great, 75ff.; growth of, 139ff.; defined, 185; its full nature, 187ff., 191f., 196ff., 199; and racial differences, 200ff., 208; as schoolmaster of affections, 263ff.
Renunciation in Jainism, 117f.
Responsibility: in Vishnuism, 104f.; in Buddhism, 110.
Revelation, The, of St. John, 129, 132f., 234.
Reynolds, Sir Joshua, 21.
Riggs, 147f.
"Righteous" anger, 257.
Righteousness in Islam, 90.
Rig-Veda. See Vedas.
Rivers, 203.
Rochefort, de, 139f., 150, 153, 180.
Romans, 42, 169, 172, 203.
Roosevelt, 198.
Roper, 25.
Roth, 143.
Royce, 63.

Rules for the fighting mood, 259ff.
Russell, 167.
Russia: war of, with Japan, 13.
Sabæans, 88.
Sacred Books, use of, vii.
Saddharma-Pundarika, 111.
Sakra, 115.
Samoa, 153, 168, 169.
Saoshyant, 81, 180f.
Satan, 158, 181.
Saussaye, de la, 144.
Savior in Zarathustrism, 81, 180f.
Schoolcraft, 150, 153, 156, 167, 178, 200.
Schultze, 140.
Science, influence of, 240.
Scourging, 142.
Sects: in Islam, 89. See Tolerance.
Self: appreciation of, 250f.; assertion of, 208; morbid attention to, 18; depreciation of, 249f.; discipline of, in Buddhism, 112; interest in, 14, 16, 24, 66, 69f.; mastery of, in Jainism, 114; review of, 53ff., 56.
Semangs, 45.
Semitic religion, 148, 217f., 227f. See Judaism.
Senegambia, 142.
Senoi, 45.
Sex: and neuroses, 15f.; struggle with, 244f., 248.
"Shell shock," 12f., 15f.
Shih King, 120ff., 124f.
Shinto, 201.
Shu King, 120ff., 124f.
Sickness: 18; attributed to anger, 143, 152.
Sidis, 10, 32.
Singleness of mind, 19f.
Skeat, 161, 163, 167.
Smith, E. A., 141.
Smith, Robertson, 148, 168, 169, 187, 217f., 221.
Social life: religion as index of, 160; religion's attitude to-

ward, 174; in religion, 191f., 197.
Socrates, 25.
Sonship: in Judaism, 219ff.; in Christianity, 221.
Sorley, 57.
Sources of monotheism, 209ff.
Spencer, 155, 163, 164.
Spirits: of ancestors, 125; in Confucianism, 121f.; emotions of, 145, 159; worship of malign, 176ff.
State, the. See Government.
Statius, 187.
Steinmetz, 63.
Sthenic emotions, 17, 24ff.
Stimulation of native impulses, 245, 247f.
Stocks, racial: different pugnacity in, 203ff.
Stone Tablet of Lao-tsze, 99.
Struggle, 32f.
Suicide, permitted in Jainism, 117.
Sutrakritanga, 113ff.
Sutta-Nipata, 106ff.
Swedenborg, 37.
Sympathetic division, neural, 9.
Sympathy: and justice, 66ff. See Friendliness; Love.

Tacitus, 76.
Tagore, 174.
Tahiti, 140, 152, 162.
Tao, the Way, 96, 97.
Tao teh King, 96, 159.
Taoism, vii., 96ff., 159, 174, 181, 201, 225.
Taylor Lectures, vii.
Tempter. See Mara; Iblis; Satan.
Tevigga Sutta, 107f., 110, 112.
Thai-Shang, 99.
Thompson, 143.
Tiele, 141, 187.
Titans, 154.
Tolerance and intolerance: 84f., 172f., 225, 236; in Islam, 88f.; in Buddhism, 108f.; in Jainism, 116.
Tolstoy, 127.

Toughening, psychic, 17.
Tranquillity, 22, 105f. See Indifference.
Truth: attitude of Jainism toward, 116.
Tschwi, 149, 179, 200.
Tuelches, 150.
Tuke, 10.
Turner, 140, 153.
Tylor, 142, 144, 149, 150, 153, 156, 178, 180.

Ukko, 170.
Unaggressive peoples, 200ff.
Unangry drugs, 145.
Unangry religions: 96ff., 205; geography of, 201ff.
Useless emotions, 20.
Uttaradhyayana, 114ff.

Valhalla, 203.
Vasudeva, 115.
Vedas, 161, 162, 167, 204, 224, 245.
Veddahs of Ceylon, 45.
Vengeance: 164f.; in Confucianism. 124; Malay, 205.
Vertebrates, anger in, 34.
Vice, origin of, 3f.
Virtue, origin of, 3f., 69.
Vishnu, 102, 105. See Krishna.
Vishnuism, viii, 100ff., 158f., 174, 181, 201, 225.

Waitz, 39, 41, 140, 150f., 153, 156, 166ff., 178f.
Wakonda, 147f.
Wales, crime in, 65.
War: 170f., 173f., 204, 228; psychology of, viii, 12f.; neuroses in, 12f.; in Confucianism, 124f.; cooperation in, 36ff.; requires more than hatred, 38; as a unifier, 38; stimulates valuation, 40; as a selective force, 41ff.; its effect on victors and vanquished, 41ff.; selects governments rather than peoples, 42f.; is not the only eliminator of "the unfit,"

INDEX

42f.; political effects of, 36ff., 42f.; as supposed origin of virtues, 62ff.; in Zarathustrism, 85f.; in Islam, 91, 94f.; in Taoism, 97f.; in Vishnuism, 100ff., 104f.; in Buddhism, 107f.; in Jainism, 115; in religion, 161ff.; religion in, 166ff.; gods of, 169f.; roots of successful war, 206f.; in Judaism, 226f.; opposition toward, 237f., 265f.; World War, 12f., 37, 40.
Washington, Booker, 237.
Watson, 32.
Way, the. See Tao.
West, the: future of anger in, 231ff.
Westermarck, 53, 165, 212.
Wicked, punishment of. See Punishment.
Will: in conscience, 59; and the native impulses, 243ff.; and intellect, 243; nature of, 243, 251.
Wilson, 141, 149, 156, 179.
Women: influence of, on anger, 240f.
Word, incarnate, 86.
Worship of malign spirits, 176ff.
Wundt, 45.

Yale University, vii.
Yi King, 123.

Zah Yung King, 99.
Zarathustra, 86, 87.
Zarathustrism, vii, 77ff., 99, 120, 154, 156f., 162, 170, 174, 201, 204.
Zend-Avesta, 77ff., 145, 154, 161.
Zeus, 170.
Zoroaster. See Zarathustra.
Zoroastrianism. See Zarathustrism.
Zürich school of Freudians, 15.

For Product Safety Concerns and Information please contact our EU
representative GPSR@taylorandfrancis.com
Taylor & Francis Verlag GmbH, Kaufingerstraße 24, 80331 München, Germany

www.ingramcontent.com/pod-product-compliance
Lightning Source LLC
Chambersburg PA
CBHW061434300426
44114CB00014B/1688